Theory of the Border

THEORY OF THE BORDER

Thomas Nail

OXFORD
UNIVERSITY PRESS

OXFORD
UNIVERSITY PRESS

Oxford University Press is a department of the University of Oxford. It furthers
the University's objective of excellence in research, scholarship, and education
by publishing worldwide. Oxford is a registered trade mark of Oxford University
Press in the UK and certain other countries.

Published in the United States of America by Oxford University Press
198 Madison Avenue, New York, NY 10016, United States of America.

Library of Congress Cataloging-in-Publication Data
Names: Nail, Thomas, author.
Title: Theory of the border / Thomas Nail.
Description: Oxford ; New York : Oxford University Press, [2016] | Includes bibliographical
references and index. | Description based on print version record and CIP data provided
by publisher; resource not viewed.
Identifiers: LCCN 2016016792 (print) | LCCN 2016003957 (ebook) |
ISBN 9780190618667 (Updf) | ISBN 9780190618674 (Epub) | ISBN 9780190618643 (hard-
cover :acid-free paper) | ISBN 9780190618650 (pbk. : acid-free paper)
Subjects: LCSH: Borderlands—Social aspects. | Boundaries—Social aspects. |
Mexican-American Border Region.
Classification: LCC JC323 (print) | LCC JC323 .N34 2016 (ebook) | DDC 320.1/2—dc23
LC record available at https://lccn.loc.gov/2016016792

9 8 7 6 5 4 3 2
Paperback printed by Webcom Inc., Canada
Hardback printed by Bridgeport National Bindery, Inc., United States of America

For Arlo

CONTENTS

ACKNOWLEDGMENTS

Since this book was researched and written in tandem with *The Figure of the Migrant*, I would like to reiterate my gratitude to all those who contributed to this project as a whole. I am extremely grateful to the Fulbright Association for providing me with the means to spend a year in Canada working with the migrant justice group No One Is Illegal–Toronto and building the research for this book. This project has benefited greatly from that year and all the connections it made possible. I also thank Concordia University, the University of Toronto, and McMaster University for hosting me as a visiting Fulbright Scholar while in Canada. When I returned to the States, I was fortunate to have the support of the Wayne Morse Center for Law and Politics at the University of Oregon, which provided me with funding as well as a desk from which to continue my research on the politics of migration. The University of Denver provided some financial assistance to help with the costs of editing and indexing.

While I was writing this book, several universities invited me to speak about my research on migration and borders. The feedback and questions that followed these talks ultimately strengthened the work. For this, I thank the University of Toronto, DePaul University, the University of Oregon, the University of Redlands, the University of Colorado at Denver, and the Metropolitan State University of Denver. My own department at the University of Denver has been overwhelmingly supportive of this project. I am lucky to find myself among such generous colleagues.

I am indebted to a number of people for their support and encouragement of this project: Colin Koopman, Ted Toadvine, Dan Smith, Nicolae Morar, Robert Urquhart, Josh Hanan, Adam Israel, Adam Bobbette, Etienne Turpin, David Craig, Kieran Aarons, Julia Sushytska, and all the folks I worked with at *Upping the Anti: A Journal of Theory and Action*. I also acknowledge No One Is Illegal–Toronto for its tireless passion and hard work toward migrant justice and for welcoming me into the organization as a fellow activist while I lived in Toronto. Thank you especially to Fariah

Chowdhury, Faria Kamal, Farrah Miranda, and Syed Hussan. To Peter Nyers, for his generous feedback and continuing support for my work, I am more than grateful. During my time as the director of Post-Doctoral Faculty in Migration and Diaspora at the University of Denver, I benefited from the support of and fascinating work done by the researchers there. In the research and final production of this manuscript I am thankful for the help of Nicholas Esposito at the University of Denver, and Angela Chnapko and Princess Ikatekit at Oxford University Press. A version of chapter 1 in this book appears in chapter 2 of *The Future of the Migrant* (Stanford University Press, 2015). I am grateful for the reports from my referees and their helpful feedback. Above all, I am grateful to my wife Katie for her love and support.

Theory of the Border

Introduction

Moving Borders

We live in a world of borders. Territorial, political, juridical, and economic borders of all kinds quite literally define every aspect of social life in the twenty-first century.[1] Despite the celebration of globalization and the increasing necessity of global mobility, there are more types of borders today than ever before in history. In the last twenty years, but particularly since 9/11, hundreds of new borders have emerged around the world: miles of new razor-wire fences, tons of new concrete security walls, numerous offshore detention centers, biometric passport databases, and security checkpoints of all kinds in schools, airports, and along various roadways across the world.

Contemporary social motion is everywhere divided. It is corralled by territorial fences around our homes, institutions, and countries. It is politically expelled by military force, border walls, and ports of entry. It is juridically confined by identification documents (visas and passports), detention centers (and prisons), and an entire scheduling matrix of bordered time zones. Above all, it has become economically stretched—expanding and contracting according to the rapid fluctuations of market, police, security, and informational borders that can appear at any point whatever in the social fabric. Although there are many borders today, no systematic attempt has yet been made to provide a theory of the border that would be useful across such widely differing domains. This book aims to fill this gap.

This book provides a theoretical framework for understanding the structure and function of borders across multiple domains of social life. Borders are complex composites. Since each border is actually several borders, there is already quite a crowd. Not only is the indexical question "What is a border?" challenging enough to answer,[2] but the questions of how, when, where, and who makes the border are just as crucial and complex. Furthermore, historically the border has gone by multiple names: the fence, the wall, the cell, the checkpoint, the frontier, the limit, the march, the boundary, and so on. These are all distinct phenomena in social history, even if they often overlap with one another to some degree.

For all their differences, these types of borders also share something in common. "The border" is the name of this commonality. The border is "a process of social division."[3] What all borders share in common, following this definition, is that they introduce a division or bifurcation of some sort into the world. This definition I am proposing has four important consequences for a theory of the border that is further developed throughout this book. Thus as an introduction I would like to begin by elaborating each of these four consequences and outlining a methodology for their general application to the study of borders, or limology.

THE BORDER IS IN BETWEEN

The first consequence of a border theory defined by the social process of division is that the border is not reducible to the classical definition of the limits of a sovereign state, offered by many early theoreticians.[4] This is the case not only because the techniques of social division precede the development of states historically, but because even as a division between states the border is not contained entirely within states. The border is precisely "between" states. Just as the cut made by a pair of scissors that divides a piece of paper is definitely not part of the paper, so the border, as a division, is not entirely contained by the territory, state, law, or economy that it divides. While the technologies of division themselves may differ throughout history according to who wields them, when, where, and so on, the cut or process of social division itself is what is common to all of its relative manifestations.

This is an important consequence for a theory of the border since it means that the study of borders cannot be approached solely according to any one type of division or social force—between territories, between states, between juridical and economic regimes, and so on.[5] This is the case because what is common to all these types of borders is the status of the "between" that remains missing from each of the regimes of social power. What remains problematic about border theory is that it is not strictly a territorial, political, juridical, or economic phenomenon but equally an aterritorial, apolitical, nonlegal, and noneconomic phenomenon at the same time.

For example, take the border between states. The border of a state has two sides. On one side the border touches (and is thus part of) one state, and on the other side the border touches (and is thus part of) the other. But the border is not only its sides that touch the two states; it is also a third thing: the thing in between the two sides that touch the states. This is the fuzzy zone-like phenomenon of inclusive disjunction that many theorists have identified as neither/nor, or both/and.[6] If the border were entirely reducible to the two states, nothing would divide them—which can't be true. For example, if a piece of paper is cut down the middle, there remains something in between the two pieces of paper that is not paper and that divides the two pieces. Similarly, in between the two sides of the cut that touch each of the states is the division itself, which is not a state nor part of a state. Thus states infinitely approach the limit in between them in the sense best described by the mathematical concept of "limit" in calculus. States approach the limit (border) but never reach it or totalize it once and for all because the limit is a process that infinitely approaches the point of bifurcation, like the slope of a tangent. Border theory is the study of this limit.

However, just because the "cut" of the border is not reducible to any given regime of social force or power does not mean that it is in any way a negative process. The "in-betweenness" of the border is not a lack or absence. The border is an absolutely positive and continuous process of multiplication by division—the more it divides social space the more it multiplies it. It is thus important to distinguish between two kinds of division: extensive and intensive. The first kind of division (extensive) introduces an absolute break—producing two quantitatively separate and discontinuous entities. The second kind of division (intensive) adds a new path to the existing one like a fork or bifurcation producing a qualitative change of the whole continuous system. The bifurcation diverges from itself while still being the "same" pathway.

Although borders are typically understood according to the extensive definition, this is only a relative effect of the intensive kind of division. Borders emerge where there is a continuous process that reaches a bifurcation point. After this point, a qualitative divergence occurs and two distinct pathways can be identified. The result of this bifurcation is that the border is experienced as a continuity by some and as a discontinuity by others. For some people, such as affluent Western travelers, a border may function as a relatively seamless continuity between two areas. For others, such as undocumented migrants, the border may appear as a discontinuous division across which they are forbidden to pass and from which they are redirected.

Figure I.1: Bifurcation.

In both cases what remains primary is the continuous process that actively maintains the border and enforces it as a filter that allows one path or road to continue on ahead and another to be redirected elsewhere through detention, deportation, or expulsion (figure I.1). In other words, the border is an active process of bifurcation that does not simply divide once and for all, but continuously redirects flows of people and things across or away from itself. The border or social division in between territories, states, and so on only appears as lack or discontinuity from the binary perspective of the presupposed social bodies that are divided. From this perspective, the border appears conceptually as a secondary or derivative phenomenon with respect to territorial, state, juridical, or economic power.

However, the problem with this extensive definition of the border is that it presupposes precisely what it proposes to explain. If individual societies are defined as delimited territorial, political, juridical, or economic fields of power, and borders are the various divisions these societies create, how did these societies come to be delimited or bordered in the first place? In other words, a border seems to be something created not only by the societies that divide them within and from one another, but also something that is required for the very existence of society itself as "a delimited social field" in the first place. In this sense, the border is both constitutive of and constituted by society.

A society without any kind of border, internal or external, is simply what we could call the earth or world: a purely presocial, undivided surface. Accordingly, society is first and foremost a product of the borders that define it and the material conditions under which it is dividable.[7] Only afterward are borders (re)produced by society. This is another important consequence for the theory of the border as a continuous division. If we want to understand the border, we should start with the border and not with societies or states, which presuppose its existence. The border has become the social condition necessary for the emergence of certain dominant social formations, not the other way around. This is not to say that *all* social life is the product of borders. There have always been social movements and communities that have been able to ward off social division and borders to some degree.[8] Indeed, since the continuity of motion is primary and bifurcation or division is secondary, the primacy of borders is only primary in relation to a certain set of historically dominant modes of social organization: territorial, statist, juridical, and economic. In this sense, the theory of the border developed here is not a universal theory of the border, but a *historical* theory of how the border has been made to work. The aim of the theory is to reveal the mutable and arbitrary nature of four dominant border regimes—not to impose them by reproducing them—but to destabilize them by interpreting them according to the very thing they are supposed to control: movement.

Material border technologies are the concrete conditions for the principles and ideas of social life. However, the border is not only in between the inside and outside of two territories, states, and so on, it is also in between the inside and the inside itself: it is a division within society. This is one of the key consequences of the in-betweenness of borders that has been important for recent border studies. As Chris Rumford points out,

> Border studies now routinely addresses a wide range of complex "what, where, and who" questions. What constitutes a border (when the emphasis is on processes of bordering not borders as things)? Where are these borders to be found? Who is doing the bordering? It is still possible to ask these questions and receive a straightforward and predictable answer: "the state." This is no longer a satisfactory answer. Seeing like a border involves the recognition that borders are woven into the fabric of society and are the routine business of all concerned. In this sense, borders are the key to understanding networked connectivity as well as questions of identity, belonging, political conflict, and societal transformation.[9]

Accordingly, recent border theory has become significantly multidisciplinary. As David Newman writes, "For as long as the study of boundaries was synonymous with the lines separating the sovereign territory of states in the international system, the focus of research was geographical. As our understanding of boundaries has taken on new forms and scales of analysis, so too the study of the bordering phenomenon has become multidisciplinary, with sociologists, political scientists, historians, international lawyers and anthropologists taking an active part in the expanding discourse."[10] However, as border theory has included new scales of analysis,[11] it has also, according to Newman, "experienced difficulties in fusing into a single set of recognizable parameters and concepts."[12] This book thus proposes a set of philosophical concepts that will allow us to theorize the border at many different levels of in-betweenness.

THE BORDER IS IN MOTION

The second major consequence of a border theory defined by the social process of division is that the border is not static. In part, this is a consequence of the fact that the border, as a continuous division, is in between and thus not reducible to any stable, fixed side. The practical consequences of this are that the border is a zone of contestation. The border is always made and remade according to a host of shifting variables. In this sense, the border should not be analyzed according to motion simply because people and objects move across it, or because it is "permeable." The border is not simply a static membrane or space through which flows of people move. In contrast to the vast literature on the movement of people and things across borders, there is relatively little analysis of the motion of the border itself. Even many so-called theorists of flows, fluidity, and mobility continue to describe the border in primarily extensive and spatial terms: as "border-scapes . . . shaped by global flows of people,"[13] or as "the material form of support for flows,"[14] whose mobility or fluidity is purely "metaphorical."[15]

The movement of the border is not a metaphor; the border is literally and actually in motion in several ways.[16] First, the border moves itself. This is especially apparent in the case of geomorphology: the movement of rivers, the shifting sands and tides along coastlines, the emergence and destruction of ocean islands, volcanic transformations of mountain ranges and valleys, the redistribution of the soil itself through erosion and deposition caused by wind and water, and even the vegetative shifting of tree lines, desertification, and climate changes. The border also moves itself in not so obvious ways, such as the constant state of erosion, decay, and decomposition to which every physical object on earth is subject to. This includes the crumbling of mortar that holds walls together, rains and floods that rot wooden fences, fires that burn down buildings and towers, rust that eats holes through fences and gates, erosion that removes dirt from underneath a building, and so on. Every physical border is subject to the movement of constant self-decomposition.

Second, the border is also moved by others. This is especially apparent in the case of territorial conflicts in which two or more social parties negotiate or struggle over land divisions; political and military conflicts over control of people, land, and resources; juridical repartitions of legal domains or police municipalities; and economic reforms that directly change trade barriers, tariffs, labor restrictions, and production zones. Borders with large zone-like areas may persist as sites of continual negotiation and movement, for example between Israel and Palestine. In a more restricted sense, this is the process that Jacques Ancel describes as *frontières plastiques*: an equilibrium between social forces.[17] But the border is also moved in not so obvious ways, like the continual process of management required to maintain the border. Without regular intervention and reproduction (or even legal or economic deployments), borders decay and are forgotten, taken over by others, weakened, and so on. Borders are neither static nor given, but reproduced. As Nick Vaughan-Williams writes, "None of these borders is in any sense given but (re)produced through modes of affirmation and contestation and is, above all, lived. In other words borders are not natural, neutral nor static but historically contingent, politically charged, dynamic phenomena that first and foremost involve people and their everyday lives."[18]

The common mental image many people have of borders as static walls is neither conceptually nor practically accurate. If anything, borders are more like motors: the mobile cutting blades of society. Just like any other motor, border technologies must be maintained, reproduced, refueled, defended, started up, paid for, repaired, and so on. Even ethnic, religious, or national borders have their technologies: the control over who is allowed in what café, in what church, in what school, and so forth. Furthermore, this is not a new phenomenon that applies only or largely to contemporary life;[19] borders, as I hope to show in this book, have always been mobile and multiple. Management in some form or another has always been part of their existence.

Therefore the distinction between natural and artificial borders posed by early border theorists[20] cannot be maintained. This is the case not because borders today are radically different than they used to be, but because throughout history "natural" borders as borders were always delimited, disputed, and maintained by "artificial" human societies. A river only functions as a border if there is some social impact of it being such (i.e., a tax, a bridge, a socially disputed or accepted division). Additionally, so-called artificial borders always function by cutting or dividing some "natural" flow of the earth or people (who are themselves "natural" beings).

see page 21

THE BORDER IS A PROCESS OF CIRCULATION

The third major consequence of a border theory defined by the social process of division is that the border cannot be properly understood in terms of inclusion and exclusion, but only by circulation. In part this follows from the movement of the border. Since the border is always in between and in motion, it is a continually changing process. Borders are never done "including," someone or something. This is the case not only because empirically borders are at the outskirts of society *and* within it, but because borders regularly change their selection process of inclusion such that anyone might be expelled at any moment.

Furthermore, the process of circulation and recirculation performed by borders is not under the sole control of anyone, like the sovereign. The power of the border to allow in and out is profoundly overdetermined by a host of social forces: the daily management of the border technology (the motor), the social acceptance or refusal of the border (the drivers of the border vehicle), and the subjective whims of those who enforce the borders (to accept bribes, and so on). The techniques of border circulation only have the strength that society gives them.

In practice, borders, both internal and external, have never even succeeded in keeping everyone in or out. Given the constant failure of borders in this regard, the binary and abstract categories of inclusion and exclusion have almost no explanatory power. The failure of borders to include or exclude is not just a contemporary waning sovereignty of postnational states;[21] borders have always leaked. The so-called greatest examples of historical wall power—Hadrian's Wall and the Great Wall of China—were not meant to keep people out absolutely. Rather, their most successful and intended function was the social circulation of labor and customs.[22] Today this remains unchanged with the US-Mexico border wall.[23] In fact, one of the main effects of borders is precisely their capacity to produce hybrid transition zones.[24] Thus "it is the process of bordering," as David Newman writes, "rather than the border line per se, that has universal significance in the ordering of society."[25]

But border circulation is not just the ongoing process of dividing; its technologies of division also have a direct effect on what is divided. What is divided must be recirculated, defended, maintained, and even expanded, but at the same time what is divided must also be expelled and pushed away. Division is not simple blockage—it is redirection. What is circulated does not stop after the division—it comes back again and again. The border is the social technique of reproducing the limit points after which that which returns may return again and under certain conditions. The border does not logically "decide"; it practically redistributes. Since the border is never done once and for all with its divisions, some people who are expelled come back again from inside (undocumented workers) and others from the outside (border crossers). But since the border is not a logical, binary, or sovereign cut, its processes often break down, function partially, multiply, or relocate the division altogether. Instead of dividing into two according to the static logic of sovereign binarism, the border divides by movement and multiplication. The border adds to the first division another one, and another, and so on, moving further along. Instead of "the sovereign who decides on the exception," as Carl Schmitt writes,[26] we should say instead that it is "the border that circulates the division."

THE BORDER IS NOT REDUCIBLE TO SPACE

The fourth major consequence of a border theory defined by the social process of division is that the border cannot be understood in terms of space alone. This consequence follows from the fact that the border is in between social spaces and states. In between two spaces is not another space—and so on until infinity. If this were the case, as Zeno argues, movement between spaces would be eliminated: there would be nothing but static space. Movement cannot be explained by spatiotemporalization.[27] Similarly, the border cannot be explained by states and presupposed spatial orderings. The border is not the result of a spatial ordering, but precisely the other way around—the spatial ordering of society is what is produced by a series of divisions and circulations of motion made by the border. The border defines society (from the Latin *finis*, boundary, limit), not the other way around.[28] Unfortunately, as Linn Axelsson observes, "there is a tendency to privilege space and spatialities in the geographical analysis of borders."[29] "The spatial turn," as Chris Rumford writes, "may work to subordinate borders to spaces, as if the former were somehow dependent upon a prior spatial ordering."[30] This can be clearly seen in the following geographical definitions of "borders as dividers of space,"[31] "bounding [as] drawing lines around spaces and groups,"[32] or borders as "the limits of state space."[33]

Social space occurs when the mobile flows of humans, animals, plants, and minerals stop and loop back on one another.[34] Society is not individuals ceaselessly moving on their own away from one another, but occurs when their motions reach a certain limit and return back on themselves in villages, cities, states, and so on.[35] In other words, social space is the product of a flow that has turned back on itself in a loop or fold (figure I.2).

The process by which these lines are multiplied and (re)circulated back on one another is the process of bordering that produces social life. Society and space do not preexist the delimitation of mobile flows. This argument requires further explanation and is developed in the next chapter.

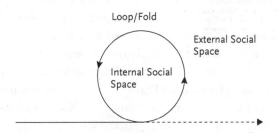

Loop/Fold

External Social
Space

Internal Social
Space

Figure I.2: Loop Space.

These four consequences for thinking the border as a process of division are crucial. Methodologically, however, the multiplication of levels of border analysis continues to pose a serious challenge for any theory of the border. As Corey Johnson and Reece Jones observe, "the expansive understanding of borders and boundaries in recent scholarship has enriched border studies, but it has also obscured what a border is."[36] If, as Étienne Balibar states, "borders are everywhere," then they are also nowhere.[37] Thus Axelsson notes, "we should be careful not to call everything a border" lest we risk "the potential loss of analytical clarity if the border concept is used too broadly."[38] Therefore a significant methodological problem for a theory of the border is how to create a concept of the border that makes sense of multiple different kinds of borders, not just geographical ones. As David Newman observes, "What is sorely lacking is a solid theoretical base that will allow us to understand the boundary phenomena as [they take] place within different social and spatial dimensions. A theory which will enable us to understand the process of 'bounding' and 'bordering' rather than simply the compartmentalized outcome of the various social and political processes."[39] In other words, what is required according to Newman is a theory of the border as a primary process and not as a derivative social product.

However, not everyone agrees that such a "solid theoretical base" is attainable or desirable. Anssi Paasi states, "A general border theory seems unattainable, and even undesirable, for two reasons. First, individual state borders are historically contingent and characterized by contextual features and power relations. There can hardly be one grand theory that would be valid for all borders. Such a theory is not problematic because the borders are unique but rather because of the complexity of borders and bordering."[40]

Truly, each and every border in history is empirically unique and composed of a complex mixture of different types of power. Perhaps the explosion of new border theories in the last ten years has not given rise to "a catch all theory," as Passi says, precisely because such a theory would have to be void of any of the empirical content specific to each border, and in doing so would render itself inapplicable anywhere. On the other hand, perhaps the recent desire for such a theory of the border has emerged precisely because of a growing frustration that the singular empirical study of specific borders lacks any larger implications, concepts, or framework outside its own parochial study. Without a transferable conceptual framework of some kind, the empirical study of borders in all their historical uniqueness begins anew with each analysis, with no consequences for future studies or other disciplines outside geography. For example, according to this empiricism, those trying to understand the division of territory between the United States and Mexico are talking about a completely different border than those trying to understand the juridical borders of immigration enforcement inside the United States. However, the idea that immigration enforcement (juridical borders) and border patrol (territorial borders) have absolutely nothing in common seems absurd, especially after their political unification under the Department of Homeland Security.

With this in mind, I would like to propose an alternative to the debate between the catch-all and empirical theories of the border. Before I do so, however, it is important to qualify three points on the relation of theory to the border. First, the purpose of a theory or concept of the border is not to explain or predict every detail of empirical border phenomena; a theory of the border aims to describe the conditions or set of relations under which empirical borders emerge. Thus the theory of the border deals both with several general sets of relations common to many borders and with the specific borders that compose these relations. The theory of the border looks at common sets of relations across—not beyond—parochial and empirical geographies.

Second, a theory of the border and its common features does not render useless the empirical study of the particular. In fact, empirical transformations often give rise to more general transformations in certain recurring sets of relations or conceptual border regimes. Furthermore, both empirical and conceptual studies can be enormously aided by a knowledge of some of the most basic recurring historical formations. Thus a theory of borders cannot claim to be empirically descriptive of all particular borders. No matter what the theory of the border, empirical study is still required to understand the historical contingency and specificity of each border in all its unique hybridity and novelty. However, such a study would benefit greatly from a broader theoretical base to compare and organize the different border regimes across the disciplines and through history.

Third, the debate between grand theory versus scientific empiricism raised in the last few years of border theory is not a new one in philosophy. In the eighteenth century Immanuel Kant formulated a similar problem in *The Critique of Pure Reason* (1781) between metaphysics and empiricism. On the one hand, "Metaphysics," Kant says, "is a speculative cognition by reason that is wholly isolated and rises entirely above being instructed by experience."[41] In other words, the knowledge of what the world is like in itself cannot have any foundation in our experience, and thus no application and no verification. On the other hand, empiricism has "assumed that all our cognition must conform to objects. On that presupposition however, all our attempts to establish something about them *a priori*, by means of concepts through which our cognition would be expanded, have come to nothing."[42] In other words, the empirical sciences bombard us with specific information, but tell us absolutely nothing about more general (a priori) conditions of knowledge under which that information appears to us as such. Thus Kant's solution to this problem is to invert it, just as Copernicus did. Let us assume instead, Kant says, "that objects must conform to our cognition" in the same way that "the spectator revolve[s] and the stars remain at rest"[43] for Copernicus. In other words, Kant proposes instead to identify the rules "that I must presuppose within me even before objects are given to me, and hence must presuppose *a priori*; and that rule is expressed in *a priori* concepts. Hence all objects of experience must necessarily conform to these concepts and agree with them."[44] Kant names this philosophical inquiry into the conditions of possible experience "transcendental idealism" or "critique." In this way he avoids both the problems of grand theory (metaphysics) and scientific empiricism.

Following this general insight, with some modification, I propose my own border methodology. What I propose is neither a grand theory (metaphysics) of the border in itself that attempts to explain all borders in advance and thus render empirical study useless, nor a purely empirical science of the border like those proposed by early border geographers including Jacques Ancel, Richard Hartshorn, Ewald Banse, Lord Curzon, Charles Fawcett, and Thomas Holdich. The goal of the theory of the border developed in this book is to develop, a solid theoretical framework that will allow us to understand *the historical* (not idealist*) conditions* in which empirical borders emerge across different social contexts.

To be clear, this book does not develop a theory of all kinds of borders across every single different dimension of reality. Such a project would be more akin to an ontology of the border and would have to explain every type of border, including the border between genres, the border between sickness and health, the border between knowledge and ignorance, and even between "things" in general. Arguably, metaphysicians have already been doing this for quite some time, and this will not give us the historical or social specificity we require for this project. Instead, the goal of this book is to provide a solid theoretical base of analytical clarity across four major social and material types of borders: territorial, political, juridical, and economic. Accordingly, this book limits its analysis to four major types of material border technologies: the fence, the wall, the cell, and the checkpoint. This book is not a theory of metaphorical or metaphysical borders;

it is a theory of the literal, material social technologies that produce social division.

Furthermore, this book does not develop a complete theory of resistance against borders nor a typology of the political subjects who have contested them. This is the case for several reasons; first, because such a theory is already developed elsewhere at length in my *Figure of the Migrant* and would be redundant to reproduce here. Furthermore, since the aim of the current book is to diagnose the historical conditions of certain dominant border regimes, and antiborder movements are not borders, they are not included in this book. The theory and history of political resistance requires the deployment of slightly different theoretical tools than those used to understand the operation of borders. A single book cannot do everything. I therefore ask the reader to forgive the arbitrary compartmentalization of border power and migrant counterpower that has resulted by not combining *The Figure of the Migrant* and *Theory of the Border* into a single six-hundred-page book on "kinopolitics," as it was originally conceived.

With respect to the present book, however, resistance still remains primary in the sense that social motions are always constitutive of borders in the first place. Social motion can never be completely or finally captured by any mixture of border regimes. All borders leak precisely because all borders are constituted by and through a process of leakage, which is only temporarily stabilized into border regimes. One important consequence of this kinetic point is that borders of all kinds have been under constant contestation and transformation by a number of different types of counter- and antiborder practices that rise and fall through history. I therefore urge the reader to supplement the present theory and history of the border with that of the migrant, developed elsewhere by myself and others.[45]

A border is not simply an empirical technology to be resisted or not; it is also a regime or set of relations that organize empirical border technologies. What I call a border regime does not transcend the material technologies that constitute it. It is their condition or relationship, not their cause, and it changes according to the way in which the material border technologies themselves are assembled. Thus the method of the present study is materialist in the sense in which it understands borders as regimes of concrete techniques and not primarily as ideas or knowledges that emerged independently from social and material conditions.

The theory of the border this book provides thus follows roughly in the critical tradition of philosophy in the following sense. There are conditions under which empirical borders emerge but, in contrast to Kant, they are not *possible* conditions; they are *real* conditions that are profoundly social and historical. In other words, there is not one universal set of a priori concepts that explains the existence of every border and all borders. There are rather several different sets of relations or regimes according to which most (dominant) social borders have operated. These logics are not transcendentally idealist in the Kantian sense of how they appear to consciousness, but neither are they purely empirical since they are not simply things or objects in the world. They are transcendentally empirical, historical, or material in the sense in which they describe how several groups of empirical border technologies are related and function as *regimes of social motion and division*. Thus we might call this method a "critical limology," or the theory of the real conditions for the production of social borders.[46]

I have divided this critical limology into two parts. First, I develop a formal or conceptual theory of the border as a kinetic structure in chapter 1. This is the most minimal theory of "what a border is," in its most abstract sense. Although this theory is presented first in this book for the purposes of helping the reader organize and define the different critical border logics that follow, this general theory of the border is practically last insofar as it is only discovered as the outcome of the critical study of border regimes as they have emerged in history. Once it is found, however, it can be seen at work throughout various different historical regimes. In this sense, it should be understood in a kind of conceptual future anterior, as that which will have been at work as the real conditions of territorial, political, juridical, and economic border regimes. In the second part of this critical limology I conduct a study of each of these four major border regimes as they have emerged historically and continue to coexist in contemporary border technologies. This second part constitutes the main body chapters of this book.

ON HISTORY

The history of the border has so far largely been a history of states.[47] In much of the scholarship and in popular discourse, borders tend to be defined as the outer territorial borders of states and identified with abstract lines and clearly demarcated boundaries. Not only is this untrue of premodern borders, but it continues to remain untrue for modern borders as well. The border as a social process of division is not reducible to state power, as was argued in the previous section, and certainly not reducible to an abstract line. Rather, the border is what divides. It is a process that states try to harness, but that often eludes them. Not only does the border precede the state historically since humans have been making borders for thousands of years before states existed, but it also precedes the state logically as the technical delimitation required in the first place for the social division called "the state" to exist at all. A history of the border cannot be reduced to the history of states or walls. Accordingly, there remains a rich history of the border that has been overshadowed or entirely ignored by the exclusive study of state borders and abstract lines.

This book thus provides a new history of the border. It is a history of social formations, including states, as the products of the bordering process. However, this book is not a universal history of the border that shows the vast intertwining of every type of border at every historical point and to every degree. It is also not able to be sensitive to every historically related term throughout.[48] The aim of this book is more modest: to provide an analysis of four major material border techniques during their period of historical dominance and to provide a conceptual, movement-based definition of them. It is not meant to be a representative or complete social history of power, movement, or all empirical borders that have existed. Rather, it is meant to be a philosophical history that extracts from empirical history the concepts sufficient to elaborate a critical limology useful for contemporary analysis.

Admittedly, this book presents a Western selection of this history. One of the unfortunate sacrifices made for the historical breadth of this book has been its geographical narrowness. By trying to theorize as closely as possible several major border regimes, I have had to reduce the study down to its most dominant expression in Western history. One of the consequences of this method is that it risks giving the appearance that these are the only manifestations of border regimes, the only ones that matter, or the only possible ones—none of which is the case. In fact, by focusing on the most dominant historical border regimes, my aim is to show the opposite: that since these regimes appear historically and not necessarily or developmentally, they could have been, can be, and might still become otherwise than they are—both historically and geographically. In this way the present work reveals the possibility of resistance to these dominant regimes, even if it does not recount all the major historical strategies of border resistance put forward in *The Figure of the Migrant*.

There are three major reasons for developing a theory of the border through a history of the border. First, doing so allows us to conceptualize the historical conditions under which different types of social border technologies have been produced. There is a tendency for border scholars to begin the history of the border in the nineteenth century when border studies began and to explain borders as the outer land limits of nation-states. However, borders did not originate in the nineteenth century. Furthermore, concepts of national and military defense offer little insight into the original division that produced the nation-state in the first place. The history of the border is more complex and goes by various names. The border appears everywhere that there is a material technology of social division. There are thus different types of borders at different times in history relative to the social conditions and forces specific to their division. This book presents a select history of four major types, their material conditions, and forces of social motion: the territorial, political, juridical, and economic forms of social division.

Second, the theory of the border and the history of its transcendental and technical emergence allows us to analyze contemporary borders. This is possible because the history of borders is not a linear or progressive history of distinct ages; rather, it is a history of coexisting and overlapping social forces of division. The borders of history do not simply emerge and disappear. As concrete border technologies, the basic technical structures of fences, walls, cells, and checkpoints persist, mutate, combine, and coexist in new social contexts and with new materials. As transcendental regimes, borders also persist, mutate, and combine to different degrees throughout history. Thus in order to understand contemporary borders and respond to them appropriately, we need to understand the emergence and coexistence of all types of borders and the conditions under which they emerged historically. John Williams describes something similar to this in his concept of "neo-Medievalism" in which the history of pre-Westphalian borders "may give us some clues as to what to expect" with respect to post-Westphalian borders, since many medieval borders were "social places that [existed] independently of sovereignty."[49] However, unlike a purely empirical and predictive method, this book is not looking to predict new empirical border technologies but aiming to understand the transcendental social conditions of past and present ones. Often what contemporary border theorists identify as new technologies and forms of bordering are simply recombinations of old regimes and technologies that have been around for hundreds or thousands of years.[50] A history of borders may keep border scholars from reinventing the wheel of border theory every time a so-called new technology comes out.

Third, the diagnosis of historical and contemporary border regimes also provides the strategic tools necessary for changing the current regimes. Understanding how a border works allows one to make more effective tactical interventions into its modification or abolition. The kinetic thesis of this book argues that borders have no ahistorical or universal social necessity and are thus open to further change or destruction. However, this book does not provide a normative theory of what we ought to do instead of creating these kinds of borders. Instead, its theoretical framework makes possible, only by contrast to these regimes, a kinetic study of the types of social alternatives possible.[51]

Transcendental "condition" does not mean causality or necessary determination. The analysis of contemporary borders that this book presents is not one of total causal explanation; rather, it is a transcendentally descriptive analysis. It begins with what has been produced and tries to understand its material and historical conditions. The aim is not to explain the causes of all borders, but to offer better descriptions of the conditions, forces, and trajectories of their historical emergence and coexistence in the present from the perspective of its bifurcating motion.

CONCLUSION

The theory of the border proposed in this book thus overcomes three problems. First, it overcomes the problem of statism that reduces all border phenomena to geographical nation-states, which ignores the constitutive and kinetic processes of social bordering. Second, in doing so it also overcomes the opposite multidisciplinary problem of dissolving borders entirely into society: "everything is a border." This book strictly limits its limology to the material technologies of social division. Finally, this book overcomes the third problem of limited historicity. If borders are not strictly defined as state borders, then the historical analysis of borders must begin much earlier than the nineteenth century, when national-state borders began to sediment. In response to this problem the present work provides a social history of borders beginning with the first human societies and leading up to the present. In fact, one of the central theses of this book is that contemporary borders are largely hybrid structures composed of a mixture of different historical bordering techniques.

This introduction has provided a general methodological orientation to the theory of the border. Chapter 1 begins with a more formal definition of what a border is. Once we understand what and how a border is, Part I of this book will be complete. We will then be prepared to develop a historical theory of the when and where of borders in Part II on limology.

PART I

Theory of the Border

CHAPTER 1

Border Kinopower

The history of the border is a history of social motion. Instead of defining the border as a secondary or derivative product of societies—primarily defined by states—in the introduction we defined the border by its primary features: its movement of bifurcation and circulation. Accordingly, if the border is not merely a derivative product but a primarily productive process, then a theory of the border also requires a reinterpretation of society itself as a process of movement and circulation. From border security and city traffic controls to personal technologies and work schedules, human movement is socially directed. Therefore the theory of the border is not a theory of the border *in abstracto* or derived from a presupposed notion of society, but a theory of social motion from which society itself is derived. Thus the history of the border is a history of vectors, trajectories, (re)directions, captures, and divisions, written exclusively from the perspective of the material technologies of social division. In other words, it is a "kinopolitical" history—from the Greek word κίνο, *kino*, movement. The kinopolitical analysis of the different types of social motion and their forms of circulation is the only history proper to the border as a form of motion since every other history reduces the border to a derivative phenomenon.

see page 7

In particular, the border is defined by two intertwined social motions: expansion and expulsion. This chapter defines and lays out the logical structure of this social motion, while the chapters of Part II analyze the historical conditions that give rise to it, and Part III shows how the concepts developed in Parts I and II help us to better understand the complex dynamics of contemporary US-Mexico border politics.

Another possible way to conceptualize the idea of expansion by expulsion is as a radicalization of Marx's concept of "primitive accumulation." Marx develops this concept from a passage in Adam Smith's *Wealth of Nations*: "The accumulation of stock must, in the nature of things, be previous to the division of labour."[1] In other words, before humans can be divided into owners and workers, there must have already been an accumulation such that those in power could enforce the division in the first place. The superior peoples of history naturally accumulate power and stock and then wield them to perpetuate the subordination of their inferiors. For Smith, this process is simply a natural phenomenon: powerful people always already have accumulated stock, as if from nowhere.

For Marx, however, this quotation is perfectly emblematic of the historical obfuscation of political economists regarding the violence and expulsion required for those in power to maintain and expand their stock. Instead of acknowledging this violence, political economy mythologizes and naturalizes it. For Marx the concept of primitive accumulation has a material history. It is the precapitalist condition for capitalist production. In particular, Marx identifies this process with the expulsion of peasants and indigenous peoples from their land through enclosure, colonialism, and antivagabond laws in sixteenth-century England. Marx's thesis is that the condition of the social expansion of capitalism is the prior expulsion of people from their land and from their juridical status under customary law. Without the expulsion of the people, there is no expansion of private property and thus no capitalism.

While some scholars argue that primitive accumulation was merely a single historical event from the sixteenth to the eighteenth centuries, others argue that it plays a recurring logical function within capitalism itself: in order to expand, capitalism today still relies on noncapitalist methods of social expulsion and violence.[2] However, the thesis in Part II of this book is notably different from these views in two important ways. First, the process of dispossessing people of their social status (expulsion) in order to further develop or advance a given form of social motion (expansion) is not unique to the capitalist regime of social motion. We see the same social process in early human societies whose progressive cultivation of land and animals (territorial expansion) without the material technology of fencing also expelled (territorial dispossession) a part of the human population. This includes hunter-gatherers whose territory was transformed into agricultural land, as well as surplus agriculturalists for whom there was no more arable land left to cultivate at a certain point. Thus social expulsion is the condition of social expansion in two ways: it is an internal condition that allows for the removal of part of the population when certain internal limits have been reached (carrying capacity of a given territory, for example), and it is an external condition that allows for the removal of part of the population outside these limits when the territory is able to expand outward into the lands of other groups (hunter-gatherers). In this case territorial expansion was only possible on the condition that part of the population was expelled in the form of migratory nomads, forced into the surrounding mountains and deserts.

We later see the same logic in the ancient world, whose dominant political form, the state, would not have been possible without the material technology of the border wall that both fended off as enemies and held captive as slaves a large body of barbarians (political dispossession) from the mountains of the Middle East and the Mediterranean. The social conditions for the expansion of a growing political order, including warfare, colonialism, and massive public works, were precisely the expulsion of a population of barbarians who had to be walled out or walled in by political power. This technique occurs again and again throughout history, as Part II of this study develops in further detail.

The second difference between previous theories of primitive accumulation and the more expansive one offered here is that this process of prior expulsion or social deprivation noted by Marx is not only territorial or juridical, and its expansion is not only economic. Expulsion does not simply mean forcing people off their land, although in many cases it may include this. It also means depriving people of their political rights by walling off the city, criminalizing types of persons by the cellular techniques of enclosure and incarceration, or restricting their access to work by identification and checkpoint techniques. Expulsion is the degree to which a political subject is deprived or dispossessed of a certain status in the social order. Accordingly, societies also expand their power in several major ways: through territorial accumulation, political power, juridical order, and economic profit. What is similar between the theory of primitive accumulation and expansion by expulsion is that most major expansions of social kinetic power also require a prior or primitive violence of kinetic social expulsion. The border is the material technology and social regime that directly enacts this expulsion. The concept of primitive accumulation is merely one historical instance of a more general social logic at work in the emergence and reproduction of previous societies.

However, Marx also makes several general statements in *Capital* that support something like this thesis. For Marx, the social motion of production in general strives to reproduce itself. He calls this "periodicity": "Just as the heavenly bodies always repeat a certain movement, once they have been flung into it, so also does social production, once it has been flung into this movement of alternate expansion and contraction. Effects become causes in their turn, and the various vicissitudes of the whole process, which always reproduces its own conditions, take on the form of periodicity."[3] According to Marx, every society, not just capitalist ones, engages in some form of social production. Like the movements of the planets, society expands and contracts itself according to a certain logic, which strives to reproduce and expand the conditions that brought it about in the first place. Its effects in turn become causes in a feedback loop of social circulation. For Marx, social production is thus fundamentally a social motion of circulation.

Part II of this book is a radicalization of Marx's concept of primitive accumulation and social periodicity under the concept of "expansion by expulsion." However, before we can elaborate on the consequences of such a concept for the phenomenon of historical and contemporary borders, it needs to be further defined according to the more general method followed by this book: the analytics of social motion, or "kinopolitics."

KINOPOLITICS

Kinopolitics is the theory and analysis of social motion: the politics of movement.[4] Instead of analyzing societies as primarily static, spatial, or temporal, kinopolitics or social kinetics understands them primarily as regimes of motion.[5] Societies are always in motion:[6] directing people and objects; reproducing their social conditions (periodicity); and striving to expand their territorial, political, juridical, and economic power through diverse forms of expulsion. In this sense it is possible to identify something like a political theory of movement. However, a political theory of social motion based on movement and not derived from stasis, time, or space also requires the definition of some conceptual terms important for this analysis. The core concepts in the definition of social motion are "flow," "junction," and "circulation," from which an entire logic of social motion can be defined and in which expansion by expulsion and migration takes place.

Flow

The conceptual basis of kinopolitics is the analysis of social flows. The key characteristic of flows is that they are defined according to their continuous movement. In this sense, the philosophical concept of flow parallels the historical development of the fluid sciences, aerodynamics and hydrodynamics.[7] In fluid dynamics, a flow is not the movement of fixed solids analyzed as discrete particles, as it is in solid mechanics; the presupposition of the fluid sciences is continuum.[8]

The history of the study of borders also developed through the study of flows. For early seventeenth-century demographers and even border scholars today, measuring the movement of human populations across borders is much more like measuring a continuous and variable process than it is like measuring a fixed solid body. This led many early border geographers in the nineteenth century, such as Friedrich Ratzel, Jacques Ancel, Thomas Holdich, and Charles Fawcett, to describe the border itself as a zone-like or plastic phenomenon shaped by and limiting human flows.[9] Modern demography, a branch of human geography, and the study of borders (political geography) were influenced by statistical science, which made possible for the first time the study of large amounts of variable data— often over time—based on theories of probability and chance. Statistics is the study of change and chance, of unpredictability. It is the science of making probable the unpredictable. Since the limits of a continuous flow cannot be totalized, flows had to be measured in an entirely new way: statistics.[10] Faithful to its etymological origins in the root (stat-), statistics emerged as the statist capture of human flows, and political geography as the study of the state's borders.

Beyond the birth of statistics and human flows across borders, we also find during the seventeenth century an explosion of scientific descriptions of flows of all kinds: flows of food, flows of money, flows of blood, and flows of air. In 1614 the Italian physiologist Sanctorius founded the study of metabolism, the science of transformative biological flows, recorded in *Ars de Statica Medicina*. In his 1628 book, *Exercitatio Anatomica de Motu Cordis et Sanguinis in Animalibus*, William Harvey conducted the first controlled experiments on and popularized the idea of pulmonary circulation as originating in the heart, circulation previously thought to originate in the liver.[11] In 1686, the English astronomer Edmond Halley published the first map of the trade winds in the southern hemisphere. In 1671 Isaac Newton invented a mathematics of flows in *Method of Fluxions,* now called differential calculus. Jean-Baptiste Moheau synthesized many of these studies in 1778 and brought them to bear directly on human mortality in *Recherches et considérations sur la population.* This was the century of the sciences of the variable, of the continuous, of flux.[12] This legacy continues today. Borders still define the limits and transition points of human flows. If the border is the political ground of our time, the flow is our conceptual starting point.

However, measuring "a" flow is difficult because a flow, like a river, is indivisible and continually moving. Thus there is never only one flow or any total of flows, but a continuous process, a multiplicity. A flow is by definition a nonunity and nontotality whose study can never be completed because it keeps moving along to infinity like a curved line. However, regional stabilities composed of a certain confluence or flowing together of two or more moving streams do exist.[13] One flow does not totalize or control the other, but the two remain heterogeneous, like a mixture without unity. Confluent flows are heterogeneous and continuous but also overlap in a kind of open collection without unity. In this conceptual sense, flows are not only physical, metabolic, or statistical but also social. The political philosophy of borders is precisely the analysis of social flows: flows across borders, flows into detention centers, counterflows (strikes), and so on.

A flow is not a probability; it is a process. A political philosophy of flows is an analysis of their bifurcations, redirections, vectors, or tendencies—not their unities or totalities. The science of probability assumes that a flow is a percentage of 100 (i.e., a totality): $x / 100$. A *percent*age presumes a knowledge of the whole such that the *per-* is a part of the known *cent-*, or whole. But a flow is not a part in a whole; it is a percentage of infinity: x / ∞. For this reason flows include chance, uncertainty, and events. Every point already presupposes a process that it marks. A point is simply a relay—both an arrival and departure point for further movement.[14] This also explains why social flows are poorly understood in terms of inclusion and exclusion. Nothing is done once and for all: a flow is only on its way to something else. One is never completely included or excluded but always inclusively excluded or exclusively included: hybrid.[15] Movement, as a continuous flow, is always both/and: it is an inclusive disjunction.

Finally, flows are just as difficult to study as they are to control. They are not controlled by blocking or stopping them, but rather by redirecting or slowing them down. The effects of border walls, for example, are not as much about keeping people excluded or included as they are about redirecting movements and changing the speed and conditions of crossing. The US-Mexico border wall, for example, has more than three thousand documented holes in a constant state of rotation between repair and reopening. The Israeli security fence is breached with underground passageways and supply lines that are similarly destroyed, moved, and rebuilt time and again. Every systemic aim for totality is confronted with the continuity and nontotality of flows that leak from its periphery. The control of flows is a question of flexible adaptation and the modulation of limits. Accordingly, the politics of movement is first and foremost defined by the analysis of continuous movement, changes in speed, and the redirection of flows.

Junction

The second basic conceptual term of kinopolitics is the junction. If all of social reality comprises continuous flows, junction explains the phenomenon of relative or perceived stasis. However, this relative stasis is always secondary to the primacy of the social flows that compose it. A junction is not something other than a flow; it is the redirection of a flow back onto itself in a loop or fold. In this way the junction is distinct from a confluence. A confluence is an open whole of overlapping and heterogeneous flows, but a junction occurs when a single flow loops back over itself. A junction remains a process, but a vortical process that continues to repeat in approximately the same looping pattern—creating a kind of mobile stability or homeorhesis.[16] A junction is the joining together of a flow with itself. The point at which the flow returns to itself is an arbitrary one, but also one that constitutes a point of self-reference or haptic circularity that yokes the flow to itself (figure 1.1).[17]

The junction then acts like a filter or sieve that allows some flows to pass through or around the circle and other flows to be caught in the repeating fold of the circle. The movement of the captured flow can then be connected to the movement of another captured flow and made into all manner of mobile technologies: a vehicle for travel, a tool for moving the ground, or a weapon of war. But the yoking of the flows also augments them, not necessarily by moving them faster or slower but by putting them under the control of something else: a driver. The driver is not necessarily a person but the given point at which the flow intersects with itself. Although the flow is continually changing and moving around the loop, the driver appears to remain in the same place. In this sense, the driver absorbs the mobility of the yoked flow while remaining relatively immobile itself: a mobile immobility, an immobility that moves by the movements of others.

The concept of the junction stands in contrast to the concept of node, developed in spatial location theory and the geography of movement. For example, Lowe and Moryadas define movement as the routes between prior discrete nodes. Movement is purposive, and "each bit of movement has a

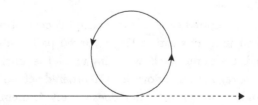

Figure 1.1: Junction.

specific origin and destination.... Our schema is predicated on the existence of nodes prior to the development of networks and movement.... Without nodes, why is there movement, and where is it consigned?"[18] *Theory of the Border* offers an alternative to this sort of static and spatialized theory, which has been thoroughly critiqued elsewhere.[19] In fact, one could easily invert Lowe and Moryadas's question and ask, "Without movement, how did nodes or stable points emerge in the first place?" Placing the fixed nodes first means that movement is always already yoked to an origin and destination, so there is no junction. Bergson argues that we will never understand movement beginning with immobility. My argument is that movement cannot be understood as a route between presupposed origins and destinations, and that junctions are not fixed nodes given in advance of movement.[20] Junctions, as the joining of flows, are secondary to the continuous movement of those flows.

As with flows, junctions are social. Every society creates its points of relative stability in a sea of turbulence. The house is a territorial junction, the city is a political junction, the commodity is an economic junction, and so forth. With respect to migration, a border wall is a junction of rocks, metal, and wood harnessed together into a relatively fixed vehicle whose drivers are mounted at its checkpoints, fixed on its survey towers, or surveying its perimeters in a patrol vehicle. The border is also a yoke or filter that allows some migrants to pass through with only minor inconvenience, others to obtain work under illegal and exploitive conditions, and others still to be caught and held for years in detention centers without charges. On the other side of the border, migrant labor flows are then harnessed through work junctions into a vehicle for production, profit, and social subordination. The flows that do not pass the border junction can end up in the detention junction harnessed into a vehicle of profit for private prison contractors and private security forces responsible for deporting them. Many kinds of political junctions yoke and direct social motion. Kinopolitics is a study of the function and typology of these junctions.

Circulation

The third basic conceptual term of kinopolitics is circulation, which connects a series of junctions into a larger curved path. This curved path continually folds back onto itself, wrapping up all the junctions together. Circulation is the regulation of flows into an ordered network of junctions, but flows are indivisible, so circulation does not divide them but rather bifurcates and folds them back onto themselves in a series of complex knots.

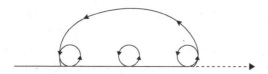

Figure 1.2: Circulation.

Since flows are continuously variable and the junctions are vortical, circulation is dynamic. It acts less like a single ring than like an origami object that brings together multiple folds, changing the neighborhoods of the junctions each time it folds. Even to remain the same, circulation has to keep changing at a relatively stable rate. Since flows have no absolute origin or destination, neither does circulation; it always begins in the middle of things (figure 1.2).

Circulation, just like flows, is not well understood by using the concepts of exclusion and inclusion. The conceptual basis of circulation is that something goes out and then comes back in again and again. It is a continuum. In this sense, circulation is both inside and outside at once. It is a multi-folded structure creating a complex system of relative insides and outsides without absolute inclusions and exclusions, but the insides and outsides are all folds of the same continuous process or flow. Each time circulation creates a fold or pleat, both a new inclusion and new exclusion are created.

However, circulation itself is not reducible to just these two categories. The aim of circulation is not only to redirect flows through a network of multiple junctions but also to expand them. Just as flows are yoked into vehicles through junction, so are junctions folded together through circulation. The junctions remain distinct, but flows tie them together. Through circulation, some junctions act together (by connecting flows) and become larger; others separate and become weaker. Circulation turns some junctions away and merges other junctions together in an expanding network. As a circulatory system increases the power and range of its junctions, it increases its capacity to act in more and more ways. It becomes more powerful. Circulation is more complex than movement in general or even harnessed movement (junction); it is the controlled reproduction and redirection of movement. Just as Marx locates the circulation of capital in the three basic circuits of money, production, and commodities in *Capital*, other forms of social circulation also have their circuit subsets. A circuit is the repeated, and often expansive, connection between two or more connected junctions.

However, within these larger circulations are smaller subcirculations, or circuits that constitute circulation. Border politics is also a circulation in which we can locate at least three circuits. The first is the border circuit, which itself is composed of three movements: (1) Migrants *cross* the border. But the border is a junction, a vehicle of harnessed flows. The border acts as a sieve or filter since it allows capital and the global elite to move freely, but, like a yoke, catches the global poor. (2) A flow of migrants crosses the border, legally or illegally, and if the migrants have lost their status they are *apprehended* by the drivers of the border junction—the border patrol. The flow of migrants might also cross and then be caught far from the border later on. Space/proximity is not the primary issue. The militarized, legalized, and political border creates the criminal act itself. It interpellates the mobility of the migrant as illegal. All immigration enforcement becomes "border enforcement." (3) The captured flow of migrants is harnessed to the enforcement apparatus and then turned or sent back across the border via *deportation*. The deported migrants are released and begin the cycle again. The border circuit is thus cross, apprehend, deport, cross (C-A-D-C). Each cycle in the circuit generates money, power, and prestige for immigration enforcement and justifies its reproduction and expansion.

The second circuit is the detention circuit, which can begin from the crossing of migrants but can also begin as a relay from the border circuit during apprehension. The detention circuit is also composed of three basic parts. (1) Migrants cross the border and are apprehended. (2) Instead of being quickly deported, they are harnessed into a different junction—the prison, detention, or camp junction. The flow of migrants is expanded into the detention center. The detention center, as a junction, is also a vehicle that harnesses or extracts mobility from the migrants through their labor,[21] their occupancy, and consumption of their own incarceration: food, water, clothing, medical care, and so on (this generates private profits that are heavily subsidized by the government). In the United States, for example, "Of the detainee population of 32,000, 18,690 immigrants have no criminal conviction. More than 400 of those with no criminal record have been incarcerated for at least a year."[22] (3) Once the maximum degree of mobility has been extracted from this flow—sometimes many years of detention—migrants are then deported. Once they are deported, the circuit can begin again or pick up like a relay into the next circuit. The detention circuit is thus apprehend, detain, deport, apprehend (A-DT-D-A).

The third is the labor circuit. Again, this circuit is also composed of three parts. (1) A flow of migrants crosses the border either legally or illegally. This could be after detention-deportation (DT-D), or apprehension-deportation (A-D), or the initial crossing (C). (2) The migrants are then harnessed by a labor junction, which aims to extract as much movement from the migrants as possible. Employers and the economy can extract more if the migrants have no status than if the migrants are legal, through the suppression of unions, threat of deportation, reduced wages, and dangerous work conditions. In this case the capitalist is the driver of the work vehicle, moved without moving. The movement of the migrant's labor pulls the vehicle along under the yoke of the capitalist. (3) From the labor junction, the migrant may return across the border, then return again to work, and so on until one of the other circuits begins through capture, detention, or deportation.

However, the labor circuit aims to indefinitely extend the extraction of movement from the migrant flow and harness it into the many junctions of the economy. Instead of folding back into the detention center, the flow is extended in the largest loop of the three: the indefinite labor circuit. The aim of this circuit is to reproduce an economy of disempowered migrant labor that props up the empowered labor and wages of citizens. The labor circuit is thus: cross, work, cross, work ... deport, cross (C-W-C-W ... D-C). The movement within and between these circuits is the circulation of border politics.

These are only three circuits of one type of circulation. As we will see, the border circuit is much more hybrid than this. Now that we understand more precisely what social motion is—flows, junctions, and circulations—it is easier to outline the kinetic components of the specific form of social circulation under consideration in the book, which is bordered expansion by expulsion.

EXPANSION BY EXPULSION

Expansion by expulsion is a logic inherit in all social circulation and requires the division or social bifurcation made by the border. However, the dual nature of this logic of expansion by expulsion also requires a dual exposition of our previous three social kinetic concepts: flow, junction, and circulation.

Conjoined and Disjoined Flows

A distinction exists between two types of flows: conjoined flows and disjoined flows. A flow, as previously defined, is not a single static thing but a process of fluid, indivisible movement. A conjoined flow is always harnessed or directed in a *limited* circuit of movement. It is still a continuous movement, but it is also redirected according to the aims of a larger

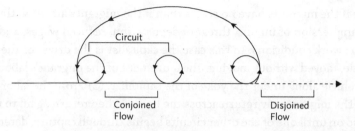

Figure 1.3: Conjoined and Disjoined Flows.

vehicle and driver that have curved the flow for some particular task. The conjoined flow is the flow in between two or more junctions that connects them into a circuit.

A disjoined flow is not part of any larger vehicle, or if it is, it still remains open to redirection and connection to other flows without junction. In short, conjoined flows form closed and limited circuits between junctions, and disjoined flows are open to new connections (figure 1.3).

Limit and Nonlimit Junctions

There are also two types of junctions: limit junctions and nonlimit junctions. Limit junctions are the final junction in a circulatory system (previously described as social borders). The limit junction or border is the junction after which flows are unbound or enter into a new social circulation. The limit junction is a filter and redirector of flows. Once a flow moves through a series of circuits and reaches the limit, it is either expelled or recirculated back across the previous circuits. There are two kinds of limit junctions: exit junctions and entrance junctions. The task of the exit junction is to actively expel, destroy, or unbind flows. It both removes flows from circulation and detaches or disjoins flows from other noncirculating junctions. It also redirects circulation back to previous circuits. Entrance junctions are filters that allow some flows to enter into circulation and others to be blocked or redirected. However, limit junctions are not always located at the spatial limit of societies. They can appear inside or outside a social area because, as kinetic social techniques, they are responsible for the junctions that define society in the first place, the kinetic conditions for social interiority and exteriority. Accordingly, entrance and exit junctions can also coexist in the same material phenomena: boundary markers, city gates, military operations, border patrol, customs offices, and so forth.

The nonlimit junction, or simply "junction," is part of a circuit within circulation. At the end of each circuit a flow can either start over or move on

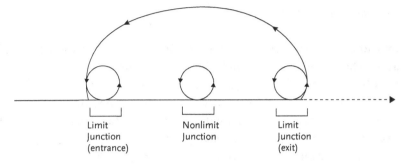

Limit
Junction
(entrance)

Nonlimit
Junction

Limit
Junction
(exit)

Figure 1.4: Limit and Nonlimit Junctions.

to another circuit until it reaches a limit junction (figure 1.4). These junctions do not filter what comes in or out of a circulatory system.

Circulation and Recirculation

There are two types of circulation: circulation and recirculation. Circulation is a regulated system of flows and junctions, including one or more internal circuits. Circulation has two poles, or limit junctions, one at each end: an entrance junction that allows flows to enter and an exit junction that allows or forces flows to leave. Circulation moves from entrance junction to exit junction, passing through one or more series of conjoined circuits. In this way circulation expands itself by allowing in more and more new flows and harnessing them to more junctions within the circulatory system. Once these new flows reach their limit, they are either expelled or recirculated. Accordingly, recirculation moves from exit junction to entrance junction across all the previous circuits. Recirculation then secures and orders what has already been harnessed (figure 1.5).

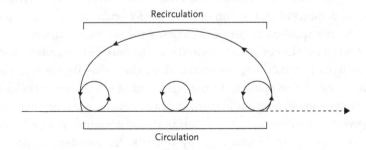

Recirculation

Circulation

Figure 1.5: Circulation and Recirculation.

Expulsion is a social movement that drives out, the deprivation of social status.[23] Social expulsion is not simply the deprivation of territorial status (i.e., removal from the land), it includes three other major types of social deprivation: political, juridical, and economic. It is not a spatial or temporal concept but a kinetic concept insofar as we understand movement extensively *and* intensively. Social expulsion is the qualitative transformation of deprivation in status, resulting in or as a result of extensive movement. Furthermore, the social expulsion of the migrant is neither essentially free nor forced. In certain cases, some migrants may decide to move but they are not free to determine the social conditions of their movement or the degree to which they may be expelled from certain social orders. Nonetheless, expulsion is still a driving out insofar as it is not freely or individually chosen but socially instituted and compelled. If a junction is the yoke of flows into a vehicle, including a driver, then the expulsion of certain flows is a direct result of the limit-junction vehicle. It is this last exit junction that utilizes its vehicle of harnessed flows to drive out other flows, or to abandon part of the vehicle itself. Expulsion is a fundamentally social and collective process because it is the loss of a socially determined status, even if only temporarily and to a small degree.[24]

Expansion, on the other hand, is the process of opening up that allows something to pass through. This opening up also entails a simultaneous extension or spreading out. Expansion is thus an enlargement or extension through a selective opening. Like the process of social expulsion, the process of social expansion is not strictly territorial or primarily spatial; it is also an intensive or qualitative growth in territorial, political, juridical, and economic kinopower. It is both an intensive and extensive increase in the conjunction of new flows and a broadening of social circulation.

Kinopower is defined by circulation, but this circulation functions according to a dual logic. At one end, social circulation is a motion that drives out, or disjuncts flows within or outside its circulatory system: expulsion. This is accomplished by the exit junction—the last junction, which is one of the circuits of the circulatory system but also outside this system, in charge of redirecting and driving out certain flows through exile, slavery, criminalization, or unemployment. At the other end of circulation is the entrance junction—an opening out and passing in of newly conjoined flows through a growth of territorial, political, juridical, and economic power. Expansion by expulsion is the social logic by which some members of society are

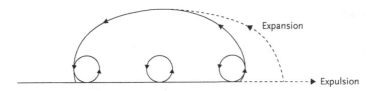

Figure 1.6: Expansion by Expulsion.

dispossessed of their status so that social power can be expanded else-where. The migrant is the subjective figure whose movement is defined by this logic, as was elaborated in *The Figure of the Migrant* (figure 1.6).

For circulation to open up to more flows and become more powerful than it was, it has historically relied on the disjunction or expulsion of mi-grant flows. In other words, the expansion of power has historically relied on a migrant surplus. While this thesis and the theory of social expansion by expulsion is defended at length in *The Figure of the Migrant*, the theory of the border or limit junction is not. While *The Figure of the Migrant* focuses on the kinetic processes of (re)circulation, conjunction, and disjunction, the *Theory of the Border* focuses instead on the specific process of the limit-junction technologies required for social motion. Thus we now turn to a closer look at the social kinetics of these border or limit junctions.

THE BORDER

The social limit junction, or border, goes by many names in border stud-ies: the limit, the mark, the boundary, the frontier, and so on. There does not seem to be any scholarly consensus regarding the differences and similarities among these different designations. Even the Oxford English Dictionary muddles the definition of these terms by defining them in almost identical or circular ways that simply reference one another. For example, according to the OED, a "boundary" is a "limit" or "boundary-mark," a "frontier" is a "border," and a "limit" is a "border, boundary, or frontier."[25] If we want to clarify the concept of "the border," it is first important to clarify its definition and ambiguous relationship to these terms. Each of these words is not only distinct, but each has a specifically kinopolitical meaning that reveals the basic and common structure of the border as a limit junction of social circulation. The mark, the limit, the boundary, and the frontier each describe a specific kinetic function of the border.

The first social motion or function of the border is to mark a bifurcation point in a continuous flow: something that can be returned to after the division, a gravesite, a spiritual site, a shelter, a fertile valley.[26] After this bifurcation point the mark introduces an inclination into the social flow. Once the flow moves away from the point, it also begins to establish a curve by "walking around" the perimeter.[27] As a social junction, the border is a flow folded back over itself, and the mark is the first half of this inclining fold. But the mark is not made once and for all. Marking is made precisely by the process of walking and rewalking (marching), constituted through a continual and mobile circulation of a march. Thus the border in its basic kinopolitical conception is not a static object but, at a certain point of inclination, an operation of marking and walking outward and around.

To mark something is also to do damage or leave behind a wound, no matter how small. A mark is a kind of division: a symbol carved in a tree, a chiseled rock, a dammed river, a sign made of felled wood inserted into the earth; even the mark of footprints in the soil leaves a wound in the earth. In this sense, the mark is an offensive sort of motion. It marks a memory or trace in the earth through violence so that it may march out and back around on itself (figure 1.7).

The aggressive or offensive function of the mark is attested to in the border processions of the Greeks, Romans, and Europeans. For the Greeks, one of the best-known border processions is that of the Heraia.[28] In this ceremony the priestess of Hera was drawn in a chariot by a team of yoked (junctioned) oxen from the center village, where humans lived, to the border where Hera's sanctuary was located. The procession march used a sacred plow to dig a single furrow—turning the earth back on itself

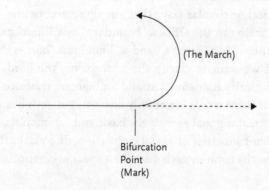

Figure 1.7: The Mark.

(*boustrophedon*)—through the countryside (*chora*). In this way the processional path "was an effective way of marking the fundamental axis of the territory."[29] Once arrived at the outer perimeter, the Greeks would sacrifice the oxen to secure Hera's blessing of fertility and mark the border with its blood.

A similar border procession was taken up by the Romans. Every February 23, Romans celebrated the "Terminalia"—for the Roman god Terminus,[30] the god of borders—by marching around in a large group to sanctify the regional boundary markers. According to the Roman geographer Siculus Flaccus, the bones, ashes, and blood of a sacrificial animal, and crops, honeycombs, and wine were placed in a hole at a point where estates converged, and a stone was driven in on top.[31] As Ovid writes, "Terminus, at the boundary, is sprinkled with lamb's blood . . . [and] sheep's entrails."[32] In this way, the border was marked and remarked by an annual march. The marks or border stones were literally covered in blood from the cutting open of animals and the binding of their vital flows into a dead junction marker, inside a rounded hole.

Practiced by medieval Europeans, the Christian ritual of "beating of bounds" descended from the Roman Terminalia. Priests would march a crowd of young boys around (the perambulation, to walk around) with green birch or willow boughs to literally beat the parish borders so that the young boys would carry on the knowledge of the borders.[33] At other times the boys themselves were literally whipped or violently bumped against the border stones to make them remember. Thus the mark was not only on the earth but on the body and in the mind—although always tied to a violent wound or beating. In all these cases, and especially in the case of the military march explored in chapter 3, the mark is an offensive force frequently associated with an expelling force. The march around the marks chases away the evil spirits, pushes out foreign intruders, and in the military march (common to almost all societies) becomes a moving mark, expelling as it goes.

The first function of the border is to mark a point of inclination in the earth's flows. Once this first point is marked, it is possible to march outward in a returning path back to the original mark. However, the mark also leaves something behind in its wake: the limit.

The Limit

The second function of the border is its limit. The limit is the path or track left behind by the mark or march.[34] Making a mark and marching to the perimeter is not sufficient to constitute a border. The border also requires that the path or track left by the march be protected, defended, and enforced. The path is the regularization or redoubling of the march that ties all the marks back together. Since the march is fundamentally mobile, it cannot be at all places and times—it circulates back and forth. It is precisely this ambulatory effect that leaves a gap in its wake or circuit. Once the march goes out and actively marks out an area, there will be places it does not reach and moments when it is absent. The limit is the defensive border function that fills the gaps left behind by the offensive march, hence the necessity of the annual renewal of the Roman Terminalia, the Greek Heraia, and others. If the mark opens up a cut or wound, the limit keeps it open. If the march circulates at the perimeter, the limit fills in the gaps of its circuit. If the border is a junction or loop of a fold back on itself, the limit is the second half of this loop that returns to the original mark and creates a complete circuit (figure 1.8).[35]

The defensive nature of the limit is attested to in Roman history. The Romans built limit (*lime*) structures not where they were ready to attack or advance, but precisely where they were *not* free to attack or where there was a gap in their military coverage. For example, Hadrian's Wall is primarily a supportive structure that was located behind the furthest path that marching soldiers were able to mark out and maintain through warfare. Like many other border fortification structures, these walls included a long foot trail for the border patrol,[36] who walked the path of the limit and watched for signs of the enemy. While the mark marches forward in a potentially widening motion, expelling or cutting through what lies in the way, the limit follows the path or gap left behind and secures the expansion of the march.

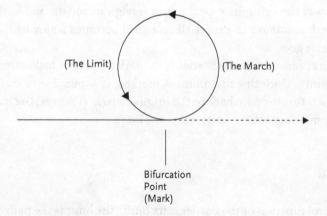

Figure 1.8: The Limit.

Thus the border not only requires the initial mark into the earth but also the defense of this mark through the plugging of the path or gap left behind. But the limit does not defend against everything; it also allows some things to pass through at the boundary.

The Boundary

The third function of the border is the boundary.[37] The boundary is not the same as the offensive march outward to mark or cut up the earth or body, nor is it reducible to the defensive patrol of the path or gap or trail left behind the marking march. Rather, the boundary is the kinopolitical process of binding or compelling part of the outside to the inside. It is a process of introducing social flows into (re)circulation or a social orbit. The word "compel" literally means "to force into motion together," from the Latin word *com* (together) + *pellere* (to set in motion, drive). Just like the mark and the limit, the boundary is not a neutral process, but a fundamentally forceful one of driving, thrusting, or striking. With one motion, the border expels people and objects through the force of an offensive mark/march, and with another motion it compels a portion of people and objects into a social kinetic bond. The limits of this bond are then patrolled and selectively expanded. This is the triple motion of the border that is required for the production of society: expulsion, compulsion, and expansion.

However, the boundary is not only the binding or compelling of disjoined flows into conjoined social circulation, the boundary is also a bending or recirculation of already conjoined flows back into circulation.[38] Once the flows of social motion reach the border, the boundary is the process that recirculates or bends them back into social circulation. Thus the kinetic meaning of the word "bound" as directional or vectorial: "homeward bound." To be bound is to be in the continual process of being socially recirculated and directed through the junctions of society. In this sense, binding should not be understood as a static process of unvarying fixity, but as a continual orbital motion of redirection and recirculation. The boundary functions as a passage across, around, and through the border (figure 1.9).

In the same way that the mark and the limit do not necessarily occur at the same place, at the same time, or even function according to the same concrete technologies, so the boundary should not be mistaken as primarily a kind of space or interiority. Like the mark and limit, the boundary is always in motion.[39] The binding function of the boundary is attested to historically by various barbarian groups. For example, the word "boundary" emerged from Germanic barbarian groups that used "bands" of bandannas,

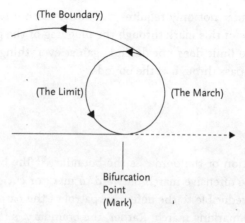

Figure 1.9: The Boundary.

ribbons, and banners (all from the Germanic root *band-*) to literally and symbolically tie the people of the social group together through visual identification markers.[40] Barbarian tribes and war bands were often highly heterogeneous in composition. Newly conquered groups would be assimilated and allegiances shifted often. Given the mutability of their social organization, the carrying of banners or wearing of different bands around their bodies served to create a mobile and flexible boundary or social orbit, hence the historical importance for the Germans and the Romans of the fundamentally collective nature of the boundary festivals. The border was not only the mark and limit of society, it was also the social force that tied the flows and junctions together with the binding of festival ribbons, banners, and bands, creating a social bond.[41] The Terminalia, as Ovid writes, brought both sides of the border together in a single social bond to make offerings to Terminus.

But the boundary does not bind or recirculate everything into its orbit; it also leaves out others at the frontier.

The Frontier

The fourth function of the border is the frontier (figure 1.10). The frontier is not the strictly spatial exterior of some static wall, but rather the foremost part of the border's process of continual motion. All three functions of the border's motion—expulsion (mark), expansion (limit), and compulsion (boundary)—produce or come up against the disjoined flows that define the frontier. The process of expulsion actively creates disjoined flows, the process of expansion then secures their disjunction, and the process of

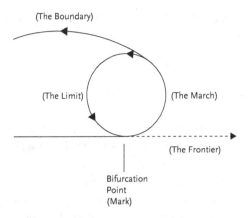

(The Boundary)

(The Limit)   (The March)

(The Frontier)

Bifurcation
Point
(Mark)

Figure 1.10: The Frontier.

compulsion binds some of them to society, leaving others out. The foremost part of the border is thus the disjoined flows that the border works on. Accordingly, the frontier, just like the other border functions, is not static at all, but constantly undergoing disjunction and conjunction. As the border moves, so does the frontier—as demonstrated by the "moving zone of settlement" described in Frederick Turner's famous text *The Frontier in American History* (1953).[42]

But the frontier is not always "outside"; it is both an internal and external process of disjunction. Wherever social flows are being expelled or disjoined, a frontier begins to emerge. For example, the existence of millions of undocumented migrants in the United States creates an internal frontier where these people are legally and politically expelled from certain social mobility and services even though they are "included" in the territory. Furthermore, the frontier does not have to be spatially contiguous with the so-called territorial borders of the state, as in the classic example of the eighteenth-century western frontier of the United States. The frontier can be any place where a colonial power is expelling a native people. As Franz Fanon writes, "The colonial world is a world cut in two. The dividing line, the frontiers are shown by barracks and police stations."[43]

The disjoined nature of the frontier may explain why so many border theorists describe the frontier as a kind of "zone."[44] A zone, no matter where it occurs, exists as a kind of gird or belt—not a line—of disjoined flows around the conjoined ones. It is a process of constant disjunction and indetermination: a "zone of experimentation," as Isaiah Bowman states;[45] "the meeting point between savagery and civilization," as Frederick Jackson Turner writes.[46] Except "savagery" does not only appear on the outside but from within "civilization" itself, as social division multiplies, self-destructs, and turns against itself.[47]

A KINOPOLITICAL HISTORY OF THE BORDER

The mark, the limit, the boundary, and the frontier are all distinctly different concepts within border theory, and yet they are all functions of the border's kinopolitical operation, based on the logic of expansion by expulsion. Now that the social kinetic logic of the border has been laid out, albeit relatively abstractly, we can now turn to analyzing the four major historical border regimes according to this logic in Part II. Each of these major regimes has a marking or offensive function, a limit or defensive function, a boundary or binding function, and a frontier or foremost zone of disjoined flows that it confronts. However, since the theory of this frontier zone of disjoined flows is elaborated at length in *The Figure of the Migrant* under the concept of migratory expulsion, this book focuses solely on the first three kinetic functions of the border.[48]

The quality, quantity, and type of border regime vary greatly, but all reemerge and coexist in contemporary border politics. This is why it is difficult to understand contemporary borders or movement by any one single domain, that is, territorial, political, juridical, or economic. Contemporary limology is a mixture of all of these. Thus an understanding of each as it emerges historically is necessary before delving into contemporary admixtures. Accordingly, the historical elaboration of this limology is developed next.

The four types of borders presented in the following chapters are not meant to be exhaustive or exclusive, but rather coexistent to varying degrees through history. However, each type of border power does have a historical period in which it emerged most strongly, or is expressed most dominantly. To be clear, the transformation and advent of the forms of border kinopower considered in these chapters is not linear, evolutionary, or progressive. Their transformation is not linear because kinopower is always a mix of its different types: emerging, receding, and re-emerging in history. Their transformation is not evolutionary in the sense that the new form does not abandon the previous one. Finally, their transformation is not progressive because there is no end or goal that kinopower strives for. Borders are always circulating movement in multiple ways at once.[49]

While general dates mark the years in which a given form of border kinopower flourished most dominantly, this does not mean that the other forms of kinopower were not already in action to some degree during that same time. For example, even in the earliest forms of human organization there was already the formation of territorial fencing, a degree of political centrality (the village, the shrine/temple), juridical norms and techniques of punishment, and economic exchange. However, among these different border regimes of circulation some are more dominant than others at different times. This book will examine only four types of border kinopower (the fence, the wall, the cell, and the checkpoint), and only during their major periods of dominance. Future work remains to explore all of their diverse admixtures and hybrid technologies.

PART II

Historical Limology

CHAPTER 2

The Fence

The first type of border is the fence. The fence is not only an array of concrete border technologies with some architectural similarity, but also a border regime or a set of kinetic conditions for social motion. Before there is a concrete technical object called "the fence," there is a kinetic social regime of fencing. In particular, the fence is a border regime that produces a centripetal social motion: the movement of flows from the periphery toward the center. Historically, centripetal social motion first emerged as the dominant form of motion with the earliest human societies beginning around 10,000 BCE—roughly during the period Gordon Childe refers to as the "Neolithic Revolution."[1] From Africa, the flow of *homo sapiens* made their first settlements in the Fertile Crescent and began farming around 10,000 BCE.[2] In general, most human beings changed from being nonsedentary hunter-gatherers to being increasingly settled agriculturalists.

Although it may sound strange, "settling down" is the first kinopolitical event. Without a relatively settled social area or territory, there is little need to redirect social motion back on itself into stable junctions. Without settlement, social motion simply follows the flows of wild game and weather patterns. Thus settlement and sedentism is poorly understood as the lack of movement.[3] Sedentism is not immobility; it is the redirection of flows, the creation of junctions, and the maintenance of social circulation. Sedentism is movement achieved by other means. When one no longer follows the flows, the problem becomes how to capture them so they will not move along without you, or rather, how to cast a net to capture them as they move by. Neolithic societies engaged in a wide range of social motion (daily, seasonal, interannual, generational, and so on) that required the invention of a particular border regime to capture the flows of the earth: the fence.

Historically, the first dominant form of kinopower is the movement to delimit an area of the earth as socially distinct. It creates a territory. While the earth is composed of continuous flows of water, soil, rock, and organic life, the territory is the social delimitation of these flows back onto themselves into junctions. Territorialization is the process of turning the earth back on itself to create relative stability in its flows.[4] Territorialization turns the soil back over itself in the creation of human graves, it turns the rock over itself into houses, and it turns organic life back over itself in the selective breeding of plant and animal agriculture. The surface of the earth has no center, but the territory creates one. The center does not preexist, but must be socially made by gathering the earth's continuous flows and turning them back over themselves into a fold or loop. "The surface of the territory is mobile and fluid."[5] In this sense, territorial border power is defined by a kind of gathering inward or centripetal social force. The fence is the material technology that cuts into the earth and redirects its flows toward a center that did not preexist the cut.[6]

THE KINETICS OF THE FENCE

The kinopolitical definition of the fence has two basic features.[7] The fence is first and foremost a strike or cut into the earth (digging, puncturing, carving out): the pit. Second, the fence adds something to the cut or hole to create a verticality rising above the earth: the pile. The fence cuts or tears into the flows of the earth in order to redirect them vertically. If, according to Bernard Cache, the most basic expression of architecture is "the frame" in the sense that all houses are composed of the basic elements of bottom, sides, and top, then the fence produces the first architectural function: separation. According to Cache, "The architectural frame fulfill[s] at least three functions, whatever the concrete purpose of the building might be. . . . The first function is that of separation. Its functional element is the wall. . . . But architectural space is not this general form of simultaneity; it is a space where coexistence is not a fundamental given, but rather the uncertain outcome of processes of separation and partitioning. The wall is the basis of our coexistence. Architecture builds its space of compatibility on a mode of discontinuity."[8] Thus architecture, according to Cache, should not be primarily conceived of in terms of space (simultaneity) or time (succession), but as the outcome of mobile processes of partitioning and "delimitation," or bordering.[9] The other two functions of the architectural frame (selection "the window" and distribution "floor") are built off of the primacy of this division in motion. The house is thus built from the intersection of several fences.

Accordingly, early human societies are filled with pits and piles to cut and store the earth's flows. The pit is perhaps the first vessel—a vessel for the dead. The dead, as Lewis Mumford observes, "were the first to have a permanent dwelling: a cavern, a mound marked by a cairn, a collective barrow. These were landmarks to which the living probably returned at intervals, to commune with or placate the ancestral spirits."[10] Following the most general kinetic definition of the fence, we can say that prehistoric burial sites were some of the first borders. Entombment cuts into the earth in order to create a mound or junction for the dead. The resulting mound rises above the level of the earth and marks a redirection of the earth's flows into the first limit junction between life and death. The grave is the limit junction beyond which one enters another world of pure undivided flows: the frontier of the spirit world. Just as Mumford claims that "the city of the dead antedates the city of the living,"[11] so we can also say that the borders of the dead antedate the borders of the living. Accordingly, a history of the border must begin with the first border, the border of the dead.

From prehistory to the present, burial borders continue to mark an important social division. "The first greeting of a traveler, as he approached a Greek or Roman city, was the row of graves and tombstones that lined the roads to the city."[12] The greatest monument markers of Egypt were their tombs: border markers or gateways to the realm of the dead modeled directly from the mound. Throughout history the cemetery is marked off from other areas in society with some kind of border. The original kinetics of burial remain roughly the same: the cut into the earth (the pit) and the centripetal storage of flows (the pile). The border fence thus historically and kinetically precedes civilization, architecture, and the city.

According to Mumford, early human societies were formed not only by the regular return to the burial fences that marked the territory, but to areas of the earth that were particularly sacred: "The first germ of the city, then, is in the ceremonial meeting place that serves as the goal for a pilgrimage: a site to which family or clan groups are drawn back, at seasonal intervals, because it concentrates, in addition to any natural advents it may have, certain 'spiritual' or supernatural powers, powers of high potency and greater duration, of wider comic significance, than the ordinary processes of life."[13] These sacred areas were marked or marked off by all manner of fences: mounds, stakes, monoliths, and so on.

The kinopolitical function of the fence is thus centripetal; it brings the periphery into the center. But the fence does not simply redirect a flow; it contains it. The fence opens a pit and centripetally contains a pile. This is the sense in which the fence is the dominant border regime of early human societies, whose social motion was primarily centripetal and vessel based.

"The Neolithic period," Lewis Mumford observes, "is pre-eminently one of containers: it is an age of stone pottery utensils, of vases, jars, vats, cisterns, bins, barns, granaries, houses, not least great collective containers like irrigation ditches and villages."[14] During the course of the Neolithic period human beings initiated the largest harnessing and circulation of the earth's flows in history at that point. For the first time they redirected the flows of seeds and plants from the wind and rivers into their own fenced-in circuits: corrals, gardens, pens, houses, villages, graveyards, and so on. This effort required not only junctions (containers) of all kinds to hold their flows, but also limit junctions to forcibly accumulate, defend, and bind groups of junctions together into social circuits. Three types of fences are thus needed to centripetally funnel (the corral), protect (the palisade), and maintain (the megalith) the accumulation of flows in these social containers.

THE CORRAL

The first type of fence is the corral. The first function of the corral is to mark or cut into the earth and march out around the perimeter. The corral is thus an offensive or expulsive type of fence insofar as its primary function is to go out, often outside the village, and expel large herds of animals from their grazing areas and centripetally funnel them into a pit or sunken enclosure for capture or killing. The corral is not only a technical structure but also the social kinetic regime of forcing centripetal motion.[15] In its most basic centripetal operation of corralling it also includes the chasing of animals over cliffs or into caves, pits, traps, or nets, and has likely been around as long as humans have hunted. In its most technically accomplished manifestation, Neolithic corral fences have been given the name "kites." From the ground many kite corrals do not seem to be distinguishable from a single row of stones. From above however, their wide, triangular kite-shaped funnel is strikingly apparent. Thus, kites were not discovered until 1927 by an Iraqi airmail pilot; over three thousand kites have now been discovered.

Some scholars interpret the kites as hunting traps, while others believe they were used to defend domestic herds in times of danger.[16] Still others argue that they were used as Neolithic corrals for capturing wild goats and cattle undergoing domestication.[17] In all these cases the kinetic function of the corral remains the same: the centripetal accumulation of motion. Although kites were originally discovered in the Middle East, many as old as 7000 BCE, and in Central Asia,[18] the kinetic function of the corral has a long legacy in herding and corralling techniques used historically around the world, including northern Europe,[19] central Asia,[20] North America,[21] and South Africa.[22] Human corralling is still used today in various border patrol techniques, explored in Part III of this book.

The kite fence is composed of three basic social kinetic features. First, it cuts into the earth to create a large open pit. Second, it piles stones around the pit to create a surrounding mound that conceals the pit and deepens it. Third, it cuts two long arms into the earth that radiate outward in a triangular or widening direction and either piles them with stones in a low wall or stakes rows of wooden poles in the ground, hung with rags. These fences function not only to herd or hunt ungulates, but also to designate the use of large areas of territory by certain people. The corral serves not only to mark the outer limits of a people's centripetal border power, but also to enact this power through the expulsion of animals from the wild toward a central point of accumulation.

The operation of the corral fence was successful precisely because of this expulsive power. For example, a group of hunters or herdsmen expel a herd from their grazing lands and force them to run in the general direction of the kite's open arms. As the herd runs, it avoids running into the kite arms and is thus funneled along the arms of the kite, some of which extend for over thirty miles.[23] The grade of the land is selected and even modified with earthen ramp mounds such that the wider end of the kite arms are elevated above the enclosure pit at the apex, by a few meters to over 100 meters in diameter, so the animals do not see the enclosure pit approaching.[24] Furthermore, the heads or apex of the kites are curved or shaped like a sock so that even if the animals see the structure they do not see it as directly at the apex of the kite arms.[25] Because of the forced speed of the animals running, their group movement, and the centripetally directed motion, their flow is largely conjoined into a single apex. The corral fence is thus a kinetic process of chasing the outside in. Once this general kinetic technique of corralling emerged historically, it was repeated in various ways throughout history to create an offensive centripetal border from ancient military techniques, to modern manhunting techniques, to contemporary kettling techniques.

THE PALISADE

Once a flow of animals or plants has been captured from the outside, it must be contained and protected. Thus the second function of the border is defensive: the limit. After the march is done, it leaves behind a trail going back to the campsite, home, or village. This is where we find the emergence of a second type of fence: the palisade or stake fence. The palisade is a pole or pile secured in the earth.[26] In its most basic kinetic definition, the palisade is composed of two motions. First, it creates a series of pits or cuts in the surface of the earth; second, it fills the holes with vertical stakes or poles. Sometimes these stakes are connected together with horizontal sticks, grass, or earth, and sometimes they remain vertical by the sheer force of the earth. In both cases, and in contrast to the corral fence, the palisade remains a predominately defensive sort of fence. The palisade concentrates on protecting the plants, animals, and human flows that have been centripetally accumulated in the village or home. The palisade captures a centripetal motion and defends it. Accordingly, we find a series of stake fences at the limits of all kinds of domestic and village structures of Neolithic societies.[27]

The Domestic

The walls of the first freestanding houses were originally not technically distinguishable from the myriad of stake structures that proliferated during the Neolithic period. Even mud-covered huts are still based on the initial wood palisade frame in the wattle-and-daub style. This is because the kinetic function of the house is not radically different from that of the palisade. The house is a centripetal technology, a vessel junction or container for human beings and the flows they have been able to amass. It is, as archaeologist Dušan Borić describes it, a literal "capturing of the landscape."[28] The house is more than a concrete technical object; it is a social border technology.[29] In this sense the house is kinetically similar to a palisaded version of the corral pit for the collection of centripetally directed flows: a cut into the earth, surrounded with stakes, with a small opening on one side (the door). Even during the Paleolithic period early houses contained postholes that were likely used to maintain wall structures and support ceilings.[30] Thus, before animal and plant domestication, the first stake fences were the walls of the home.

The palisade fencing of the home and its usage as a centripetal container function to mark it off from other homes and other people's storage vessels.[31] In the creation of nucleated palisaded housing, a border tension is thus created between the collective production of shared labor in the gardens and fields and the private appropriation of crops as they are accumulated behind the palisades of the individual houses.[32] "The very fabric and practices of the house created Neolithic society because [it] involved bonds, dependencies and boundaries between people."[33] Thus the palisade fence emerges as one of the first border technologies for the early division of labor between commonly worked and grazing lands and personally worked garden spaces, and the designation/protection of something like personal or nucleated property. Opposed to earlier communal cave structures that were used for collective storage and shelter, early palisaded houses divided or cut up groups of people and stocks of food. As Rousseau writes in the *Discourse on the Origins of Inequality*:

> The first person who, having palisaded [*enclos*] a plot of land, took it into his head to say, "This is mine," and found people simple enough to believe him, was the true founder of civil society. What crimes, wars, murders, what miseries and horrors would the human race have been spared, had someone pulled up the stakes or filled in the ditch and cried out to his fellowmen, "Do not listen to this impostor. You are lost if you forget that the fruits of the earth belong to all and the earth to no one!"? But it is quite likely that by then things had already reached the point where they could no longer continue as they were.[34]

The palisade is the technology that cuts into the earth, creates a junction or storage of flows, but also creates a limit junction that divides people and ownership into nucleated groups.

Outside the home, the palisade fence was also used to contain and defend plants and animals in the form of the animal pen and garden. There were several social kinetic functions of these numerous fences outside the home where they increasingly emerged: (1) to centripetally accumulate and defend a selection of living plant and animal flows; (2) to mark off communal versus personal garden and pen junctions; and (3) to demarcate personal property using fence lines or general enclosures.[35] The palisade is more than a mere mound; it is a defensive structure of fastened stakes. Wherever a wild or predatory animal can eat a crop, attack a person, or eat a domestic animal, the palisade appears. But this defensive structure also has the function of dividing the motion of plants, animals, people, and labor from one another socially. Thus the palisade is not only a centripetal defense of human stock from the wild frontier of disjoined flows, but also an internal division between humans—contributing to possible divisions of labor and social inequalities.[36] With the invention of the palisade, Neolithic villages thus began to take on the kinetic social geometry of an interrelated or coordinated circulation among discrete palisaded junctions—homes, pens, and gardens, making possible the emergence of an increasingly centralized interior.[37]

The Sacred

The palisade not only defends a division or cut between the social circulations of human, plant, and animal flows inside and outside an enclosure, it also protects a division between the living and the dead, what is above (visible) and what is below (hidden). Accordingly, the palisade fence also emerges around the sacred limit junctions of early societies in at least two ways. First, the burial palisade is a defensive technology for keeping animals from digging up the remains and keeping people from trampling or accessing the burial site. In some cases, fortified burial sites even become defensive fortresses against attack from other animals and humans. Second, the burial palisade creates a sacred site of ritual where all manner of communications, sacrifices, sanctifications, divinations, and so on may take place between the living mortal and the celestial ancestor. The word "sacred" is defined precisely by social division: to "set apart, exclusively appropriated to some person or some special purpose."[38] Thus one of the first technologies for the production of the sacred is the border fence, specifically the palisade. Without the ability to divide and set apart, and even defend (as the term "sacrosanct" suggests), there could be no sacred. The sacred does not produce the border; the border produces the sacred by limiting the conjunction of flows: of life, death, plants, animals, and so on.

The sacred palisade takes many architectural forms around the site.[39] The palisade can encircle the mortuary zone, can stand behind it, or might form a trapezoid around the perimeter. In addition to these arrangements, it can also form a short avenue between posts converging on a mortuary area or a long passageway leading up to the site.[40] These sacred palisades are often called henge enclosures, timber circles, or even "superhenges." Such sacred palisades include the recently (2008) discovered twenty-foot palisade surrounding Stonehenge; Goseck Circle; Durrington Walls, which was composed of four large concentric circles of postholes holding extremely large standing timbers; Mount Pleasant, which was an egg-shaped enclosure with five concentric palisade rings (sixteen hundred timbers) with cross-shaped aisles leading to the center with two one-meter-wide entrances through the palisades; Woodhenge, which had six concentric oval rings of postholes with a center holding the remains of a likely sacrificed child; and the Sanctuary, which had two concentric stone and timbers circles and a timber building. According to Thomas, in other palisades, such as those at Bryn Celli Ddu, it seems highly likely that they marked various astronomical events.[41] In other locations palisades themselves were considered sacred as "distinctions between inside and outside, above and below ground, left and right, back and front as a means of dividing up the things of the world."[42] In some but not all cases, this is evidenced by different sorts of sacrificial depositions (animal bones versus pottery) made between the base of different palisades.[43]

The Community

The palisade creates a division not only between nucleated homes and sacred sites, but also between entire groups of people or communities. Neolithic communities between 10,000 and 4,000 BCE were largely composed of small groups of several dozen families in palisaded mud longhouses surrounded by small gardens and animal pens, but in addition to these fences there was also an increasing proliferation of palisades that encircled entire groupings of houses. This is not a universal feature, but gradually became more common from the seventh to fourth millennium BCE. However, by no means should we imagine early villages as static entities always and entirely bounded by fences.[44] Neolithic villages were not always permanently occupied at all times of a year or beyond one or two generations at a time. Early humans were often quite mobile and traveled often. In many cases, palisaded enclosures, occupied and unoccupied, produced the "idea of permanence and order"[45] and a "tethered mobility."[46] Furthermore, palisades sometimes preceded communal occupation, and other times came afterward or were transformed back and forth.[47] Increasingly, however, over thousands of years people began to return more and more frequently to the common location of the village and to border the village site with larger and larger palisaded enclosures that delimited a certain community of persons.

Thus many early semisettled communities were, in part, the product of the palisade in the following three ways. First, to build a palisade around several houses, pens, gardens, or graves, was a massive collective enterprise that required hundreds of hours of labor, often from hundreds of people. Accordingly, early communities were the result of a border regime that required the coordination of an increasingly large number of persons. The larger the group of people that could be assembled together in one place under a single will, the larger, the more prestigious, the more powerful the palisade that could be built with their power. The community palisade is thus first a social monument or testament to the social kinetic power of a community of persons to divide themselves from others and from the surrounding territory. No other animal has the capacity to cut the earth that deeply or to establish a division this strong. The community palisade was the largest border that had been created in history up to this point. No doubt early people viewed these massive projects with a certain pride and awe at their own collective power based on their population, and wished to maintain and increase it.

The second way in which the palisade produces the community is through increasingly complex practices of social cohesion and coercion. For example, to dig two to six concentric ditches hundreds of feet in diameter and several meters deep, then fill them with hundreds of large timber poles, is no small task and required the creation of a social order not present in Paleolithic societies. Since Neolithic populations were also not yet large enough to have a division or specialization of labor (or slave population) large enough to accomplish this task on their own, we must assume that most of the population must have participated in the construction of these enormous palisade enclosures. The palisade actualizes or brings into existence the social order through the practice of bordering. To create the community, defined by those included in the enclosure, a massive collective effort had to be enacted through the construction of the first major public work: the border. Once the palisade was completed its power could then be retroactively attributed to "the community," which was made and defined by the inside and outside of the border. In the future, the border could then be attributed to the ancestors and other spiritual entities including chieftains and "heroes" like Gilgamesh. In this way the border fence was the material condition for the possibility of early human communities. While their labor process was temporally primary, the being of an exclusive community was possible only because of the retroactive power of the material fencing to define them as such. Only once a material border was produced could future generations then experience themselves as part of a preexisting and exclusive community. To what degree the original versus reproductive labor of border construction was coerced by social force, physical violence, or spiritual commitment is likely to have been variable and is largely unknown, but some large and powerful collective will was absolutely required to build and produce a palisade enclosure large enough to surround several houses.

Given the relative lack of warfare between Neolithic communities, village palisades were unlikely to be built for military defense.[48] This is not to say that were not defensive structures. They defended against all sorts of large predators and other animals, as well as the vision of others. As archaeologist Alasdair Whittle suggests, palisaded enclosures were more likely motivated by other concerns.

> These were great collective enterprises, which drew people from wide areas around into feats of pooled labour, and then into active use of the sacred spaces thus created. Given the context, I find it hard to envisage a system of political coercion, and much more satisfactory to suppose a sense of sacred obligation, with shame as the sanction for failure to participate, generated by still active memories of earlier enclosures, concepts of ancestors, and notions of time. These monuments renewed the past in the present. They enhanced respect for ancestors by drawing people into public, shared rituals of a formalised nature.[49]

Since many of these community palisades were not large enough to hold all the animals or houses of the village, they may have been used more as collective special gathering sites for community ceremonies that created cohesion between members.[50] Thus even if the community palisade did not literally surround all the houses of the village, the division of an enormous, collectively constructed limit junction in the center still functioned to produce community cohesion and likely coerced according to certain social norms, traditions, and distinctions between right and wrong.[51]

The third social technology included in the community palisade is the apparent desire for identity formation and division from other social groups. This is attested to not only in the community-based construction and occupation within these fences, but in the fact that many of the ditches that marked the palisade circuit were filled with the community's dead ancestors. As archaeologist Robin Skeates writes, "The ritual elaboration of the ditches as liminal boundaries, in which the bones of the ancestors were embedded, may also have enhanced distinctions between 'insiders' and 'outsiders.' "[52] Thus the palisade remained a defensive structure in the sense that it created a selective division between clan lineages: those who were allowed into the inner circle because their ancestors were part of it, and those who were not allowed in. In this way a "stronger sense of shared identity"[53] was produced by the palisaded enclosure, but also an increasingly larger social division between larger and larger groups of people.[54]

THE MEGALITH

The third function of the border is the boundary. After the corral march has gone out and centripetally expelled the disjoined flows of the earth such as wild animals, and the palisade limit has encircled and defended these flows in their various container junctions, the boundary centripetally binds and bands those who circulate within the territorial community. During the Neolithic period when this type of border was first invented, this territorial boundary took the form of the megalith (from the ancient Greek μέγας (*megas*), meaning "great," and λίθος (*lithos*), meaning "stone"). Although the megalith reappears again and again throughout history to create a similar boundary function, it first emerged as kinetically dominant during the Neolithic period.

The megalith boundary is neither an offensive border nor a defensive border, but a point of centripetal attraction and accumulation that marks an inward-directed motion. These enormous stones lodged in the ground exert a social force that draws in and binds people into their surrounding area. In its most basic kinetic function, the megalith is composed of two basic motions: to strike or cut a pit into the earth and to erect a vertical junction so large that it will exert a social force of attraction and accumulation for generations to come. Megaliths marked the first important sites that early humans continued to return to again and again. This is quite different from the palisade fences that were built to protect megaliths, and more different still from the multiple and nucleated houses, pens, and garden structures that were not nearly as singular or central as the tombs, temples, and territorial stones that almost universally outlasted any palisade fence. Not only was the function of the megalith to mark a point of continued centripetal return or social circulation, but the megalith also marked a border between different regions of circulation. For example, territorial road megaliths marked the farthest regions of social circulation, temple megaliths marked the furthest interior region of social circulation, and the tomb interior marked the most inner and restricted region of social circulation. Accordingly, it is important to distinguish between the social kinetic function of these three distinct centripetal boundaries: the tomb, the temple, and the territory.

The Tomb

The tomb is the first megalithic boundary. In all likelihood human burial mounds were the first singular sites that ambulatory humans began to return to with any regularity. They are certainly the most numerous megalithic structures.[55] In this way, the tomb is the first centripetal attractor of social motion. In order to express the importance and magnitude of these first social returns, almost all of the earliest-discovered human burial mounds were marked with large stones. The tomb megalith thus has three social kinetic functions. First, it cuts into the earth and creates a mound junction, but then binds or doubles the mound made by the buried body by adding a large vertical stone (monolith) or series of stones (polylith). The kinetic purpose of this is to literally fold the earth over onto itself and create a junction or point of local redirection or blockage. However, the megalith is not simply a stone placed atop the mound, it is the insertion of a dramatic "unnatural" verticality that opposes the horizontalism of the earth's constant disjoining forces of gravity, erosion, and decomposition. In the face of the earth's powerful forces of continual disjunction and death, the megalith attempts to halt or slow this process by turning the earth's flows against itself: erecting an unearthly verticality or spiritual entity that cannot die.

Thus the beginnings of human societies are bound by a rejection of the disjoined and destructive flows of the earth and the attempt to create a permanent band or symbolic individual on the earth that will resist the earth's movement. In fact, this *petranthropos* is quite literally indicated in the names given to various cairn megaliths in other languages. For example, in Inuit they are called *inunguak* or "imitation of a person."[56] In Near Eastern Neolithic cultures large stones or stacks of stones were painted and worshiped as spirits and gods.[57] The tomb megalith thus marks a boundary beyond which the flows of the earth will not be destroyed.

The second social kinetic function of the tomb megalith is to mark the border between the flows of life and death. The stone or stones buried in the earth create a division between above and below, between the living and the dead. In fact, the megalith itself duplicates the original burial. Just as the human body is half buried, dead, and invisible, and half unburied (the mound), alive (in the memories of the survivors), and visible (as the vertical stone), so the megalith tomb is also partly buried under the earth, dead, and invisible, partly unburied, alive, and visible as the immortal protruding stone. The burial stone is thus between the living who remember and the dead who remain underground.

The third social kinetic function of the tomb megalith is to create a centripetal social circulation in the form of a seasonal, annual, or generational return of the survivors to the stone in remembrance. In the world of the earth's unpredictable changes, one can always return to the stable center for orientation or as a touchstone whose orbit one cannot leave without abandoning the guiding and authentic force of the ancestors. Especially in the case of collective or mass tombs that are added to, tombs became the first stable social residences and established a social unity among all of the decedents whose ancestors shared this necropolis, this city of the dead. The boundary is the point on the border where the flows are recirculated and bound into a differential repetition, a continual return. Without the tomb to bind the ancestors together and into a stable territorial limit junction, circulation and recirculation lack a point of return and kinetic repetition. Accordingly, most other Neolithic megaliths are either modeled on the tomb megalith (dolmen), originated as one, or became one.

The Temple

The second megalithic boundary is the temple. Megaliths that begin as tombs frequently become temples, shrines, or other sacred areas. At other times a temple can emerge without a tomb. In addition to the three kinetic functions of the tomb megalith, the temple megalith adds three more functions. First, the temple boundary creates a common bond between worshipers as they pass on religious content and forms to subsequent generations and from founders to followers.[58] Thus the temple megalith or shrine not only creates a centripetal circulation of people around the stones or back and forth between different temples, but also dictates a very specific set of collective worship movements whose transmission ties the followers back to an original center. In fact, this is visually demonstrated in the very arrangement of the temple stones themselves into concentric rings of ditches and stones around a central zone. Almost every megalith temple in the Neolithic period attests to this.[59] Accordingly, the kinetic social force of the temple is to bind the community together and to the territory in a central zone, just as it binds the stones themselves together in a circle and into the earth.

Second, by creating a centripetal zone of spiritual accumulation, the temple stones also mark a boundary division between followers and nonfollowers, unifying the identity of the believers and dividing them from the nonbelievers. Accordingly, in their spiritual function temple megaliths also create a boundary division between the sacred and the profane and mark a movement or passage between them. This is not only an effect of the palisade fence that keeps the presence of the nonbelievers or nonsacred from the inner circle, but more primarily an effect of the very site-specific nature of the stones themselves. The very fact that the sacred takes the form of a site-specific boundary marker cut into the earth already marks some difference between the sacred site and the nonsacred site. Furthermore, their specific location in the earth frequently aligns with a singular celestial connection such as the solstice. The territorially binding structure of the temple megalith thus lays the conditions for a whole new form of social motion: the pilgrimage. The pilgrimage is necessary precisely because the believer is cut off kinetically from the stones, yet still bounded in its centripetal orbit, and periodically pulled back to its center and its spiritual, astronomical, or magical connection with the divine. In this sense one could say, as Lewis Mumford does, that the collective centripetal pilgrimage is one of the first social motions.[60]

Third, the temple megalith makes possible a territorial boundary division between priest and layperson. The inner circle of the temple megalith not only divides followers from nonfollowers, but also makes possible the creation of a specialized group of priests who have some special access to the stones, or through the stones to the ancestors, spirits, or celestial observations, if one knows how and when to use the stones. Evidence from many Neolithic temples shows that occupancy around the stones, when it existed, was often although not always quite small.[61] This may indicate a small, dedicated group of priests that would have stayed at the temple year round or several years or generations in a row, and may have had some special access to the divine. For example, Euan MacKie suggests that small villages like Skara Brae near megalith temples like Brodgar and Stenness may have been homes for a theocratic class of wise men who engaged in astronomical and spiritual ceremonies.[62]

The Territory

The third megalithic boundary is the territorial marker. The territorial boundary frequently marks the furthest reaches of an actively bordered territory. Similar to the tomb and temple megaliths, many territorial boundary markers were at one point, are, or may become a burial or sacred site; thus several of the social kinetic functions are the same. However, the territorial megalith (or stela) also adds three of its own unique kinetic functions to the others.

The first kinetic function of the territorial megalith is that it creates a centripetal force of attraction that binds or links together several other centripetal borders. For example, many tombs in the Neolithic Near East were intentionally placed near the roadside so that pilgrims could visit them easily.[63] Conversely, other Neolithic roadways were created by walking between the tombs and temples already created. In this way roadside megaliths were linked to one another in a series of centripetal accumulations. As Uzi Avner observes, "Travelers in all periods were exposed to many dangers and invoked the protection of the gods by means of various religious acts."[64] Thus we find in the Neolithic Sinai "an extraordinarily large number of cult sites of all types [that] have been located along these roads."[65] In fact, "The entire system of ancient roads [in Sinai] was in place by the fourth millennium, and almost every path used in the desert today was created thousands of years ago."[66] Whether the road or the megalith came first or both were part of an increasing border feedback loop, these territorial megaliths were the main centripetal attractors that were bound to the roadway and to one another through the roadway.

The second kinetic function of the territorial megalith follows from the first. Once a series of tombs or shrines has been erected and bound together through the roadway, these territorial megaliths begin to function like a perimeter or gateway around a territory. The territory is thus bound at its farthest limits by both its dead ancestors and its gods. It is the first mark a foreigner sees before entering. On one side of the megalith is the traveler who passes along the perimeter of a community of people who have died there; on the other side are the living descendants of the ancestor. Thus the territory is not simply the territory of the living but the territory of the dead marked by their vertical tombs and with the symbols and sacrifices regularly brought to them.[67] In this way the living and the dead are bound together, and to a delimited section of the earth, by the territorial megalith. If anything like a larger territorial border existed in the Neolithic period, it was certainly not marked by physical walls or gates but by gateways or boundaries of passage across which one walked into another community's bound territory.

The third kinetic function of the territorial megalith is informational or directional. Whether the megalith is or was a tomb or shrine, many territorial megaliths also provide information or direction to another communal attractor: a sanctuary, a spring or water source, the direction of another megalith or cairn, or a solstice marker.[68] They could also simply bear the band or banner of a given community in the area, thus rendering their territorial occupation visible.[69] For example, cairns or megaliths are quite common on hilltops because they can be seen from a distance and indicate a territorial claim or other informational content. Thus territorial megaliths are not strictly isolated from one another, but tied together into a network of mobility and directional reference toward or away from centripetal community occupations or use sites. Throughout history this same form of territorial megalith (stones buried in the ground) appears again and again from anthropomorphic Mongolian boundary statues called *balbals*, Mesopotamian stelae, and Greek boundary stones called *horos*, to modern road and border markers.

CONCLUSION

The fence is not only a material border technology first invented by Neolithic peoples, but part of a larger border regime of centripetal social force. In its most basic social kinetic definition the fence cuts into the earth and fills the hole with a vertical pile (dirt, wood, stone, and so on) in order to redirect a flow into a vertical limit junction. As a limit junction or border, the fence secures three basic kinetic functions required for social motion and circulation. First, it functions as a mark to centripetally expel the wild flows of the earth inward toward the corral of the pen, garden, or village. Second, it functions as a limit to expand and defend its centripetally accumulated stock with palisades. Third, it functions as a boundary to compel and symbolically bind several social junctions together into a single circulatory social system.

The fence introduces the first major kinopolitical divisions into the flows of the earth. It divides the earth from itself and creates the first social borders between people. However, the border regime of the fence is no mere relic of the past. Once it was invented by early humans, it persisted throughout history wherever we find the social practice of cutting up the body of the earth and compelling it into a centripetal accumulation: corrals that hunt down and capture disjoined flows (dragnets, manhunts, kettling); palisades that erect defensive stake structures to protect a kinetic stock (houses, plots of land, military limits); and megalith practices of verticality and directional signage that mark the boundaries of a territory (road signs, memorial sites, sacred sites). To be clear, fencing was not a border that emerges from a centralized power; it was a periphery or centripetal segmentation that creates the conditions for a socially central power in the first place. Only then did it become possible, as we see in the next chapter, for a centrifugal border power to emerge as dominant during the ancient period.

CHAPTER 3
The Wall

The second type of border is the wall. The wall, like the fence, is not only a set of empirical technologies for expanding, expelling, and compelling social movement, but also a regime of social force. Just as the border fence functions according to a centripetal motion that directs social motion inward, defending and binding it into various junctions, the wall regime also has its own kinetic logic. But this does not mean that the fence disappears. The wall appropriates or is added to the fence regime in a way that transforms its technologies and creates a new form of dominant social circulation.

In particular, the wall creates a centrifugal social motion that consolidates the centripetal accumulations of the previous fence regime into a central point and redirects them outward with a new force. Historically, centrifugal motion emerges as the dominant form of motion alongside the rise of the cities and ancient empires of Mesopotamia, Egypt, Rome, and Greece beginning around 3000 BCE, roughly during the period Gordon Childe refers to as the "Urban Revolution."[1] During this time humans began to independently transition from fenced-in agricultural villages to walled-off urban centers. Childe lists ten defining features of these urban centers: large populations, division of labor, the social appropriation of agricultural surplus, monumental architecture, ruling classes, writing, sciences (arithmetic, geometry, astronomy, calendars), sophisticated art styles, long-distance trade, and the state.[2] To this list we should add walls.

If settling down is the first major kinopolitical event, then urbanization is certainly the second. If the kinetic problem for Neolithic societies was how to capture the wild flows of the earth and bend them back onto themselves in the form of a delimited territory (the corral, the palisade, and the megalith), the kinetic problem for ancient societies is how to consolidate all of these dispersed local accumulations of social motion into a single center and redirect them outward through warfare, military defense, and transportation. In other words, once a variety of territorial circulations have been established through junctions, circuits, and limits, how can the life of these territories be further delimited into a distinctly political form of life—unified, centralized, and mobilized into a single megajunction? Thus the sedentary nature of urban life should also not be understood as a form of immobility. Ancient borders were not defined by fixed lines on a map but by political power. Urbanism only appears to be immobile from the perspective of the driver of the social vehicle who moves without moving: the king, the immobile motor. The wall is the border regime or motor that transforms all of society itself into a mechanism of transport in the service of centralized rule.

The wall creates a centrifugal or centralized social motion that is political in the kinetic sense in which it emerged alongside politics, as invented by the centralized cities of the ancient world—in Mesopotamia, Egypt, Greece, and Rome. The English word "politics" derives from the Greek word *polis*, meaning "city," which derives from the Proto-Indo-European root *pelə-*, meaning citadel or fortified high place. Politics required the city, and the city required the wall. It is not political society that builds the border, but the border wall that is the kinetic condition for the existence of political life itself. Without walls, ancient cities were quickly destroyed or conquered. Politics is thus first and foremost a kinetic logic whose division produces a distinctly political kind of life in the fortified city. The wall is what marks, limits, and bounds the social motion of political life.

THE KINETICS OF THE WALL

In order to further interpret the political meaning of the wall, we must first define the social kinetics of the wall. Just as the centripetal motion of the fence has two defining functions based on its kinetic definition, (1) to cut into the earth's flow, and (2) to centripetally fill the hole with a vertical junction, so the kinetic definition of the wall has two functions based on its split meaning and basic architectural motions: (1) to create bricks, and (2) stack them.[3] The wall is first of all related to a regime of military government and consolidated rule over the palisade fences that divide the people. The wall is the rule or government that unifies all the various divided subgroups into a higher unity while at the same time retaining the partition fences and organizing them into "bricks."[4] As Deleuze and Guattari write,

"The [fenced-in] blocks subsist, but have become encasted and embedded bricks, having only a controlled mobility."[5] The brick is a fenced-in mobility under centralized rule.

The old territorial fences become the building blocks of the wall that unifies them. As Kafka writes in "The Great Wall of China," to build a wall one must begin in a fragmentary way by creating human and territorial "bricks" or sections of wall. Accordingly, a social brick should not be understood simply as a baked ceramic building block, although it is this as well. A brick, in its social and kinetic definition, has several features. Like ceramic material, the brick is produced through a process of standardization. Ceramic bricks are made by digging up the earth and shaping it into blocks that are relatively identical in form and content. Ancient empires accomplished the same thing with people, as Kafka suggests. With the emergence of ancient cities and empires, the different regional groups, divided by their territorial fences, were put into a system of communication, taxation, transportation, trade, and monetization that standardized their relative social motions. They increasingly spoke a common language, traded, were taxed in similar currency, and so on. Second, just as the first kiln fired ceramic bricks (invented in 2600 BCE),[6] required a division of labor between the miners who dug up the clay or stone, the makers who shaped and fired them, and the masons who assembled them into walls, so the ancient empires instituted a similar division of labor on the people more broadly: priests, scribes, doctors, farmers, miners, sailors, soldiers, and so on. Third, a brick is marked or stamped with the symbol of centralized political rule. Ceramic bricks were frequently stamped with the same symbol that politically unified the people and branded the slaves and temples of the empire: the sign of the king, emperor, or city.

Kinetically, a single central model or mold is created of which all bricks are copies. All the bricks are copies that emerge and radiate outward centrifugally from this single mold. While the model remains relatively static and fixed, the finished bricks become mobile repetitions distributed to the periphery of the city. The wall is not a conceptual metaphor. Real material (clay) is molded according to a single central apparatus and then moved to the periphery of the city as a wall. The geometry of this movement is attested to clearly in Euclid's *Elements*: "A circle is a plane figure contained by a single line [which is called a circumference], (such that) all of the straight-lines *radiating towards [the circumference] from one point* amongst those lying inside the figure are equal to one another."[7] All the heterogeneous lines radiating outward become equal to one another by virtue of the limit of the circumference and the mold of a single common point: the center, from whence they originate. "To draw a circle," Euclid writes, all we need is "any center and radius."[8] When the radius is moved by rotation around the center, a circle is produced. To describe a wall, all we need is a central mold and a radial periphery the wall encircles with homogenous bricks.

The second kinetic function of the wall is the stacking of these social bricks. This function is different from the first inner processes of standardization, division, and marking of bricks.[9] If the first kinetic function of the wall was to create bricks through centralized rule (centrifugal social force), the second function is to assemble those bricks by stacking them. Stacking is a different motion than the piling found in Neolithic structures (the burial mounds, the stacked rocks of the megaliths, and so on). The pile or mound is the assembly of relatively heterogeneous or roughly shaped objects like stakes, stones, or earth. The stack, however, is a highly ordered horizontal or vertical assembly of standardized units resulting in a relatively smooth and highly ordered facade. This distinction between the pile and the stack wall is even given moral status by Greek historians like Plutarch, who contrast those who build walls by "heaping and piling up pell-mell every kind of material" with those who build virtuously, as if "'wrought on a golden base,' like the foundation of some holy or royal building . . . and adjust everything by the line and level of reason."[10] A cairn is a relatively ordered pile of stones, a fence is a relatively ordered pile of stakes or timber poles, but a wall is a highly ordered stack of bricks, built, as Plutarch writes, "according to reason." The "golden base" is the center from which the wall radiates upward and outward centrifugally, following the central command line of reason.

The emergence of walls is certainly a matter of degree without sharp historical breaks. For example, as early as 7000 BCE the protocity of Jericho was already making sun-dried mud bricks and vertically piling relatively homogenous stones into city walls and houses. However, these bricks were still very roughly shaped, did not require significantly skilled labor, and were not symbolically marked with the unifying seal of the king. Furthermore, Jericho and a few other cities were the exception to the rule. The vast majority of Neolithic villages did not start using bricks until around 3000 BCE, as they became cities.[11] However, if we were to locate an approximate break or shift in limological technologies, we could look to the invention and dominance of the kiln-fired brick, which closely parallels the rise of the cities and politics—the wall is their limological condition.[12] As archaeologist M. L. Smith writes, "For urbanism baked bricks seem to have been a precondition."[13]

The kinetic process of stacking thus presupposes the formation of highly standardized bricks, either pure ceramic or highly chiseled stone. The harder the bricks (high kiln temperatures plus bitumen) and the more standardized the bricks, the better their fit and collective strength in the wall and the smaller the gap between them that can be exploited by the enemy. Stacking thus accomplishes the following kinetic aims: (1) it minimizes the degree of mobility between the bricks by pushing them as close together as possible; (2) it creates a single continuous and smooth surface that controls both the movement of the enemy (smooth, hard walls are harder to scale and puncture) and the movement of the city or state (smooth, hard walls are also harder to escape from); and finally (3) it allows for a dramatic extension of vertical and horizontal motion of border walls that is not possible by piling alone. Even the largest Neolithic megaliths are dwarfed by the stacked bricks of the Egyptian pyramids, the Sumerian Ziggurats, and Roman temples and towers. Without the stacking of bricks, there would have been no ancient empires.

The kinetics of the wall are thus defined by two functions: the standardized, divided, and symbolized measurement of human and territorial flows (the brick) and the organized assembly of these bricks into a continuous surface (the stack). This continuous surface presupposes a centralized social force capable of directing the mining, firing, and stacking of bricks, but also radiates outward from this same power center: the temple, the palace, and the Acropolis (Greek ἄκρος, *ákros*, "highest, at the extremity"). For example, "The Assyrians required thousands of slaves to knead and mould the clay, fire the kilns, and build their walls, which in turn involved further punitive expeditions against vassal states which had not fulfilled their quotas of forced labor."[14] This in turn caused other states to want to build walls, which required more slave labor, which required more warfare, and so on, in a feedback loop of social circulation requiring ever-expanding outward circuits of slave raids, centralized command, and larger walls. This is the sense in which the wall is a centrifugal social force—organized, assembled, and directed outward from a centralized power. But like the fence, the wall also has three distinct limological aspects: the mark, the limit, and the boundary, all of which work on the disjuncted flows of the barbarian frontier. Accordingly, the remainder of this chapter will develop these three aspects as they are expressed in three major types of ancient wall technologies: the military wall, the rampart wall, and the port wall.

THE MILITARY WALL

The first type of wall is the military wall, defined by the marking and marching function of the border. The military wall is historically expressed in three major border technologies: soldiers, surveyors, and siege towers.

Each functions according to a centrifugal and offensive social force that creates bricks of homogenized matter, stacks them in a compact formation, and marches them outward to expand social kinetic power at the periphery.

The Soldier

The first major military border technology is the creation of soldiers. This may sound strange since we often think of walls as made primarily of stone or clay and other inanimate material. However, before the creation of the first fired-brick walls (2600 BCE) came the creation of a specialized body of weaponized and armored men in military service to a central leader (at least by 3000 BCE, in Sumer and Akkad).[15] The soldier is the human brick stacked into the military wall. As Lewis Mumford writes, "The earliest complex power machines were composed, not of wood or metal, but of perishable human parts, each having a specialized function in a larger mechanism under centralized human control."[16] Soldiers do not simply enforce the border but physically constitute the border itself as they march forward in the military extension of the city or state. The soldier is thus a human wall not only in the sense in which it marches outward (centrifugally) bearing the mark (flag, crest, and so on) of its political center, but also in the kinopolitical sense in which it functions as a standardized and ordered border technology. It is thus more likely that the idea for building a fired-brick wall was inspired by the standardization and military formation of the soldier rather than the other way around. The human machine comes first, then the fired-brick wall becomes the substitute for soldiers. As Aristotle writes, "The strongest wall will be the truest soldierly precaution."[17] The wall stands so that the soldier does not have to.

The soldier is first constituted as a human brick in the sense that he is standardized into a homogenous military block or unit under central command. In Assyria soldiers were divided into units of fifty to two hundred men.[18] In Egypt one source from a battle in 1274 BCE reports that soldiers were members of a fifty-man platoon or *sa*.[19] In Rome legionaries were grouped into *manipuli* and then into *centuriae*.[20] An army is a wall or "column" (rank and file) of ordered units of soldiers. The column is first one of soldiers and only later architectural. Each individual is placed in its homogeneous block, and each block is stacked into its military formation—like the segments of a column. This is not a metaphor.

Once an agricultural surplus is accumulated in a central granary it becomes possible to create a standing or unproductive professional division of soldiers, typically fed from the granary, to further defend the granary, temple, or palace and enforce the centralized will of the king or leader.[21] In this way soldiers are one of the few uniquely unproductive professions whose job it is to destroy. But insofar as their physical bodies are the technical product itself, they are productive of the military body or "metabolic vehicle."[22] Their training into ordered bricks or units is precisely the productive process of which their own bodies are the standardized product. The standardized body of the soldier was, from the beginning of ancient warfare, "hardened" with armor, specifically with the invention of the shield. With the invention of the standardized shield and armor the first armies of shielded soldiers could then be marched and mobilized into battle as a smooth and mobile war wall. Just as many ancient Roman kiln-fired bricks bear the symbolic mark of the imperial consuls or emperors,[23] so do many ancient soldiers' shields and armor bear the symbolic marking, crest, flag, or colors of the centralized power.

The soldier is then organized into a stack of human bricks in the military configuration and directed outward from a command center. The defining military formation used by almost every major army of the ancient world was the phalanx.[24] The phalanx, from the Greek word φάλαγξ, meaning both the bone of a finger or toe and a group of people standing or moving closely together, is a human wall of soldiers, composed of a tightly grouped unit of soldiers with shields and weapons. The soldiers overlap as tightly as possible to create a continuous shield wall and restrict enemy penetration. The Greeks and Romans also used an even more defensive version of the phalanx called the *testudo*, or tortoise formation, in which the first row of the phalanx square faced its shields forward and the rows behind put their shields up (to defend projectiles), sacrificing mobility for defense. The military is a moving human wall.

In battle the two competing walls of soldiers collide and try to break through the other's wall. As its name suggests, the phalanx is the hardened core of the outstretched expanding imperial appendage of power. Where it goes, the border extends its grasp. Accordingly, the ancient concept of the border was not restricted to the idea of a geographical limit. For ancient city-states and empires, the border was strictly kinopolitical: where the king and his army can go, there is the border. Thus the border is mobile, fluid, metabolic, and synonymous with the process of the military march and what it is able to mark out as it moves. For example, after military conquest the Romans would mark out the new territory with a system of administrative wooden stakes, appropriately called "palisades," literally "city stakes" from the Latin *palus* (stake or pole), from the PIE root **pelə-* (citadel).[25] These marks in progress often constituted the future borders of a new town (city).

The soldier wall also marks a central point in the city from which it marches outward to the periphery, extending the border. According to Mumford, in the center courts of many ancient cities we find "the first housing for such military functionaries, the barracks,"[26] and broad streets in cities like Ur or Lagash designed precisely for the centrifugal march of the soldiers and their centripetal return of loot (treasure and slaves) to the city.[27] The architecture of the early city—its walls, roads, and institutions— made it, as Mumford says, "a container of organized violence and a trans- mitter of war."[28] Once the military border of soldiers is marched out of the city, they mark the countryside with the blood of battle, steel, stones, camps, or new cities, and then return back to the center: the city-bunker.[29]

Geodesy

The second major military border technology is the invention of geodesy and the creation of surveyors. Surveyors emerged as the instruments of military science by which a centrifugal state power marked its center and measured its borders. Land surveying, as Leroi-Gourhan writes, is the means by which "the farthest confines of the earth are connected by the symbolic radii of the wheel of distances."[30] Geodesy, the division and mea- surement of the land, is a wall technology in the sense that it creates a stan- dardized bricking and ordered stacking of the earth. It creates a horizontal wall that divides the surface of the earth into standardized mathematical parcels and orders them into a contiguous property border. It presupposes a centralized and hierarchal division of labor and specialized training for scribes and military scientists and marks the earth with an abstract survey line. It then orders these parcels together into a total and continuous area under centralized administration and centrifugal rule.

Aerial images of farming plots along the Nile River, the Greek city of Miletus, and Roman colonial towns all reveal precisely the grid image of the wall. Border walls are made of more than clay and stone; they are the geo- metrical grid plan thrust onto the earth itself. Geodesy turns the earth and social life into a grid wall and then builds vertical walls on top of it in the form of temples, palaces, city walls, houses, and so on.[31] The survey wall is thus a military wall because ancient surveyors were almost always military engineers whose work was concerned with the security of the city-state (property law and taxes, public works, and political borders).

Ancient geodesy is a centrifugal kinopower in the political and archi- tectural sense. Politically, its conditions of emergence are the centralized political powers of ancient kings and rulers who used geodesy to measure and divide various aspects of their land for the security of the state. Architecturally, geodesy emerged as a metric science of lines, angles, and polygons (not curves) that all presuppose a point or axis (the place where two or more lines meet) and from which they radiate. As Lewis Mumford observes in the rise of the ancient city, "Male symbolisms and abstractions now become manifest: they show themselves in the insistent straight line, the rectangle, the firmly bounded geometric plan, the phallic tower and the obelisk, finally, in the beginnings of mathematics and astronomy, whose effective abstractions were progressively detached from the variegated matrix of myth. It is perhaps significant that while the early cities seem largely circular in form, the ruler's citadel and the sacred precinct are more usually enclosed by a rectangle."[32]

The geodetic military wall is attested to in several major ancient empires and early civilizations. In Babylonia, border stones called *kudurus* recorded the exact geometrical measurement, in cubits, reeds, rods, and cords, of landed property because border disputes under King Hammurabi were common.[33] For these purposes Hammurabi created some of the first military engineers and mapmakers to keep track of these records and mark the continually shifting borders of property, military kingdom, and world in latitudes, weights, and measures. A cuneiform tablet (circa 1300 BCE) from Nippur, Mesopotamia, lays out the measurements of all the regional fields, canals, townships, and royal land in square and polygonal units, with the palace at the center.[34] This can be seen in the Babylonian pictorial and symbolical representations of cultivated land as a rectangle of fifteen squares.[35] These measurements were important for the collection of taxes and the construction of buildings. Thus the Akkadian word *kisurrû* means both "border" and "outline or plan of a building."[36] From the beginning, there was a connection between borders and architecture. The ancient Babylonians even invented a measurement for calculating the quantity of standardized bricks in a given area, including a measure called the "brick garden," holding 720 bricks.[37]

In Egypt, geodesy was also directly linked to the military enforcement of taxation and squared property borders. As Herodotus writes,

The priests also said that this king [perhaps Sesostris II of Egypt (1897–1878 BCE)] divided the country among all the Egyptians, giving each an equal square plot. This was the source of his revenue, as he made them pay a fixed annual tax. If some of anyone's land was taken away by the river, he came to the king and told him what had happened. Then the king sent men to look at the land and measure how much less it was, so that in the future the owner would pay the due proportion. It seems to me that land survey started from this and passed on to

Greece. The concave sundial and the division of the day in twelve were learnt by the Greeks from the Babylonians.[38]

Egyptian scribes were sent out to flooded lands to keep a measure of the floods and changing property areas using a survey instrument called a *merkhet*, an "instrument of knowing," consisting of a holder with a short plumb line and plummet.[39] With the help of this instrument, Egyptian surveyors achieved incredible accuracy. For example, the measurements of the Great Pyramid are almost exactly square at the base (440 royal cubits).[40] From this central point, the peak of the pyramid, the grid radiates out centrifugally in a cardinal axis to the celestial poles. Badawy points out this same orthogonal and axial structure—two main streets crossing at right angles in the center—in the military fortresses built on the Nile in the Twelfth Dynasty. Fairman also points it out in Egyptian towns already enclosed in brick walls during the Negada II period:[41] "On the stone palettes of the late pre-dynastic and early dynastic times, towns are shown as circles or ovals, surrounded by stout walls and often provided with buttresses. This perhaps explains the otherwise inexplicable hieroglyph for a city, an oval or circular enclosure, whose crossroads (if they are crossroads) divide the city into four quarters. If this is in fact a symbolic plan, it would be the best possible symbol for the classic city."[42] Thus, fortress, camp, tomb, and city have a common base in Egyptian military regimentation.[43] The connection between religion and geodesy is also made clear in the statue of the god Pa-en-hor from Abydos that holds a rolled measuring cord in his hand.[44] Geodesy was the mathematics of the celestial tombs of the Pharaohs, and it was the military art of constructing some of the largest desert fortress-cities (*mnnw*) like Buhen of the New Kingdom.[45]

The Greeks, as Herodotus notes, believed they learned geodesy from the Egyptians. But for several reasons, both geographical and military, we see Greek geodesy of the grid-wall type most clearly in the city planning of the colonies outside Greece, where centralized planning was more prevalent.[46] For example, after an enormous fire at the end of the sixth century BCE, the Greek colony of Oblia was rebuilt from scratch by the centrifugal military planning of Greek colonists as a grid wall of stacked uniform squares. However, not all grid-planned cities were in Greek colonies. After the second Persian invasion of Greece, the military general and politician Themistocles began rebuilding the city of Piraeus in 493 BCE as an ultrafortified military harbor surrounded by enormous walls, *neosoikoi* (ship houses), and an enormous long wall stretching all the way to Athens. Under the militarization of the Piraeus, Hippodamus was called on to redesign the entire city as a rectilinear grid wall or brick city. "The city itself," as Mumford observes, "was composed of such standardized block units: their rectangular open spaces, used for agora or temple, were in turn simply empty blocks."[47] Following this same military wall model, Hippodamus redesigned his own city of Miletus in 479 BCE and later took part in the military grid planning of the Greek colony at Thurii in southern Italy.[48] Strabo reports that such rectilinear planning often began at a single central point and radiated outward in the cardinal directions into grids. For example, in the military city of Nicaea, "built [as a defense] against the barbarians who dwelt higher up the country"[49] because it was "mountainous and fortified by nature," was "quadrangular," with "four gates. Its streets [were] divided at right angles, so that the four gates may be seen from a single stone, set up in the middle of the Gymnasium."[50] Aristophanes similarly depicts the ideas of another fifth century BCE Greek surveyor, Meton: "With this straight ruler here I measure this, so that your circle here becomes a square—and right in the middle there we have a marketplace, with straight highways proceeding to the centre, like a star, which, although circular, shines forth straight beams in all directions."[51]

However, unless the Greeks were designing an overmilitarized city like Piraeus, they tended not to impose the military grid wall against their own people, since it was extremely unpopular. For the most part, the grid wall functioned as a colonial weapon against barbarians. As such, it became almost universal among Greek colonies by the third century BCE:[52] "The standard gridiron plan in fact was an essential part of the kit of tools a colonist brought with him for immediate use. The colonist had little time to get the lay of the land or explore the resources of a site: by simplifying his spatial order, he provided for a swift and roughly equal distribution of building lots. . . . Within the shortest possible time, everything was brought under control."[53]

Among ancient civilizations, the military function of the grid wall is most strikingly apparent in the Romans. Not only did early Romans follow the Greek tradition of marking out the borders of a new town by plowing a furrow around and through it symbolically repeated in the Greek festival of Helenia and Roman festival of Terminus, but they also divided the inner area into square plots around a central axis (*cardo*).[54] "The surveyor of state lands which were to be allocated would start at a chosen point and plot a *limes*, or dividing line, in each of the four directions planned, which often corresponded approximately to the four cardinal points. The squares which these delimited . . . were called *centuriae*, 'centuries,' because they theoretically contained 100 plots of the early size of smallholding."[55] Similarly, when Virgil depicts Aeneas founding a city in Sicily, he writes, "Aeneas marks the city out by ploughing (*sulcus primigenus*); then he draws the homes by lot"[56] and begins to institute law and political order from his central court. The founding of a new city and the centrifugal political division of land go hand in hand.

However, Roman borders were not fixed or absolute. As limologist Jacques Ancel writes, "The empire is a power, not a territory."[57] Accordingly, the division of land (border geodesy) arises from conquest, as the Roman surveyor Siculus Flaccus explains: "As the Romans became the masters of all nations, they divided up the land captured from the enemy among the victors."[58] "War," he writes, "created the motive for dividing up land" because the spoils were given to the soldiers who had seized it.[59] These same rectilinear land divisions often became the city plan for the new colonies that followed in the wake of the army's military march.

This was accomplished through the use of military *agrimensores* (*ager* "territory," + *mensor* "a measurer"): Roman surveyors. *Agrimensores* not only measured land, they also marked borders and planned the construction of new colonial cities as the military marched across the land. Measure, mark, plan: the holy trinity of the grid wall. Accordingly, Roman surveyors were a crucial part of the expanding imperial army. On their military march they were responsible for measuring and planning the army's camp (*castra*) each night. The surveyors would first "stake out the center line of the camp (*decumanus maximus*) crossed by its axis (*Cardo maximus*). These two lines formed the basis of two pathways bisecting the camp, the *via principalis* about 30 metros wide. All the various *strigae* (or rectangular spaces where the tents were to be erected) were marked off, as were the corners of the square of oblong camp."[60]

In the center of the camp the general's tent served as the basis of operations from which orders were centrifugally directed outward. After this military tent city was erected, it was quickly fortified with a wall (*vallum*) of stakes and earth around its perimeter and redoubts (*castella*) and the gates and four corners. When the army moved forward the next day, the camp was left behind as "Caesar's camp." "When the Roman Empire ceased expanding and entered upon its phase of settled occupation, it was simply a matter of making permanent structures out of temporary camps; architecture out of fieldworks."[61] By repeating this strategy as it marched, the Romans were largely responsible for the colonial implantation of the military grid wall across all of western Europe and Britain and eventually to their subsequent colonies around the world.

Siege Tower

The third major military border technology is the siege tower. The siege tower is quite literally a mobile military border wall (*turres ambulatoriae* or *turres mobiles*). The siege tower looks as if it is part of a city wall that has broken loose by centrifugal force and flung itself head-on into the enemy's city walls. Ancient warfare could perhaps be called "the clash of walls": of phalanx walls, of grid walls, and siege walls. In particular, the siege wall conjoins the previous two walls by combining the human soldier wall with the military architecture wall. These wheeled walls could be up to ten stories high and contain hundreds of stacked soldier bricks and weapons like battering rams or drawbridges at various levels throughout, like the *helepolis*, the taker of cities. The walls themselves were mostly built of wood and covered with interlocking metal plates or leather hides to protect them from catching fire. Once the siege tower reached the enemy's city wall, it either used its weapons to destroy it or used its bridges (*sambucae*) to put soldiers across the border. Smaller siege walls like the tortoise (*testudine*) or vine arbor (*vinea*) were totally enclosed structures that protected siege engineers while they tried to penetrate the city wall. As a military wall, the siege wall's power marks the expanding and mobile political border.

THE RAMPART WALL

The second type of wall is the rampart wall, defined by the defensive limit of the border. The rampart wall is historically expressed in three major border technologies: the citadel, tower, and the territory. Each functions according to a centrifugal and defensive social force that conjoins bricks of homogenized matter and stacks them in a compact formation around a protected center. Thus the rampart (from *emparer*, to defend, fortify, surround, seize, take possession of) is a dividing wall that defends by surrounding.[62] The rampart accomplishes not only a centripetal division between inside and outside like the territorial fence, it is a redivision or repossession that "reacts back on the hunter-gatherers, imposing upon them agriculture, animal raising, an extensive division of labor, etc.; it acts, therefore, in the form of a centrifugal or divergent wave."[63] The rampart is a dividing wall that connects back with itself in a looped junction to surround the city or territory with fortifications. Although we often think of border walls as emerging at the outer limits of a territory, the earliest clay-brick walls actually emerged from the center and moved centrifugally outward.

The Citadel

The first type of rampart wall is the citadel. The citadel, or "little city," likely grew out of previous palisade fences around sacred sites that were meant to create social divisions between living and dead, terrestrial and celestial, the community and foreigners, and even provide safety against evil spirits or predatory animals. The citadel wall is different from the palisade fence in several important ways. First, the earliest walled citadels functioned not only as centripetal conjunctions of flows (of sacred objects, dead ancestors, foodstuffs, and so on), but as centrifugal controls over the outflow of social kinetic stock by an increasingly powerful chieftain, ruler, or king. The early citadel was the first megajunction or holding point where agricultural surplus could be withheld from the villagers. "He who controlled the annual agricultural surplus exercised the powers of life and death of his neighbors."[64] In this way, the sacred site also becomes the fortified stronghold: each refortifies (ramparts) the other.

Since "shrines occupied the central place in preliterate villages in Mesopotamia," as Childe reports,[65] at some point the stronghold and citadel wall must have emerged from them. From Uruk to Harappa, almost all Mesopotamian cities had a walled citadel, even if the rest of the town had no walls or permanent structures.[66] Within the citadel one finds three types of baked-brick walls whose height and thickness are significantly out of proportion to the military means that then existed for assaulting them: the palace, the granary, and the temple.[67] Therefore, although the early citadel likely emerged from the defensive sacred palisade,[68] it increasingly protected two intertwined political and sacred social forces and centrifugally controlled social circulation according to a single ruler-god or priest-king like Gilgamesh.

> Of ramparted Uruk the wall he built,
> Of hallowed Eanna the pure sanctuary. . . .
> Is not its brickwork of burnt brick?[69]

The citadel thus precedes the city, but from this "little city" politico-religious kinopower slowly expanded its citadel wall outward in all directions. Accordingly, the invention of the city wall is first and foremost a centrifugal extension or refortification (rampart) of the citadel wall. The two walls are the expression of the same central kinopower. The city follows the same logic of centrally concentrated and controlled mobility that the citadel does, but in this refortification the citadel remains the "political nucleus . . . dominating the entire social structure and giving centralized direction to activities that had once been dispersed and undirected, or at least locally self-governed."[70]

In Egypt the rampart walls of the pyramids and temples were rivaled only by those of their military fortresses as they slowly expanded their citadel walls outward down the Nile River. After the march wall of Egyptian soldiers marked out new land through warfare, a new city-fortress marked the limit to which the next flow of soldiers could return defensively. The series of city-fortresses down the Nile River could then be used as relay points in the supply line back to the centrifugal command center. The march wall goes out, and the limit wall fortifies and returns, completing the border circuit and defending it. During the Middle Kingdom (2052–1786) the sole purpose of border citadels was to defend the provision of accommodation and supplies for frontier troops.[71] These were not offensive walls. With Sesostris III's creation of city-fortresses along the West bank of the Nile and along the Nubian border, the rampart technology of the ancient Mediterranean world reached its apex in 1860 BCE. The city-fortress of Buhen, for example, covered 140,000 square feet and held over thirty-five hundred people, including administrators for the whole region.[72] The rampart itself included a moat ten feet deep, drawbridges, bastions, buttresses, battlements, loopholes for archers, and a catapult.[73] As cities, these fortresses were orthogonally planned as concentric extensions of the innermost ramparts (citadels) of a central square or rectangular building.

In Greece most city walls surrounded a central temple-citadel (acropoliss) that functioned as a defensive refuge with military and food supplies, the shrine of the god, and a royal palace. When the military march reaches its limits or must retreat to the center, it hastens a retreat to its most secure and minimal limit: the acropolis. From the central point of this military/temple/palace, the city also radiates outward and around. As "the Athenian" describes it in Plato's *Laws*, "We will divide the city into twelve portions, first founding temples to Hestia, to Zeus and to Athene, in a spot that we will call the Acropolis, and surround with a circular wall, making the division of the entire city and country *radiate from this point*."[74] Later in the same dialogue the Athenian again makes clear the kinopolitical primacy of this center point by arguing that it should be the only walled rampart of the city because a city wall "never contributes anything to a town's health, and in any case is apt to encourage a certain softness in the souls of the inhabitants. It invites them to take refuge behind it instead of tackling the enemy and ensuring their own safety by mounting guard night and day,"[75] as is done by the Spartan soldier wall. However, he admits, "If men are to have a city wall at all, the private houses should be constructed right from the foundations so that the whole city forms in effect a single wall."[76] This position, rejected outright by Aristotle,[77] is perhaps the strongest ancient statement of kinopolitical identification between the acropolis-city and the rampart wall. For the Athenian military architecture, urban planning, political power, and religious practice become identical with the social kinetics of the wall diagram. Given the military history of

Athens and its penchant for building enormous walls (the long walls and the Piraeus), it is not surprising that Plato, an Athenian, attributes this position to "the Athenian." Furthermore, it is not surprising that Athens, birthplace of Western philosophy, also gave rise to Socratic philosophers who often defined philosophy and wisdom itself as an "impregnable walled stronghold."[78] The mind is the citadel-wall of the city-body.[79]

The Territorial Wall

The second type of rampart is the territorial wall. The territorial-limit wall is a defensive wall, but not in the sense in which the citadel operates as an inner and ultimate limit. The rampart is bounded by two limits: an inner ultimate limit after which the people are exterminated, and an outer indefinite limit that follows behind and supports the conquering military march wall of the phalanx, *castrum* grid, and siege wall. Like all border limits, the territorial wall does not define a permanent or fixed place, but a defensive buffer zone or supply line that retraces the military march. Territorial walls are not meant to stop all movement across the border, but to surveil, patrol, and provide resources for military border walls. They are defensive walls in the sense in which they provide support and service for the border, a place where offensive military operations might fall back to temporarily as a refuge, like an outer citadel. In other words, the border wall has two sides: the side that faces outward (the military wall) and the side that faces inward (the rampart wall). This was demonstrated above in the case of Egyptian city-fortresses, but is most apparent in the ancient society with the most extensive system of territorial limit walls (*limes*), the Romans.

As the Roman military marched forward from the center centrifugally, its *agrimensores* would measure, mark, and plan the *castra*. The line of the march, from *castrum* to *castrum*, defined both the territorial borders in progress of the empire and the supply roads that connected the *castra* to one another and back to Rome. These supply lines were then developed into a vast system of roadways that also functioned as borders between towns and property. Although related, the *agrimensores* manuals clearly distinguished between the territorial limit or *limes* and the purely abstract straight lines of surveying that have no width, or *rigors*.[80] The rigor is the surveyor's *mark*, but the *limes* is the path, track, or zone of the supply route connecting the *castra* together in the service of, and not identical to, offensive military operations.[81] As Piganiol confirms, the "*limes*, in the time of Domitian and Trajan, was a military road in the *service of* offensive policies.

From the time of Hadrian, it was a frontier line whose significance was more juridical than military".[82] Thus the *limes* were not fixed lines with zero width, but routes, zones, vectors, rivers, paths, or tracks that were constantly in motion and negotiation.

This is the case even with more fortified *limites* like Hadrian's Wall, the Devil's Wall, and Antonine's Wall. None of these walls were built to stop movement or be an absolute border between Romans and barbarians. Even in the case of the largest and most fortified, Hadrian's Wall, it could not possibly have defended against a full-scale barbarian attack,[83] although it was probably effective in holding off smaller invasions.[84] The wall was easily scaled, and its thirty-two guards per mile would have been easily defeated long before any help could come from Eboracum, Lindum, or Deva.[85] The real military walls of soldiers and *castra* were all stationed on the offensive (barbarian) side of the wall and well beyond it, engaged in battle, not defending the wall.[86] Thus, according to the later Byzantine historian Procopius, there is a technical distinction between two types of Roman troops: the *limitanei* (who man the *limites*) and the *comitatenses, palatini*, and *scolae* (who fight in battle).[87] The *limitanei* were patrol troops that were prepared to temporarily hold off the barbarians, not heavy infantry or cavalry intended for military expansion and conquest.[88] In fact, like the citadel, the *limites* may have been much more effective at retaining flows of colonized labor and producing Roman subjects through restricted mobility than they were at preventing barbarian invasion.[89]

The Roman *limes* were territorial walls insofar as they were routes or supply paths that had been fortified into long stretches of wall, punctuated by outposts, forts, and *limitanei*. For instance, the *Limes Germanicus*, the "Devil's Wall," was a massive 173-mile-long wall with palisades and ditches. It supported a chain of approximately fifty-five auxiliary forts, connected together by "a sophisticated road system ensuring legionary reinforcement from garrison towns in the rear."[90] Far from static, it underwent significant modification over 148 times under emperor Antoninus Pius.[91] Although the building of these incredible territorial border walls may seem like a testimony to the strength of the Roman Empire, it is in fact the opposite. The building of such extensive territorial walls only becomes necessary once the military wall has reached its maximum march and needs to retreat to its limits, and restrain its own colonial population from defection.[92] As Roman historian Cunliffe puts it, "By the second century CE the core—the Roman Empire—had grown so quickly that it had engulfed its periphery without fully integrating it."[93] The rampart wall appears when the military wall has reached its limit.

THE PORT WALL

The third and final type of wall is the port wall, defined by the passage across and through the border's boundary. As the military wall marches outward and the rampart wall fortifies the path or route left behind, the port wall compels or binds flows into a regime of recirculation by controlling their passage across the border. It is the type of wall that imports, exports, deports, reports, and transports. If the wall has two sides—the military and the rampart—the port is between the two and ensures their communication. It draws on both military force for taxation and the rampart for security. Accordingly, a port can occur at any wall with a controlled gate or opening where flows can port over from one side to the other. The wall supports a passage and regulates the circulation and mobility of various social flows at each concentric level. There were at least three major types of ports in the ancient world: transports, city ports, and territorial ports.

Transport

The first port wall is the transport wall, which regulates the circulation across borders. The historical rise of centrifugal kinopower and the transportation revolution emerge together. The two require each other. Without an expanded system of transportation and roads, it is difficult for a central administration to centripetally collect resources, people, and taxes from the countryside, and difficult to centrifugally enforce military control, adjudicate property disputes, and engage in long-distance trade and border defense. On the other hand, without a central administration it is not possible to enforce the division of labor necessary for the creation of a military large enough to force peasants to build roads (corvée), create military engineers to plan them, or enforce roads as borders. Thus it is not society that first creates the border, but a kinetic border regime of centrifugal force that is the mutual condition for the concrete technical objects of the road, the military, taxation, kingship, society, and so on, which all presuppose one another.

The transportation wall is the kinotechnical object that allowed the states of the ancient world to create a series of social divisions between the temple, city, countryside, and periphery, and that facilitated the resonance between them. Transportation in the ancient empires combined the centripetal force of accumulation and the centrifugal force of administration into a continual circulation between inside and outside. Orders and laws from inside (kings, pharaohs, emperors, princes, and so on) flowed

out across the borders and towns; things and people returned and reso-
nated in accordance with the military power of the of the divine king. This
is attested to from Mesopotamia to Rome. All ancient empires built military transportation systems of roads, bridges, and waterways that all led
back to the central city. For most of history, the road has served a primarily military function directly related to state warfare: the rapid movement
of troops and the supply of construction materials.[94] "Transportation," as
Lewis Mumford writes, "was the most dynamic element in the city, apart
from war."[95] But the two are related: they share the same centrifugal heart,
as Paul Virilio observes: "Transport is at the heart of the State apparatus
just as it is at the heart of war."[96] The ability to centrifugally expand the
border, to mobilize troops (the military walls), and to build defenses (the
rampart walls) fundamentally depends on transport. It is this attempt to
overcome the kinetic paradox of centrifugal power that Kafka so beauti-
fully depicts in "A Message from the Emperor": that centralized rule is the
victim of its own immense size, limited by the time it takes to traverse
its own borders. In Kafka's story the emperor sends a message, "but the
crowds are so vast; their dwellings boundless" that the message never ar-
rives.[97] In other words, the aim of centrifugal kinopower depends precisely
on the power to come and go between the center and periphery as it wishes,
when it wishes.[98]

Social transportation (foot trails, rivers, and ocean transport) predated
the ancient period, but the emergence of ancient kinopower invented a
whole new transport technology and border regime. Ancient kinopower
was not satisfied with natural passages alone, but added to them a new network of centrally directed and constructed transport walls: the road wall,
the water wall, and the bridge wall.

The road functions as a horizontal wall,[99] or the rampart wall functions
as a vertical road. The two emerged together as expressions of the same
border technology around 2000 BCE: the brick and the stack. The paving of
a road is simply stacking by other means, but the rampart wall and the road
also have different border functions. While the rampart wall has a largely
defensive purpose, the road supports the passage, transport, and portage
of people and goods between borders via the border itself. Most ancient
roadways functioned not only as a means of transport from one end to another, but also as political, geographical, and spiritual borders between one
side and another. Roadways were either constructed on top of existing territorial divisions—graves, shrines, dirt paths, along rivers, and so on—or
established new social divisions as a result of their construction.

Paved roads first emerged in the center of ancient cities to mark the
politico-sacred border between the central temple and other areas of the

city,[100] and then moved centrifugally outward. This is attested to in many Mesopotamian cities like Khafaje, Babylon, Ur, Assur, and Asmar, where the first roadways were the processional brick roads, bonded with bitumen, that led to the central temple.[101] In 615 BCE, King Nebuchadnezzar described the three-layer brick processional road built by his father, Nabopolassar, as "glistening with asphalt and burnt brick. . . . Placed above the bitumen and burnt brick [was] a mighty superstructure shining with limestone," known as "the street that no enemy ever trod."[102] From this central temple road a vast network of backed brick roads eventually radiated outward into the countryside like the radiation of spiritual and military power over the periphery.[103] The Assyrian kings were also the first to assemble a road-building engineer corps, or *ummani*, as part of the military.[104] According to King Esarhaddon, the aim of this massive road system throughout the kingdom was to facilitate commerce and military control.[105] In Persia as well, roads were a necessity for maintaining military control over and extracting taxes from a landlocked empire.[106] For this purpose the Persian king Darius the Great (Darius I) built the Royal Road from Sardes on the Aegean coast to Suza near the Persian Gulf to transport commerce and war from port to port. If centralized power is only as strong as its transportation walls and "there is nothing in the world that travels faster than the Persian couriers," as Herodotus remarks,[107] then the Persian Empire was certainly one of the strongest.

Although Greece's rocky countryside and abundance of seaports meant that most transport occurred by the "wooden walls"[108] of ships, Greek brick-paved roadways still played an important border function. Beginning around 2000 BCE and peaking around 1000 BCE,[109] the paved roads of Greece supported social divisions between property, municipal, and administrative areas, as well as spiritual areas between the living and the dead whose graves lined the roadways near cities. The Y junctions or crossroads of the Greek road system became temples and shrines with statues of Hermes (god of transport) and Hecate (god of magical passage) that marked the transport border between gods and mortals, life and death.[110]

Above all, the Roman system of roads was the most extensive and advanced, built on all the previous road-making knowledge of other civilizations—Greek masonry, Etruscan cement, Carthaginian pavement, and Egyptian surveying.[111] Like other road systems, the Roman system was designed, constructed, and maintained largely by centrally governed military forces and slave labor (corvée). Where the military wall of soldiers and surveyors expanded the empire they left behind them a grid wall of *castra*, orthogonal *colonias*, and rampart *limites* that could then be connected by paved roadways capable of supporting wheeled transportation two chariots wide.[112] According to Strabo, these roadways were then marked with pillars every ten stadia to indicate the measures and distances between other roads, which radiated out from and returned to the Golden Milestone (*miliarium aureum*) in Rome—the political and spiritual center. On the stone was inscribed the distances to all the major cities of the empire in the name of the *Curatores Viarum*, Julius Caesar, the "Director of the Great Roads." In addition to paved city streets that socially divided Roman cities into neighborhoods (*vici*) or quarters (*quartus,* the division proper to the orthogonal city bricks or blocks), roads outside the city also defined municipal boundaries, as Pliny the Elder confirms.[113] These boundaries were then used to enforce taxes and control the local circulation that often paid for the roads' maintenance.[114]

The Romans were also the most advanced in the construction of other transport walls like the bridge and the aqueduct. With the increasing usage of wheeled vehicles, brick bridges became crucial and frequently connected two sides of one of the most common geographical and political borders: rivers. The bridge is a transport between and through the border itself. Roman bridges were effectively walls that traversed two sides of the river, allowing passage. The concept of the bridge wall brilliantly combines the territorial wall and the road wall by transforming the top of the wall into a site of transportation. The Roman bridge is thus superior to all previous bridges because of this insight: instead of simply traversing the river or valley laterally, it inserts a wall into it vertically. The river then passes through the wall via the supporting arches, modeled on centrifugal geometry of the circle. As a port, bridges were also a common site for the control of passage, customs, and taxation.[115] The aqueduct or water wall functions in much the same way, except the control over the hydraulic flows of water in many places also meant control over life and death. Both the bridge wall and water wall maintain divisions in social flows: who gets in, who gets water, and who dies.

City Ports

The second major type of port wall is the city port. The city port is a wall that is both continuous with the city wall and discontinuous insofar as it functions as a kind of sieve or valve that regulates the flows of the city. The citadel and city walls presuppose the port wall, just as the port wall presupposed the city walls. They are two functions of the same border regime. Thus borders are poorly conceived of as immobile or as simply stopping movement. Border walls are a political invention for the selective regulation of movement in and between the three areas of political circulation: inside, outside, and passage. The circulatory importance of the port wall is a regulated passageway between the inside and outside, through the port. The regulation of this passage keeps the concentric circles of social kinetic power in proper relation to one another without collapsing them, and makes it possible to extract a surplus from their bounded passage.

Almost as long as there have been cities, and thus politics, there have been walled passages that extracted a kinetic tax on imports and exports from the passengers. As Herodotus reports:

> Babylon then was walled in this manner; and there are two divisions of the city; for a river whose name is Euphrates parts it in the middle.... The wall then on each side has its bends carried down to the river, and from this point the return walls stretch along each bank of the stream in the form of a rampart of baked bricks: and the city itself is full of houses of three and four stories, and the roads by which it is cut up run in straight lines, including the crossroads that lead to the river; and opposite to each road there were set gates in the rampart that ran along the river, in many in number as the ways, and these also were of bronze and led like the ways to the river itself.[116]

In this way Babylon positioned itself not only as a city port but a port-city whose gates absolutely controlled all passage down the Euphrates to the Erythraian Sea. As its name *Babilli* suggests, the entire city itself was considered "The Gate of God."[117] Just as transport is the "most dynamic element of the city," so the lack of transport, as Mumford observes, "was a threat to its growth, indeed to its very existence. This doubtless accounts for the tendency of powerful cities to extend their frontiers and to destroy cities that might block their trade routes: it was important to safeguard the 'life lines.'"[118]

Not all ancient cities are able to position themselves in the middle of an enormous river, but what they may lack in flows of water they make up for in flows of goods and people who want entrance to the city. As Virilio writes, "The street is like a new coastline and the dwelling a sea-port from which one can measure the magnitude of the social flow, predict its overflowings. The doors to the city are its tollbooths and its customs posts are dams, filtering the fluidity of the masses, the penetrating power of the migrating hordes."[119] In this way, the city port also allows for the exclusion of foreigners or undesirables, and multiple internal gates allow for similar social divisions to occur within the city itself. The creation of the port makes possible the report to the central authority on the flow of goods, slaves, smuggling, merchants, and so on. This is one of the first ways of accumulating knowledge of the city's flows and more effectively controlling its boundaries of inclusion: "The openings in the city wall were as carefully controlled as the sluice gates in an irrigation system. . . . Not indeed till the city at length reached the dimensions of a metropolis was there any problem of congestion around the city's gates, causing the trading population to back up there, with inns, stables, and warehouses of their own, to form a merchant's quarter and *entrepot*, or 'port.' "[120]

The port wall is thus a combination of the rampart and the military wall. It is a human-operated wall whose offense is military control over passage, and whose defense is the fortified rampart itself. It takes advantage of both functions, which is precisely why the gates of ancient cities often have an especially hybrid social functionality: as sacred spaces (temples, chapels, sacrificial zones); as processional spaces of military ritual, art performance, spaces of public assembly; as juridical spaces of judgment, court decisions, and legal agreements; as spaces of public execution; as public markets; and as customs and taxation points.[121] These functions are all possible at the city port wall precisely because the city port functions as a boundary or liminal space of passage between legal and criminal, between life and death, between sacred and profane, between member and foreigner, and so on. Ancient city gates were special borders, distinct from military or rampart walls. This is perhaps why in Mesopotamia gates were occupied by gods different from those of the city walls, and why in Rome, according to Plutarch, the gate could not be included in the same holiness as the city wall: "Where they designed to make a gate, there they took out the share, carried the plough over, and left a space; for which reason they consider the whole wall as holy, except where the gates are; for had they adjudged them also sacred, they could not, without offense to religion, have given free ingress and egress for the necessaries of human life, some of which are in themselves unclean."[122]

The territorial port is largely a centrifugal extension of the city port to more distant locations outside the city, as indicated by the Latin word *portorium*, meaning both a right of way (*portus*) and a transport tax on movement paid at the city gates, territorial gates, roads, or bridges.[123] Just as the rampart wall has both a citadel inside the city and a citadel at the perimeter (the outpost or fort), so the port wall has both city ports and territorial ports. Since the borders of political kinopower are constantly changing, these ports are much harder to enforce across larger territories. The Romans were the closest to achieving this kind of port at Hadrian's Wall. The primary function of Hadrian's Wall was not to defend against barbarian invasion but to regulate the ports of entry into the empire and collect taxes from those who wanted to pass across its numerous gates built at each milecastle. In this way movement could be allowed to pass or not from some areas and not others. This had at least three intended effects: (1) to retain skilled or educated colonial subjects from defecting to the other side, (2) to make new colonial subjects "enjoy" being Roman by restricting their movement, and (3) to restrict the flow of information across the wall to the barbarians so they did not learn the location of camps or supply lines.[124]

CONCLUSION

The wall as a border regime introduces a centrifugal social force that links together the fenced-in flows of territorial borders and mobilizes them into a single central power. This power is then deployed offensively through the use of military walls, defensively through the use of rampart walls, and as a technology of passage in port walls. However, the border regime of the wall is no mere relic of the past. As Lewis Mumford writes: "Though the forms and functions of government have changed during the last four thousand years, the citadel has a continued existence and is still visible. From the Pastel San Angelo to the concrete bunker by the Admiralty Arch in London, from the Kremlin to the Pentagon . . . the citadel still stands for both the absolutisms and irrationalities of its earlier exemplars."[125]

The modern citadel and politics cannot be separated from their ancient kinopolitical roots in the border power of the wall. Once it was invented by ancient societies, it persisted throughout history everywhere that we find the social practice of centrally organized and controlled mobility: military marches that expand state power (national armies and federal forces), rampart technologies that erect massive walls against the enemy (border walls and military citadels), and port structures that regulate the flow of commerce and migration (international ports of entry and customs areas). But the paradox of the centrifugal power that defines the wall regime ultimately leads to the fragmentation of the periphery. Historically, this resulted in a new border regime found in feudalism and the Middle Ages, as we will see in the next chapter.

CHAPTER 4
The Cell

The third type of border regime is the cell. While the fence divides the earth into a delimited territory and the wall divides territorial life into political forms of life, the cell divides human life into individual lives. Historically, the cell emerged as the dominant border technology during the Middle Ages, but also had precursors in the Neolithic cave, the ancient inner temple, and other technologies of enclosure. The cell also has social kinetic contemporaries with the fence and the wall that not only persist but are also directed toward other ends under the redirection of a rising cellular power. For example, medieval kinopower is defined by an ongoing centripetal accumulation of territorial flows (agriculture and labor) into the towns and cities—divided by corrals (cattle and land enclosures), palisades (houses and pens), and megaliths (tombs, temples, territorial markers), but also by central or centrifugal political powers that divide society by the military deployment of soldiers, the defense of city ramparts, and regional systems of transport, roads, gates, and other ports. Unfortunately an exhaustive account of all border technologies during the Middle Ages is beyond the scope of this work. Instead, this chapter focuses exclusively on the newly dominant cellular technologies that emerged during this time.

Cellular border power emerged historically once the centrifugal forces of political kinopower unified the centripetal forces of territorial power into a new and unstable center-periphery relationship. The distance or gap in mobility and social circulation between the center and periphery (the problem of transport) created the possibility for the emergence of new centers in between. Once this occurred, these centers could then link up with one another under limited (not global or imperial) conditions. This social link bound the junctions together without merging them under a single imperial center. The legal contracts that proliferated during the Middle Ages were the kinetic links between social junctions that aimed to keep the junctions bound together but also held apart in relative autonomy.

The "parcelized sovereignty," as Perry Anderson calls it, that characterized European society from around the fifth to the seventeenth centuries creates precisely this sort of social motion as a result of the untenable center-periphery political circulation of the Roman Empire. Feudal society was one of multiple warring kingdoms, each with its own center, bound together largely by the overlapping linkages of legal contracts between and within them. The kinopower of feudalism and early modern states can no longer be understood solely according to a central empire centrifugally unifying heterogeneous territories. Medieval border technologies were thus less defined by the social divisions of a single political center than by a thousand tiny centers of "decentralized political authority, [and] scattered territories," linked together through a vast web of "overlapping jurisdictions."[1]

Cellular kinopower is a juridical power in the kinetic sense in which it is a network of binding laws that replaces the unitary political rule of the emperor. In many areas at this time, sovereignty was perceived in terms of jurisdiction over subjects, not territory.[2] Thus the same territory could have had several sovereigns.[3] Although the concept and practice of law is, in some sense, as old as human society, feudal law included a much larger range of social activities than ancient and even modern justice. As Perry Anderson argues at length in his book *Passages from Antiquity to Feudalism*, "Justice was the central modality of political power—specified as such by the very nature of the feudal polity.... It is thus necessary always to remember that mediaeval 'justice' factually included a much wider range of activities than modern justice, because it structurally occupied a far more pivotal position within the total political system. It was the ordinary name of power."[4] The dominant form of social division in the Middle Ages was thus juridical and defined by quasi-voluntary legal links between individuals. Serfs were linked to the land and the lords linked to the juridical administration of the serfs. However, the lords did not own the land either and were in turn linked as vassals to the land "in fee" by a superior lord, to whom they owed military knight service. This contract was formalized by an oath of complete fealty (conjunction) to the lord, who ceremonially held the vassal's head in his hands and handed him a clod of dirt, representing the fief he was now bound to.[5] But this granting lord was also the vassal of one or more feudal superiors, and so on all the way upward in vast *maille* of multiple alliances to a monarch. According to Anderson, the monarch "was a feudal suzerain of his vassals, to whom he was bound by reciprocal ties of fealty, not a supreme sovereign set above his subjects. His economic resources would lie virtually exclusively in his personal domains as a lord, while his calls on his vassals would be essentially military in nature. He would have no direct political access to the population as a whole, for jurisdiction over it would be mediatized through innumerable layers of subinfeudation. He would, in effect, be master only on his own estates, otherwise to great extent a ceremonial figurehead."[6]

Therefore the social kinetics of feudalism were not defined primarily by the rotational and centrifugal power of the ancient sovereign, but by the linked rotation and tensional power of the feudal suzerain among innumerable layers of subinfeudation. "The consequence of such a system," Anderson states, "was that political sovereignty was never focused in a single centre. The functions of the State were disintegrated in a vertical allocation downwards, at each level of which political and economic relations were, on the other hand, integrated."[7] This new form of social circulation therefore produced a new dominant force of motion according to Anderson: "*a dynamic tension* ... within the centrifugal State."[8] It is precisely this "disintegration in a vertical allocation downward" that defines this form of social motion as predominately juridical: a laying *down* of *law*.[9]

Tensional force is the force created by at least two junctions bound together by a rigid link. The rigid link keeps them together and apart. It decenters their motion while also strengthening it. Kinetically, both junctions are relatively autonomous centers with their own form of motion, but since their movements are held together by the tension of the link, the motion of one is always restricted by the motion of the other. Tensional motion is inelastically relativized by the motion of others. This can be exemplified by, among other things, the movement of the human arm.[10] The human arm is composed of several radial joints connected by several bone linkages. Each ball joint rotates in its own orbit with its own degrees of freedom, while the rigid linkage between them both decenters and strengthens their movement.

Socially, tensional force is expressed in the juridical connections between individuals. Each individual retains a certain degree of freedom, but relative to a vertical and horizontal network of legal ties. Each feudal vassal has a lord above and a serf below in addition to agreements with other vassals to the side. Each lord above is also another vassal with similar connections. Further, there are multiple kingdoms in which one might be a vassal or lord at the same time. Political hierarchy is nothing new, but with feudalism the top is decentered and the middle multiplies. With feudalism there is only a complex mesh of legally binding agreements holding each to the other. The churches, the lords, the vassals, the workshops, and the prisons all have their own forms of justice. Together they form a mesh of nonunified but overlapping and conflicting laws and codes: "dense, entangled, conflicting powers, powers tied to the direct or indirect dominion over the land, to the possession of arms, to serfdom, to bonds of suzerainty and vassalage . . . a myriad of clashing forces."[11] Given this vast proliferation of legal power, it is no wonder that "since the Middle Ages," as Foucault writes, "the exercise of power has always been formulated in terms of law."[12]

Accordingly, medieval borders cannot be defined as fixed geographical lines, or even zones. They are much more complex and tensional. In fact, "Justice so little holds to a [geographical] fief," as sixteenth-century political philosopher Jean Bodin observes, "that the sovereign Prince who has sold or given away a fief/feudum, of whatever nature it might be, is not to be reputed as giving away or selling the jurisdiction."[13] According to Bodin, this is because it is the "jurisdiction exercised by the prince over his subject that makes the citizen. . . . All other differences are accidental and circumstantial."[14] Juridical power, Bodin continues, is primary and alone definitive of medieval power: "Kings were first instituted . . . for the sake of justice, and this remains the essential attribute of the kingly office, as is shown by the representation of the king on the great seal, seated on his throne in the act of judgement."[15] Accordingly, in the Middle Ages there were pockets of people scattered across noncontiguous spaces who might be under the jurisdiction of multiple princes or vassals at the same time, who themselves might be beholden to two or more others, and so on.

As medieval border scholar Ronnie Ellenblum observes, there is thus "no essential overlap between the limits of suzerainty and political power on the one side and the legal, fiscal or ethnic borders on the other."[16] Each type of kinopower has its own types of borders, but they do not all line up across a single geographical space. Instead, in the Middle Ages "centers of jurisdiction" rose and fell, continually shifting a nonlinear tension between one another.[17]

THE KINETICS OF THE CELL

The kinetics of the cellular border are defined by two interrelated functions: enclosure and linkage. Unlike the political technology of the wall, which produces bricks by formal and material uniformity, exclusive divisions, and orthogonal stacking according to a centrifugal power, the cell is quite different. The first kinetic function of the cell is the construction of an enclosure. To enclose is to surround, confine, and contain. The enclosure is first of all defined by a material flow that has been turned over on itself, but in such a way that it leaves an interior within it. In this sense it is quite different from the ancient brick, defined by a solid uniformity. The enclosure not only encircles, as was the primary function of the wall (the tower, the city, and so on), but surrounds on all sides, including top and bottom. The enclosure digs out an empty space inside the brick. It takes the temple/citadel not as its center of concentric expansion, but as its very model of social mobility and multiplication. From the Greek word ναός, *naos*, which described the unknown chamber within the dark inner sanctum of the temple, comes the Latin word *cella*, the small room where the image of God stands. To enclose is first of all to surround entirely, creating a small space, room, or interiority. Second, the enclosure confines this interiority. Once an empty space has been completely surrounded with the exception of some type of opening or access point, the access point must be closed off and sealed. However, this does not imply any immobility. The movement is an intensive one: a qualitative change or transformation. Confinement exchanges external or extensive mobility for an accelerated internal or intensive mobility or change. Third, with the space surrounded and confined, the enclosure contains itself and isolates a discrete individual. The cell thus has a specifically individualizing function, which the wall does not have. The wall is composed of homogenous units, while the cell contains qualitatively distinct individuals. Accordingly, the container itself may become mobile and enter into specific relations with other self-contained entities or unique individuals.

This makes possible the second kinetic function of the cell: linkage. Once an enclosure contains separate individuals, linkage is able to bring them together without unifying or homogenizing them. The link is not simply a connection; it is a nonelastic, rigid connection that both brings individual enclosures together and holds them apart. It is a kind of mutual contract or shared agreement between individuals. Linkage does not imply immobility, but moves instead according to a linked rotational motion defined by the tensions between two or more centers or individuals. In the Middle Ages the proliferation of centers of power produced precisely this form of motion, but it did so according to three major types of border technologies: identification, confinement, and the timetable.

THE IDENTIFICATION CELL

The offensive or mark cell that emerged during the Middle Ages was the identification cell. As we have seen, the border technology of identification is quite old. Identification points are junctions that divide the social flow of bodies and places. During the Neolithic period territorial megaliths—graves, shrines, informational signs, and so on—were used to bind or bound points of entrance and exit between the territorial community of ancestors, whose bodies were similarly bound in life (with tattoos)[18] and death (funeral art) as part of the territory. These "archaic societies of the mark," as Pierre Clastres calls them,[19] were quite different from the state societies of the ancient world that similarly marked their territorial borders, but did so with the written symbol of the king or despot. The king bordered his territory with the bodies he had killed, mutilated, decapitated, and branded as the enemy.[20] Ancient territorial borders were not simply marked, but written on with the symbolic stamp of political and military power. As Plato writes in the *Laws*, "If anyone is caught committing sacrilege, if he should be a slave or foreigner, let his offense be written on his face and hands."[21] The ancient stamp is not simply a mark, but a symbolic mark that represents the political power of the king. "The scarred body supplies a visible inscribed monument or document of the king's power, equivalent to the herms [border stones], pillars, or statues, that chart the imperialist's triumphal progress and record his victories."[22] This is the meaning of the ring of Gyges story told by Herodotus and retold by Plato in the *Republic*.[23] The rings of ancient rulers like Gyges often bore a seal or stamp, which allowed the ruler to reproduce a written symbol on a mobile document that represented his power, allowing him to exert an invisible power elsewhere when he was absent.

The identification cell of the Middle Ages invented a whole new kind of identification border: the letter and passport. The marks of the body and the symbolic stamp of the ruler did not disappear in the Middle Ages, but something new was added: an enclosure or interiority that identified and individualized the bearer as a linked extension of the ruler's juridical power. This was expressed in two different types of enclosure and linkage technologies: the letter and the passport. Both function as mobile juridical borders, fundamentally tied to medieval travel and a system of identification marks that produced individuals.

The Letter

The first type of identification cell is the letter. By definition, the technology of the letter functions only in its mobility and social circulation. It must be set in motion from sender, through bearer, to receiver; its power to define and divide social bodies is inversely proportional to its size, weight, and relative fragility. For something so small, its juridical power is incredible. In contrast to the military walls of the ancient empires constituted by soldiers, surveyors, and siege towers, the identification cell seems like an insignificant junction, yet the letter allowed its bearer to pass through almost any wall, to pass untouched by any solider, and to safely traverse multiple foreign borders.

The letter is a simple junction or fold in the flows of water and cloth that contains an extremely powerful inscribed interiority. This was made materially possible by the introduction of paper (macerated cotton and linen fibers) by the Arabs of Spain, North Africa, and the Levant in the eleventh and twelfth centuries[24]—over a thousand years after its invention in China.[25] The introduction of a lightweight, highly mobile, affordable, and mechanically reproducible writing material gave birth to nothing short of a revolution in written communication, identification, administrative, and border practices during the medieval and early modern period (eleventh to seventeenth centuries). As historian Valentin Groebner notes, "Paper became the matrix, the host material, of memory."[26]

The letters that proliferated during the medieval period (letters of safe conduct and letters of recommendation) were technologies of enclosure. These were not the engraved bronze tablets or *diploma* occasionally given to certain Roman soldiers, or the ancient symbolic writ of the king. Medieval paper letters were much more supple, mobile, and interiorized. They took the writing surface of inscription and folded it back over itself, creating a secret interiority or cryptographic junction. This letter enclosure was then confined by a seal or stamp of the sender, securing and containing the contents for transport and linkage to its recipient.

These medieval letters have two juridical border functions: as technologies of identification, and as technologies of jurisdiction. As technologies of identification they link together and identify two sets of doubles. The first set is the sender and the writing of the sender in the document. One way of authenticating the validity of the sender in their absence was that letters were often safeguarded with secret passwords on which the sender and receiver had previously agreed.[27] Another was to identify the writing with what Bernard de Clairvaux specified as the criteria of the *identitatem manus*, or "identical hand," writing of the author.[28] Yet another already in use from the eleventh century was to encode *intersigna*, or concealed signs, in the text itself.[29] The medium of paper also made possible for the first time the use of authenticating watermarks. All of these techniques aimed to identify the true and legal identity of the sender or authority of the letter by linking the signs in the letter to yet another duplicate of the sender's sign, previously provided through a growing system of notation and recording that emerged in the twelfth and thirteenth centuries. These true signs aimed to disclose the legal validity of what was enclosed in the contents of the letter of safe conduct or *conductus*, or *salvocondotto*, that became the common currency of border mobility in the twelfth and thirteenth centuries.

The second set of doubles identified by the technology of the letter is that of the bearer of the letter and the contents of the letter. By far the most common way this was done was simply by reference to the identity of the authority who had issued the letter. If a bearer had obtained this letter, most likely the mere possession of the identity of the issuer's stamp or seal was enough. If further proof was needed, the contents of the letter might refer to a physical description of the bearer, his possessions, or exact route of travel. However, identification is never certain. The very technology of identification also gives rise to its opposite—dissemblance, counterfeit, and spy networks that proliferated throughout the Middle Ages.[30]

In these ways the technology of the letter produces an important juridical border that identifies and delimits the individual sender and individual bearer of the letter and links them together through the juridical mediator of the judge or authenticator. The letter quite literally defined the juridical limits of who a person was and the scope of his mobility. The letter reproduces the authority of the issuer and the legal status of the bearer as discreet legal entities: juridically linked individuals. Never again would the "legal personage" be capable of ensuring its recognition without the help of others in the growing juridical administration of mobile documents. The enclosure of the letter also makes possible an invisible transformation of identity. "These documents transformed whoever could produce a sealed letter as valid proof of personal identity into whomever and whatever the document 'certified.'"[31] Since letters or documents became the dominant legal borders of social identity, if they changed, so did the person. The letter therefore introduces a new subjective limology into social mobility.

The second juridical border function of the letter is as a technology of jurisdiction. The letter was not only used to identify persons, but to control their movement and circulation within and between multiple and overlapping juridical borders. In this way the medieval letter of conduct or recommendation was different from other communication documents used by the Greeks or Romans, which were used almost exclusively within their own political borders. Outside Greek and Roman political power were illiterate barbarians to whom a "letter of safe passage" often meant nothing. In the Middle Ages, however, juridical kinopower was mobile, and borders were fluid across jurisdictions. The border appeared when persons were attached to a lord, or a lord to a vassal by mutual written legal agreement, and not necessarily in a place or time. The juridical letter not only is thus itself a technical enclosure of folded paper, but also functions as a mobile legal enclosure around the bearer: the diplomat, *ambaxiator*, pilgrim, courier, or legally sanctioned traveler. The king's or duke's jurisdiction follows the route and person of the traveler, certifies his identify, and protects him from the "judicial encroachment"[32] of others. The march of the mobile traveler is literally the outward expansion of the jurisdictional border. Whosoever crosses borders crosses a legal border defined by the authority of the ruler whose letter grants protection.

Across the early medieval Byzantine, Lombardian, and Carolingian kingdoms, such letters were required for passage across certain borders.[33] By the late medieval period, "Such letters of introduction and safe conduct were part of daily business ... a terrain replete with borders, customs checkpoints, and tariff barriers."[34] Eventually almost every legal authority began issuing letters of conduct that promised protection through a given area for a price.[35] In this way such letters became indistinguishable from a formal tax on mobility. Some of these documents even permitted passage on the condition that travelers return and prove where they had been. For example, Prussian military pilgrims of the Teutonic Order traveled to wage war on the pagan Lithuanians in the fourteenth century, and returned with elaborate letters of recommendation from across Europe certifying their travel.[36] From this example it is clear that enforcing all these juridical borders required the deployment of a new mobile border apparatus of couriers, messengers, and ambassadors to link together disparate and cross-jurisdictional sites such that one could travel continuously across Europe. Hence the invention of the word *ambaxiatores*, which, according to Bernard du Rosier's handbook for diplomats *Ambaxiator brevilogus*, comes from the word *ambo*, meaning "both together." In this sense Rosier's *ambaxiators* function as mediating juridical linkages between enclosed persons and enclosed documents.

The Passport

The second type of identification cell is the passport. Unlike previous letters of conduct that functioned more like a costly privilege or mobility tax, the passport was an "obligation imposed by the authorities on all travelers"[37] and described in much greater detail the physical identities of the carriers. From the middle of the fifteenth century on, the growing system of registration across multiple overlapping jurisdictional circuits made possible the enforcement of mandatory identification documents.[38] In June 1464 this process of circulatory control began under the French king Louis XI, who required all provincial border towns, or circuit junctions, to have a local representative of the royal postmaster to open, consider, reseal, and stamp all documents with an official seal. Once the couriers arrived at their final destination, they submitted their passes, which were then forwarded on to the *registre de passeports* to verify the path of their journey afterward.[39] The circuit of authorized mobility was then complete and enclosed—like the passport itself. Consequently, the mid-fifteenth-century use of the French word *passport* ("to go through the door") soon appeared in other languages across Europe: *passporti* in Italian, and *passzettel* or *bassborten* in Germany.[40] Around this same time medieval cities began creating similar registers for their military contingents and requiring all rank-and-file soldiers, not just crusaders, to carry identification documents in order to keep track of and juridically punish deserters.[41] Customs checkpoints, tollgates, and other juridical borders began to require certificates providing personal details of the traveler.[42]

Related to these passports was the emergence of *bollette di sanità* (bills of health), first issued for a fee in Italy in the latter half of the fifteenth century. The purpose of these bills of health was not to merely disclose the symbolic stamp of the authority and health administrators who authorized the documents, but to reveal the enclosed or internal biological contents of an individual body and determine the legal limits of its mobility. Bills of health were first administered in Italian cities (Lucca, Milan, Parma, Padua, and Venice) and port cities, where ships had to present a bill of health that listed the other cities they had been to.[43] The new document included residence, parish and gate, name, age, physical description, destination, and reason for the trip. By the late sixteenth century Palermo authorities followed suit, requiring the name, workplace, and dates of departure and return of all travelers. In this way these new bills of health drew new borders that could not be reduced to territorial or political types and techniques. Juridical health borders pertained not only to one's territorial or political marks, but to the legal status of one's inner and individual biological markings. This border practice was common across Europe during the plague.[44]

Similar special passports were also required by beggars in the late fifteenth and early sixteenth centuries. In Bern, for example, a resolution was passed to expel all "unauthorized" beggars who did not carry a beggar's permit. These papers were carefully dated and stamped with official seals confirming in writing the details justifying the beggar's collection of alms.[45] "The Bernese ordinance on begging of 1527 required all resident recipients of alms to display official badges on their clothes, thereby making it known that their names were recorded in writing and that they were identified by the authorities as locals."[46] In Spain, similar documents, *cédula de persona*, were issued by the municipal council. In England from 1530 on all beggars were required to disclose a *sedule* (slip of paper) or *byllet* (ticket) on pain of physical punishment and legal expulsion.[47] Accordingly, these new borders produced new border crossers who simply counterfeited these documents.

Juridical borders were becoming ubiquitous across Europe, as were registration technologies and border guards. As early as 1511 King Ferdinand of Spain required the registration of all emigrants departing to the colonies. As Groebner observes, "In 1518 and 1522, royal decrees prohibited Moors, Jews, and their descendants from embarking on transatlantic passages. Absconding debtors, persons with criminal records, former clerics, or those suspected of heresy were equally barred from passage."[48] By 1552 King Philipp II, known by contemporaries as *el rey papelero* ("king of paper"), required that all *pasajeros* had to show written proof of identity, including a record of physical marks, age, and marital status, before they were allowed to leave Spain.[49] "During the course of the sixteenth century within this mesh of ducal directives and locally refined identity documents, a utopian slogan was formulated that was to determine the discourse on, individuality and identification in Europe from then on: 'Register everyone and everything.' Now it was not only royal officers, inquisitors, and border guards who would act as supervisory authorities; from the mid-sixteenth century on, municipal directives instructed innkeepers to submit a tally sheet of all newly arrived aliens to the authorities every day."[50]

Identification borders and juridical zones multiplied across Europe. In Leipzig and other German cities poor tenants were required to carry with them at all times a paper permit certifying their landlord's recommendation. In Salzburg (1579) the first and surnames of all parish members, their age and legal status, residence, descendants, marriages, and death were all recorded.[51] If the new utopian juridical function of these identification borders was not explicit enough, Jean Bodin makes it entirely clear. A universal recording system of mandatory identification is also an offensive border: a manhunting apparatus. If we register the name, status, and place of residence of everyone, why wait for a person to cross some particular point when we can simply hunt these parasite vagabonds down and expel them? According to Bodin, universal registration would "make it possible to get rid of those parasites which prey upon the commonwealth, to banish idlers and vagabonds, the robbers and ruffians of all sorts that live among good citizens like wolves among the sheep. One can find them out, and track them down wherever they are."[52] Bodin's enthusiasm was prescient. This is precisely the trajectory that the identification cell would take over the course of the coming modern age.

The second major type of border technology of juridical kinopower is the confinement cell. Just as the identification cell functions offensively to enclose and link together mandatory legal identities and jurisdictional borders, so the confinement cell functions more defensively to enclose and link together individual souls and legislate their confinement. While the march of the medieval traveler is marked by the letter and passport, the limits of the medieval body are traced in the monastery, the prison, hospital, asylum, and the quarantined city. These are the new confinement borders of medieval mobility. However, confinement does not mean immobility. The confinement cell system is "a *perpetual movement* in which individuals replace one another in a space marked off by aligned intervals,"[53] as Foucault writes. "It 'trains' the moving, confused, useless multitudes of bodies and forces into a multiplicity of individual elements—small, separate cells."[54] It is a specifically cellular mobility. Confinement cells are not only enclosures of docile bodies, but complex spaces that are "at once architectural, functional and hierarchical. [They are] spaces that provide fixed positions and *permit circulation*; they carve out individual segments and establish operational links."[55] The confinement cell adds to the ancient orthogonal grid a profound interiority "to render visible those who are inside it; in more general terms, an architecture that would operate to transform individuals: to act on those it shelters, to provide a hold on their conduct, to carry the effects of power right to them, to make it possible to know them, to alter them."[56] Each enclosed individual cell has its own centralized rotational motion linked to the others through a confined social circulation.

The Monastery

The first and perhaps most significant technique of cellular confinement that emerged in the Middle Ages is the monastery. Monasteries have always been border phenomena: at the limits of the African deserts, the dense forests of early medieval western Europe, and the desolate plans of central Spain.[57] On the mountaintop or in the desert cave, the monastery not only produces the influential model of the enclosed individual linked to others through the enclosure of the cellular monastery, but also invents a new system of legislated confinement.

Just as ancient civilizations had invented politics in the form of the polis, so "the monastery," as Lewis Mumford says, "was in fact a new kind of polis,"[58] a polis that "exercised a command over urban life, even over its architectural forms, out of all proportion to its [relatively marginal] numbers."[59] The monastery was a heavenly city, as Bernard de Clairvaux writes, the stronghold of paradise: the *paradisus claustra*.[60] This was the case because the kinetics of the cell are modeled precisely on the kinetics of the confined and dark interiority of the ancient temple and citadel. However, instead of expanding outward centrifugally, cellular power stays inside and circulates between enclosed and bordered spaces. In fact, the bordered space of the cellular enclosure had its correlate in the bordered enclosure of the soul: the two entered into a reciprocal determination. "Let all of you then live together in oneness of mind and heart," as Saint Augustine writes in his *Ordo Monasterii*, "mutually honoring God in yourselves, whose temples you have become."[61] Instead of the centrifugal temple of the ancients, monasticism multiplies, individualizes, and interiorizes the temple within: the soul. Human souls are so many cells in the house of God. As Saint Anthony writes, "Consider the pomegranate, all of whose seeds exist under a single skin, yet each seed has its own proper cell."[62] "That is why the Lord says: In my Father's house (the 'skin') there are many mansions (the distinct cells)."[63]

Instead of the centrifugal law of the ancient political leader, monasticism decenters the law and folds it back over itself into a tensional network of a thousand tiny interior self-judgments. "Judge yourself first," Augustine says in his *Political Writings*, and "then you will be able to leave the inner cell of your conscience in security and go out to someone else."[64] This reciprocal movement between the juridical cell of the soul and the juridical order of physical confinement is the kinetic essence of monasticism. It encloses the movements of the soul within the borders of the body and legislates the circulation of both within monastic spaces of confinement.

But monastic cells, like all borders, are not a static. The monastic cell is a dynamic battleground where the soul fights in confined security against the flesh, which continually encroaches on its borders. "It will be a matter of dislodging the most hidden impulses from the inner recesses of the soul," Foucault writes, "thus enabling oneself to break free of them."[65] The solitude of the cell was necessary to confront this temptation and the severity of God alone.[66] The cell thus functions as a performative stage and territory of inscription on which God's soldiers, the monks, do battle with the flesh and inscribe their victories and defeats.[67] "The images and graffiti on the walls are records of the active participants in ascetic living."[68] As an internalization of juridical borders, "monasticism came to absorb the ideal of the martyr"[69] sacrificing mortal life for spiritual immortality. As Darlene Hedstrom documents, these cellular spaces therefore function as borderlands or "intersections between heaven and earth," body and soul.[70]

The monastic cell becomes the model of social reality. Individuals are themselves enclosures, enclosed by the cell, but also put into close enough proximity to retain a social kinetic tension or "a sense of fellowship" and community, as Philo prescribes.[71]

The history of this cellular mobility begins with the invention of monasticism in Egypt in the fourth century. While the Egyptian peasantry of the third century had a tradition of solitary desert hermitage or *anachoresis* as a form of protest against tax collection and other social evils, this practice was adapted by Saint Anthony into an ascetic Christian practice in the late third century. In 370 Saint Basil linked asceticism, manual labor, and education under monastic rule for the first time.[72] Saint Athanasius brought these practices to Europe in 371, starting with several houses in Italy, and then spreading to Spain, North Africa, and southern and central France.[73] By the seventh century monasteries extended from Ireland to Africa.[74]

The goal of monastic rules like those of Saint Pachomius and Saint Basil was not to confine mobility but to invent a legislation of mobilized confinement. Monks were not simply locked in their cells, but were socially legislated in all kinetic activity: prayer, food, drink, chastity, poverty, work, study, the renunciation of wealth, and so on. Monastic rule is the constant and total rule over collective/individual motion to such a degree that the monk is not at all burdened by the practical concern of free action: kinocracy.[75] Monastic kinocracy is both collectivizing and individualizing at the same time. While eremitic monks, or "hermits," lived alone in a hut or cave, cenobitic monks, "cenobites," lived together and thus required multiple cells.[76] Alternately, the Carthusian Order, founded in 1084, combined eremetical and cenobitic life. The monks live in cells arranged along three sides of a courtyard. Each cell has a room for work, a room for prayer, a bedroom, and a miniature garden. Meals are prepared by lay brothers and are passed in through a hatch. The monks leave their cells only at night, to worship together in the monastery church.[77]

The monastic enclosure linkage is the system of laws and rank that distinguish the cells from one another. According to the Benedictine rules, there are cells for the sick (chapter 36), cells for guests (chapter 1), cells for sleeping (chapter 22), a cell for the porter (chapter 66), and so on. According to the rule of Saint Pachomius, strict laws govern each cell: "It is prohibited to enter in the cell of the neighbor without having knocked first on the door," "When everybody separates to go to sleep, no one will be allowed to leave their cell, except in case of necessity," "Do not let anybody eat anything inside his cell," a monk "will not have a cell in which he can lock himself," and so forth. Every cell has its rank and classification (sleep, work, eat, pray, heal), and they all form intervals in a continuous circulatory relay system guided by strict juridical limits.

The Prison

Cellular kinopower began with monasticism in the fourth century, but was further developed with the proliferation of prisons throughout the Middle Ages. The prison is a system of linked enclosures that socially divides, and unites by division, a collective of prisoners. Following monastic practice, the prison links together a series of cellular and individualized practices for the purpose of spiritual reform. Just like the monastic rules of Saint Pachomius, the cells are locked from the outside. This is precisely why both the monastery and the prison are called penitentiaries: places of regret and repentance. The English word "jail" further attests etymologically to its monastic origins in mountain caves, from the Latin *cavus*, meaning hollow or cave. The jail is thus the place where the law (**legh-*) has been laid down into the earth and forms a cavity (**keuə-*) or cell (**kel-*).

This is quite opposed to Roman legal thought, which considered incarceration an illegitimate punishment "dismal to the innocent, but not harsh enough for the guilty."[78] Accordingly, for the Romans the cell was simply a temporary holding place for those awaiting trial: a temporary transport zone between periphery (where individuals are captured) to the center (where justice is centrifugally administered). However, the medieval prison was a conjunction of flows into a circuit of linked enclosures aimed at producing a self-legislating spiritual interiority. As Augustine says, one must administer justice to oneself since punishment is salvation. From as early as the fifth century monastic cells were already allocated for confining and punishing erring brethren, including clergy and laymen who never took monastic vows.[79] In fact, punitive incarceration was favored by the church because of its nonviolence, which functioned as a "sweet inversion" of Christian asceticism.[80] Thus from the beginning, the prison was intended to function as a juridical "tension between misery and spiritual growth."[81] Later prisons, as Foucault notes, exhibit "clear reference to the monastic model,"[82] as the following description of the American prisoner reveals: "Alone in his cell, the convict is handed over to himself; in the silence of his passions and of the world that surrounds him, he descends into his conscience, he questions it and feels awakening within him the moral feeling that never entirely perishes in the heart of man."[83]

By the early thirteenth century the prison expanded dramatically with the increased activity of the papal inquisition, which often sentenced heretics to prison for long periods of time before even determining their guilt or innocence.[84] While ancient centrifugal borders expanded outward from a political center, medieval tensional borders expanded transversally across multiple and individualized cellular orders. In contrast to the unbridled slavery of the ancient world, juridical kinopower does not directly enslave its criminals, its debtors, its vagabonds, its aliens, its heretics; it incarcerates them and instructs them in their self-judgment. Thus the prisoner is not centrifugally directed outward as a mere body by the master, but tensionally directed inward against a divided and parcelized self: a soul *and* body fundamentally in tension. The prison creates a system of borders—between bodies and souls, types of crimes (divided into wards),[85] types of social status, and types of activities—importantly linking them all together in a mobilized confinement—a linked, rotational motion of enclosed cells.[86]

The Hospital and Asylum

The monastery also gave birth to the cellular institutions of the asylum and hospital. Monastic pharmacies stored and studied medicaments. They copied medical books and stored vast medical knowledge. Among the many cells of the monastery was the infirmary, the place where monks, travelers, the poor, old, weak, and sick were treated. As the Benedictine Rule prescribes, "For these sick let there be assigned a special room and an attendant who is God-fearing."[87] Even in the thirteenth century, after hospitals began to appear in the cities more frequently, physicians, still influenced by the Benedictine tradition, refused to treat patients who would not confess their sins. Even late-medieval secular hospitals often required patients to follow monastic rules.[88]

The hospital was a cellular system of linked enclosures. Individuals were divided by beds, partitions, and occasionally cells. They were instructed in daily life—work, meals, prayer, and so on—according to their capacity, just like monks. The Benedictine Rule even goes as far to say that "care must be taken of the sick, so that they will be served as if they were Christ in person."[89] Conversely, the sick must also behave according to "being served as a God." Thus the enclosure system of cells is aimed not only at confining but also at legislating the conduct of individuals "as if they were Christians": in effect, producing individual Christians. Accordingly, "to cure" (from the Latin *cura*, office, task, or responsibility) was a spiritual responsibility to manage the daily tensional linkage between the material borders of body, prayer, work, and sleep.

The asylum for the mad emerged from this same cellular social technology in order to harmonize the erratic movements of the soul into harmonious ones that follow their own self-adjudicated rotation. Madness was often interpreted as an affliction of the soul or demonic possession, and thus in need of confinement and an interior realignment of spiritual borders between good and evil. Thus common to almost all treatments was physical confinement. Some towns had madmen's towers (*Narrentürme*); in Paris special cells were set aside at the Hôtel Dieu. Specialized hospitals began to appear under the influence of Islam in Spain: Granada (1365), Valencia (1407), Zaragoza (1425), Seville (1436), and Barcelona (1481).[90] All of these attest to a mobilization of cellular confinement.

THE TIME CELL

The third major type of border technology of juridical kinopower is the time cell. Just as the identification cell functions offensively to mark, enclose, and link together mandatory legal identities and jurisdictional borders, and the confinement cell functions more defensively to enclose and link together individual souls and legislate their confinement, the time cell functions as the boundary system or rules of passage that enclose units of space-time-activity and link them together under the law.

The Timetable

The timetable is a border technology that both divides and prescribes the passage of social time, social space, and social activities. The timetable is a type of border distinct from the cellular social divisions of walls, doors, bars, cages, locks, guards, ward, desk, divided beds, dorms, and so on, that enclose and link together medieval motion. The timetable is the schedule that regulates and legislates the social circulation between space-time-activity cells. As Foucault observes, the timetable establishes a "temporal continuum of individuality-genesis . . . the individuality-cell or the individuality-organism. . . . And, at the centre of this seriation of time, one finds . . . the drawing up of 'tables' [and] the distribution of individuals and cellular segmentation."[91] Thus the identification, confinement, and timetable cells are mutually supportive and often coexist, but they are not the same thing. The timetable creates a unique border enclosure of social space-time.

The timetable functions as a social border in at least four ways. First, the timetable conjoins a series of time flows into a single junction: the hour.

Until the fourteenth century, time was literally the measurement of flows of water and light: the water clock and the sundial. Once these flows have been enclosed into discrete time cells, they can be filled with an interiority, bounded on either side: beginning and end.

Second, the timetable conjoins the flow of matter into a bounded space. The timetable matrix not only encloses a period of time, but encloses a space in which this time takes place. The emergence of socially regulated time in the Middle Ages was not universal, but appeared differently in different locations. There was the hour in the monastery, the hour in the university, the hour in the market, and so on. Different clocks regulated different times. Even our language today of time zones evidences the historical cellularity of space-time made possible by the deployment of multiple clocks to regulate social motion.

Third, the timetable conjuncts a series of human movements into a single junction: social activity. Within the enclosed interior of the time cell, social activity is bounded by a starting point and stopping point. If one spends too much or too little time engaged in a certain activity, one transgresses a social border or juridical limit defined by the time cell.

Fourth, the timetable encloses all three junctions of the hour, the space, and the activity together in a held tension—that is, the right thing must be done in the right place at the right time. The enclosure exists only when the tension between the three types of cells is just right. Once the time-space-activity cell is fully enclosed and individualized, it can be multiplied and then linked together with others through a series of laws. The laws do not unify all the cells, but coordinate their collective motion in tension: now do this here, now do that there. For example, the activities of the monastery, the prison, and the city market must all begin and end in their own series. If one cell takes too long or is done poorly or in the wrong space, all the subsequent cells borders are delayed and transgressed. The linkage has broken apart like a snapped gear in the mechanical clock. Thus the borders of the timetable must be enforced just like any other border: curfews in the cities, prayer and work in the monastery, and meals and visitations in the prison.

Just as the monastery is the birthplace of the cell, it is also the birthplace of the timetable: the *horarium*. As Foucault notes in *Discipline and Punish*, "The time-table is an old inheritance. The strict model was no doubt suggested by the monastic communities. It soon spread. Its three great methods—establish rhythms, impose particular occupations, regulate the cycles of repetition—were soon to be found in schools, workshops and hospitals."[92] The monasteries were, as Foucault says, "the specialists of time, the great technicians of rhythm and regular activities."[93] The *horarium* is a communal timetable that ensures that the time given by God is not wasted but held in its proper proportion or tension in service. In this way the *horarium* deploys a rhythmic control over the flows of social circulation and the periodicity of the movement between cellular circuits: prayer, work, meals, reading, sleep, and so forth.

We can see this clearly in the Benedictine rules: "How many psalms are to be said at these hours" (chapter 17), "At what hours the meals should be taken" (chapter 41), "On giving the signal for the time of the work of God" (chapter 47). In chapter 48, "On the Daily Manual Labor," for example, the Rule reads: "Idleness is the enemy of the soul. ... From Easter until the Calends of October, ... from Prime in the morning let them labor ... until about the fourth hour, and from the fourth hour until about the sixth let them apply themselves to reading. After the sixth hour, having left the table, let them rest on their beds in perfect silence.... Let None be said rather early, at the middle of the eighth hour, and let them again do what work has to be done until Vespers."

The monastic timetable lays out a bordered social division into time-space-activity enclosures and then links them together in a shared tension of monastic law. This is made possible not only by conjoining flows of water and light, but eventually by using a uniquely tensional system of mechanical time. The mechanical clock links together a series of rotational gear motions subject to a purely discontinuous mechanical form of escapement. The first mechanical escapement is produced by an alternately held tension-and-release linkage between two rotational motions: the weighted rotation of the *foliot* and the weighted rotation of the *verge*.[94] The first mechanical clock thus measured time not by the centripetal stockpile of water and its centrifugal release outward, but rather by the alternating tension and release of a link between two rotating motions. With the invention of the mechanical clock in the fourteenth century, time could be coordinated much more accurately and at smaller intervals—the half hour, the quarter hour, and so forth. The messiness of the flows of the water clock was replaced by the more appropriately linked tension device. The connection between the mechanical clock and social kinetic control is evidenced in the explicitly social automata that were built into many mechanical clocks of the Middle Ages. When the hour rang, carved wooden people would emerge from the clock tower to pray, work, sleep, and so on. Time borders are social and material borders that were built explicitly to direct the circulation of human movement.

Just as the technology of the cell spread from monasteries to prisons, hospitals, and asylums, so did the timetable. Prisons used timetables to coordinate the passage between eating cells, sleeping cells, and visiting cells. Hospitals followed the rules and timetables of the monks. Universities followed the timetable of classes, professors, times for eating, sleeping, and so on. From the fifth to the seventeenth centuries there was therefore an increasing regimentation of social circulation and boundaries through time borders, based on a timetable that did not exist on such a scale in the ancient world.

CODA: THE QUARANTINED CITY

The quarantined plague cities of Europe, famously analyzed by Foucault, also made exemplary use of the time cell in the form of mass "shut-ins." The quarantined city not only created timetables for keeping track of how long persons had been locked in their house, when to bring food to the houses, when to take the dead, when it was safe to take the possessions from a plague house, and so on, but also remodeled entire cities around cellular borders, enclosed and linked together through a system of administrative control.[95] The word "quarantine" comes from the Italian *quaranta giorni*, meaning "forty days." This is how long ships and people were made to wait outside the city of Ragusa, Italy, and then Marseille in 1383 because of concerns regarding plague transmission. This initial practice may have been related to Hippocrates's notion that the fortieth day was the critical day in the course of a disease.[96] However, since the term "quarantine" itself does not emerge until the fifteenth century,[97] when many inland cities were not using the forty-day method, it is also likely that the word reflected another strategy altogether: the cell.

The word "quarantine" also comes from the Latin *quattuor*, meaning four. From this same root comes the Latin derivative *quadrum*, meaning "square." The quarantined city is not only shut inside the city grid square but also shut in or enclosed inside the cubical (three-dimensional square) homes. The plague home is transformed into a cell by (1) surrounding it completely with boarded windows and doors, (2) confining it with locks and armed guards, and (3) containing the biological interiority of the individuals within. Thus the quarantined city is also the quadrantized city: the cellular city. From the fourteenth to the seventeenth centuries cities across Europe dealt with the plague by turning their cities into cellular enclosures. They closed up the borders of the towns, and shut in the population within their homes.

This is attested to in, among other documents, the *Orders Conceived and Published by the Lord Mayor and Aldermen of the City of London Concerning the Infection of the Plague, 1665*. Searchers were sent throughout the city, looking for signs of illness. "As soon as any man shall be found by this examiner, chirurgeon, or searcher to be sick of the plague, he shall the same night be sequestered in the same house; and ... the house wherein he sickened should be shut up for a month." If any person visited the home of any person known to be infected by the plague, "The house wherein he inhabiteth shall be shut up for certain days by the examiner's direction." "Every house visited [had to] be marked with a red cross of a foot long in the middle of the door, evident to be seen." Guards or warders patrolled the enclosed cells, providing padlocks, bars or spikes, medical personnel, medicines, food, fumigation material, and fuel for cooking—all charged at the community's expense. Lowestoft, Suffolk, for example had 263 infected families shut in at a weekly expense of £200.[98] "Most regulations required strict isolation, with doors and windows barred or nailed shut and only one opening left for passage of food and other necessities. This was often a second-story window, with supplies delivered in a basket on a rope. Even keyholes were sealed."[99] The rules for the guards were as follows:

> That to every infected house there be appointed two watchmen, one for every day, and the other for the night; and that these watchmen have a special care that no person go in or out of such infected houses whereof they have the charge, upon pain of severe punishment. And the said watchmen to do such further offices as the sick house shall need and require: and if the watchman be sent upon any business, to lock up the house and take the key with him; and the watchman by day to attend until ten of the clock at night, and the watchman by night until six in the morning.[100]

The quarantined city is thus a city under a juridical system of plague laws that parcelizes the city into a multiplicity of enclosed, boarded-up, and locked cells, linked together and monitored by an administration grid of guards, searchers, surgeons, wards, and so on. Those who escaped faced penalties, including immediate execution.[101]

The quarantined city was rigorously bordered by divisions of social time-space-activity: the time cell of the guard schedules, the time cell of the meals for shut-ins, the time cell of how long a family was locked in. Each social activity had to happen in the right place at the right time or else the borders were transgressed and the plague spread. The quarantined city resembles the monastery, the prison, and the asylum, which in turn all resemble the linked enclosure: the cell. In fact, during the plague it was the hospitals, poorhouses, monasteries, and prisons that were turned into temporary plague hospitals or, where resources were scarce, camps for the dead and dying.[102] When administration and resources were inadequate, families hid away the sick, patients tried to flee, and family members assaulted staff.

Patients were therefore often locked in and guarded. In Rome in 1656, gallows were even constructed bedside the *lazaretto* (plague hospital) to hang escapees.[103]

CONCLUSION

Although the border regime of the cell has historically precise deployments in medieval technologies, where it first rises to social dominance, it remains active in contemporary border politics as well. For example, identification technologies today are similarly concerned with an informational enclosure of individuals that links them to complex systems of controlled mobility. Today we still find technologies of confinement in schools, offices, hospitals, prisons, military barracks, hotels, detention centers, internment camps, concentration camps, and so on. The list of modern techniques of confinement is as empirically vast as they are conceptually similar: all create sites of enclosure, interiority, and linked coordination of individuals. The time cell persists as well in the form of the timetable: work schedules, bus schedules, sleep schedules, meal schedules, traffic schedules. Our lives are filled with schedules that link together enormous numbers of individuals into time-space-activity enclosures. Even minor transgressions of these borders can cause profound chaos in systems of social circulation. Thus contemporary social mobility cannot be understood without a careful analysis of cellular kinopower and the borders that identify, confine, and temporalize human movement. Even more importantly, contemporary borders cannot be understood without an analysis of the checkpoints that remain the most dominant form of modern limology, as we will discover in the next chapter.

CHAPTER 5
The Checkpoint I

The fourth and final border regime analyzed in this book is the checkpoint. The checkpoint adds a further form of kinetic social division to the previous regimes, and in particular responds to the cellular regime of the Middle Ages. While the cellular borders of the Middle Ages were primarily directed at dividing human beings into enclosed individuals, checkpoints further divided these individuals into collections of "data." Data becomes the discreet and quantifiable substratum that composes individuals: age, height, weight, location, status, and so on. Instead of using border technologies largely to create enclosed interiors that identified qualitatively unique individuals at privileged sites—juridical borders, the monastery, the prison, the quarantined city, a site of emigration, a customs house, the privileged space-time of the *horarium*, and so on—the checkpoint border takes place at any point whatever. Accordingly, the border technologies that emerge under this regime are far more polymorphic than all previous historical borders. Any space-time point can become a border.

Historically, the checkpoint regime emerged dominantly around the eighteenth century, after cellular borders had made possible the identification, confinement, and temporal enclosure of mobile individuals. Modern limology goes hand in hand with the rising power of autonomous cities and city leagues, and the declining power of feudal land tenure, vassalage, and serfdom that gave birth to a radical increase in social mobility of many kinds, from merchants to vagabonds.[1] Kinopolitically, feudalism did not dissolve as a social regime because of a lack of mobility, as is often argued,[2] but rather because of an uncontrollable excess of mobility. By multiplying cellular individuals and juridical zones too rapidly, feudal tensional force ended up destabilizing social motion through an overly complex network of conflicting juridical contracts and mobile individuals in what Eric Hobsbawm calls the "Crisis of the Seventeenth Century,"[3] characterized by widespread vagabondage and social turmoil, most notably in the Thirty Years War, 1618–1648.[4]

More so than previous historical periods, the modern period can be characterized by increasingly dramatic forms of social expansion and contraction: expansions and contractions of demand and supply in the market, expansions and contractions of births and deaths in the population, expansions and contractions of abundance and famine in the food supply, and expansions and contractions of space and time in communication and transportation. In this way the increasing oscillation of these social fields is always producing a relative social kinetic surplus or deficit according to its degree of expansion and contraction. With the increase of social oscillations (expansions and contractions) comes the importance of a new kinolimological problem: equilibrium. Where does one draw the line on the widespread social mobility of individuals, and how can new social junctions be generated just as fast as, or faster than, they are being contracted through unemployment, poverty, and other forms of social expulsion? The question of modern kinopower is no longer, "How do we juridically enclose and link oscillating flows," but rather, "How will it be possible to establish an equilibrium among social oscillations?" However, the problem with increasingly large flows of individuals is that one does not know in advance where to introduce a bifurcation or division into the continuum to achieve optimum results. There are too many individual variables. Accordingly, historically privileged border sites are no longer sufficient to ensure the continuous control and rapid redirection of social flows. The border must now be deployable at any point whatever throughout society.

The border must now act elastically to redistribute social motion divided by data points. Social elasticity is the capacity of a network of junctions to return to its normal shape after contraction or expansion. It is the social force that quickly redistributes people to fill a deficit or displace an excess to avoid social decline or collapse. The checkpoint is the set of border technologies that make possible the redistribution of a stretchable social surplus that acts like a buffer against unpredictable expansions and contractions that might disrupt a certain type of social motion. Since the modern checkpoint can occur at any point whatever, it is able to intervene quickly, often unlinked from juridical restrictions, and reorder flows. The aim of the checkpoint is not to maintain static borders (homeostasis), but to maintain a dynamic equilibrium (homeorhesis), and, when possible, expand this equilibrium. If social motion contracts, a kinetic surplus can be redirected elsewhere or confined; if social motion expands, a kinetic surplus can be expanded as a form of growth. As long as a society is capable of producing and mobilizing its surplus and deficits, it will be able to achieve an elastic equilibrium or expansion. Thus elasticity moves not from the outside to the center (centripetally), nor from the center to the outside (centrifugally), nor by rigid links between centers (tension), but rather by the redistribution of a surplus to whatever point it is needed.

This elastic force of the checkpoint is a specifically economic type of kinopower in that economics, in its kinetic sense, strives for the free arrangement and movement of things to and fro with a minimum of territorial, political, or juridical restrictions and a maximum of equilibrium. In particular, the dominance of the checkpoint emerges alongside the social kinetics described by the liberal economic concept of *Laissez faire et laissez passer*, coined by the physiocrat François Quesnay and popularized by Vincent de Gournay with the slogan *Laissez faire et laissez passer, le monde va de lui même!"* (Let do and let pass, the world goes on by itself!).[5] The social kinetics of liberal economics are clear: let the flows of social motion move and pass across all previous territorial, political, and legal borders. This does not entail the abolition of all borders, of course, but rather the creation of new elastic borders of police, security, and informational borders that, instead of blocking movement, order it according to the multiple and competing ends of dynamic social oscillation. All that is solid must melt into air! Everything must be set into economic circulation.

More broadly construed, economics is not simply the science of wealth, but an entire kinetic regime for the direction of social motion. In this way economics functions more like the management of a household (*oikonomia*) than like the management of a state (*polis*). This is precisely why Aristotle, for example, argues that the *techne oikonomike* (economics) differs from politics, just as the house (*oikia*) differs from the city (*polis*).[6] While the state is concerned with the goal of the public good, the household is simply concerned with the desirable arrangement or balance of the individual's private property. The house is not the fenced village of centripetally accumulated flows, nor the walled megajunction of the ancient city from whence power radiates centrifugally, nor the linked junctions of the cellular and monastic institutions of the Middle Ages. Economics and the household are not a centric or unifying social kinetic process.

The economy is more like a series of decentered and unlinked private households that do not, on their own, constitute a city or a feudum—all of which require centers. Households, like a series, can be added together indefinitely without ever establishing a social center or totality. Instead, the assembly of private households forms an indefinite series with a shifting point of equilibrium. The series is not a centripetal inward curve, a centrifugal circle, or a tensional link. The series is a flow between relay junctions, oscillating between constant contractions and expansions aiming toward social equilibrium. The checkpoint takes place precisely along a series of any points whatever, not only at privileged territorial, political, or juridical points.

THE KINETICS OF THE CHECKPOINT

The kinetics of the checkpoint border are defined by two interrelated functions: the point and the inspection. The first kinetic function of the checkpoint is the isolation of a point in a flow of social space-time. A kinetic point is the smallest possible discreet unit of information or data extracted from a social flow, but since flows are not reducible to points, there is no absolutely smallest point. What a point is and where a point is may change as it flows. The point is thus determinable without being fully determined. It is a point of bifurcation whose sloped tangent intersects the flow at infinity. Unlike an enclosure, which emphasizes the interiority created when a flow folds back on itself, the point has no depth or interiority. The point is not the border that identifies the depth of a legal individual, but the border that can occur at any point on the surface, like a Cartesian coordinate. The modern individual can thus be divided up into points of information on the axes of space and time. These points can then be elastically modulated and redirected according to the changing demands of social motion. The point is thus perfectly abstract in the sense in which any place and any time may become a bifurcation point, but entirely concrete insofar as it always occurs as some specific point.

The second kinetic function of the checkpoint is the inspection. The checkpoint border is not merely a series of possible points of intervention and bifurcation, but a concrete point where the subject comes under formal inspection and division by a border authority. However, since the point may be anywhere, the border authority could be anyone who can report or enforce a social division based on one or more discreet points of information. This is a significant break from previous border technologies. The border has always been mobile, but tended to appear predominately around privileged territorial, political, and legal sites—shrines, city perimeters, customs houses, and so on. The checkpoint takes the point of bifurcation common to all previous borders and gives it an autonomy of its own in order to appear anywhere and be inspected by anyone. It is a total mobilization.[7] The inspection is also different from the border techniques of medieval juridical linkage that were concerned primarily with valid identification of an author or document carrier. Valid identification almost always resulted in free mobility. However, the inspection is not only concerned with valid identification, but with the collection of new information and enforcement of further redirections, which were not given juridically in advance of the inspection itself. In other words, just as the point aims to take on an autonomy from the flow, the inspection takes on an autonomy with respect to the law. Inspection is security above and beyond the law.

Checkpoints are defined not simply by what they allow through or do not allow through; they are also defined by a dramatic increase in the use of informational technologies for actively surveying, surveilling, and registering the passing traffic. Checkpoints gather and record a variety of information from human traffic: name, age, place of birth, previous domicile, occupation, means of subsistence, and so on. They record births, deaths, and marriages, and collect census data. Finally, they use this data to inspect and control individuals as informational assemblages within the larger flows of traffic. This information is stored first in the form of the passport (walking file storage), then slowly into centralized and international databases.

Checkpoint borders try to secure the continuous circulation of large population flows. However, the checkpoint also accepts both the impossibility and the undesirability of completely controlling all movement across borders. Modern borders deal with vastly larger movements of people and things than ever before in history. Since checkpoints respond to these large and constant oscillations driven by the *laissez passer* imperatives of the liberal state and capitalist market, they try to control these flows through a multiplicity of divisions. Social motion thus becomes a continual series to be modulated and secured as probabilities using periodic checks or random searches, detaining potentially dangerous types of individuals, and so forth. If the checkpoint cannot stop all unwanted movement, at least it can stop enough of it.

The checkpoint is not simply a demarcation of territory, or a military wall around the city, or even a cellular division of the institution. The modern border is neither the curve, nor the circle, nor the linked rotation; it is the oscillation of points in an indefinite series. The checkpoint is the control over information points within a large and continuous flow of people and things. The checkpoint is a matter of what Michel Foucault has called "security":

I think we can speak here of a technique that is basically organized by reference to the problem of security, that is to say, at bottom, the problem of the series. An indefinite series of mobile elements: circulation, x number of carts, x number of passers-by, x number of thieves, x number of miasmas, and so on.

An indefinite series of events that will occur: so many boats will berth, so many carts will arrive, and so on. And equally an indefinite series of accumulating units: how many inhabitants, how many houses, and so on. I think the management of these series that, because they are open series can only be controlled by an estimate of probabilities, is pretty much the essential characteristic of the mechanism of security.[8]

In order to secure the driven oscillation of flows to and fro, economic kinopower develops three types of checkpoint borders: the police checkpoint, the security checkpoint, and the information checkpoint.

THE POLICE CHECKPOINT

The first major type of checkpoint is the police. The police checkpoint is the offensive or march border that emerged in the modern period. During this period the ancient military march of the soldier became a peaceful force for the "preservation of public tranquillity."[9] The soldier's march in battle was transformed into the policeman's march in the streets,[10] as all across Europe ex-soldiers were transformed into urban watchmen, patrolmen, police, and spies.[11] The police checkpoint became the new border wall. As police historian Alan Williams recounts:

> About 1670, acting on orders from the crown, workmen began pulling down the walls that since the fourteenth century had shielded Paris from its enemies. Their work did not so much mark a new sense of security as it did a conviction that mortar and stone had become obsolete, that the ancient walls—having already been breached—were useless, and that new strategies of defense were required. It is more than coincidence that, while men and animals struggled with the debris of fallen ramparts, the government was at work trying to create an effective urban police force. The new entity was to stand during the eighteenth century and subsequently as successor to the condemned and outmoded fortifications that had once encircled the city. It was to give the capital a more adequate barrier against danger, a security traditional ramparts had ceased to afford. Paris did not under Louis XIV become an open city; instead, it acquired, as it had under Charles V and Philippe Auguste, a new wall, one better suited to altered circumstance, one which in this case could be used against an enemy who now appeared more often within the city than without it.[12]

New enemies call for new social divisions and borders. After years of warfare Louis XIV had conquered the territory, but "Parisian authorities began to discover that an enemy dwelt in their midst, an enemy against whom walls had already proven ineffectual and whose defeat would require new measures of defense": the poor,[13] what Jeremy Bentham would later call "the mischief from internal adversaries."[14] The walls of Paris were successively torn down throughout the eighteenth and nineteenth centuries, and *grands boulevards* were erected in their place. The new borderland became the city streets; some were even named after the police (*Maréchaussée*) that patrolled them: the *boulevards des maréchaux* (Marshal's boulevard or beltway). The new, increasingly mobile enemy called for a new and particularly mobile offensive border of "police supervisions that partition society," as Foucault writes, a border that "recounts from day to day a sort of internal battle against the faceless enemy; in this war, it constitutes the daily bulletin of alarm or victory."[15] The new border calls for a new war, as Marx observes, against "the great army of beggars, most of them able-bodied men, with whom the police carries on perpetual war."[16]

In this way social flows are newly divided according to police precincts, districts, *quartiers*, beat territories, patrol routes, and so on.[17] In this sense Jacques Rancière is entirely correct to say that "the essence of the police lies neither in repression nor even in control over the living. Its essence lies in a certain way of *dividing up* the sensible."[18] Police are fundamentally a border function of kinetic social division. They divide social flows according to increasingly centralized administrative precincts and security zones, and introduce a division of persons into "citizens" and "criminals."[19] As police theorist Mark Neocleous writes, "In this sense social police is in some sense a form of border patrol—the policing of the borders of citizenship; the borders, that is, of the categories defining those who are to come under the greater control, surveillance and administration by the state. And it is by removing ... individual[s] from the category 'citizen' and placing them in the category 'claimant' or 'criminal' that the case can be made for granting the claimant/suspect fewer rights."[20] The police divide social movement and define a new system of checkpoints: inspections that can emerge at any point within social circulation. No point within social motion is outside police jurisdiction and discretion. The police checkpoint is carried out through two major kinetic forms: the police patrol and the spy.

The Police Patrol

The first type of police checkpoint is the patrol. The police patrol is the single most important police border technology of the modern period,[21] and has four major social kinetic functions: a preventative function, a kinoptic function, a kinographic function, and a circulatory function.

Preventative Function

The first social kinetic function of the police patrol is preventative; it began around the latter half of the eighteenth century. This new motion should be distinguished from two previous kinetic stages of police. The first stage is a reactionary one. Up until around the seventeenth century police had been characterized according to predominately reactionary tactics whose focus was simply to maintain or reestablish the cellular tensions between linked enclosures. "While it is true that [early police] measures were designed to prevent disorder, violence, and crime, their primary function would seem to be the reformation, by juridical means, of relations of authority and service which had been previously ensured by the customary bonds of the serf to his manor and the labourer to his master."[22] For example, when serfs would run away, riot, or refuse taxes and work, police patrols would be dispatched in order to reconnect the broken juridical links between cellular individuals and their enclosed spaces. In this first stage the police were kinopolitically restricted to the bounds of feudal law and order. The task was simply to confine and enclose an excessively mobile vagabond population, or as Hobbes puts it, to restore order to the "dissolute condition of masterlesse men, without subjection to Lawes, and a coercive Power to tye their hands."[23] Medieval police sought to bind motion into the juridical tension of a great chain of being. In this way there is a kinetically circular relationship between previous historical forms of police and law insofar as police simply refer "back to the exercise of sovereignty. The good is obedience to the law, so that the good proposed by sovereignty is that people obey it."[24]

The second historical stage of the police patrol is a more interventionist one—beginning around the mid-seventeenth century and waning around the mid-eighteenth. Instead of simply reacting to the broken juridical links between enclosed power centers and individuals, police patrols were directed at actively mobilizing a population into well-ordered social motions: to and from work, church, throughout the properly ventilated town, and so on. As Foucault writes, "From the seventeenth century 'police' begins to refer to the set of means by which the state's forces can be increased while preserving the state in good order. In other words, police will be the calculation and technique that will make it possible to establish a *mobile, yet stable and controllable relationship* between the state's internal order and the development of its forces."[25]

In this second stage police motion is not only about reestablishing the cellular borders of feudal law broken by excessive movement, but also of positively creating and arranging new rigid links between individuals and centers of enclosure in early modern states. Major centers of social kinetic power still predominate (states, churches, the aristocracy), but a new tensional order is laid out.

> In its concern with good order amidst the breakdown of the old system of authority, police held an incredibly broad compass, overseeing and administering a necessarily large and heterogeneous range of affairs. In some sense [the] police [function] was without parameters, since it was to see to everything that might be necessary to maintain order within a community. The police mandate extended to the minutiae of social life, including the means of comfort, public health, food and wine adulteration, expenses at christenings, weddings and funerals, the wearing of extravagant clothing, the behaviour of citizens at church or during festivities, the maintenance of roads, bridges and town buildings, public security, the regulation of the provision of goods and services, the performance of trades and occupations, religion, morals and manners, and the behaviour of servants towards their masters.[26]

The domain and jurisdiction of police became so broad during this time that almost everything became an object of kinetic power—even things outside the purview of the law. In this way, police government becomes increasingly interpreted as a uniquely "economic" type of power. For example, eighteenth-century German political economist Johann Heinrich Gottlob von Justi describes *oekonomie* as the science "concerned with the goods and gainful occupation of private persons."[27] But he also argues that the gains of private persons concern the gains of the state as a whole. "In other words," as Neocleous writes, "'political economy' and 'police' were not separate fields of enquiry for cameralism."[28] Police supervision and the direction over the conduct of the population during this time should thus be seen as the same as the father's rule over his household and goods.

We can see this explicitly in the work of several major French theorists of the seventeenth and early eighteenth centuries. Political economist François Quesnay describes this power precisely as "economic government."[29] Police theorist Nicolas de La Mare similarly equates "police," "economy," and "government" under the same definition of "good social order."[30] Lieutenant General of Police Jean Charles Pierre Lenoir describes policing broadly as "the science of governing men and doing them good."[31] Thus, from the mid-seventeenth to mid-eighteenth century, government is increasingly understood as the general management of "the good" in every area of life.

The important point I want to make in this brief history of police is that this "good order" was not simply the fancy of great theorists but was concretely achieved through the material mobilization of various police patrols that were required to observe social motion and keep everything and everyone moving according to a "good" circulation, down to the smallest micromovements of daily life (etiquette, posture, speed, and so on)—motions on which formal laws were often silent. This is the sense in which government, police, and economy became one and the same process of a general management of social circulation. This general management of good circulation, alternately called police, economy, or government, was aimed at achieving a social kinetic equilibrium. As Foucault argues:

> The maintenance of equilibrium is only gained insofar as each state is able to increase its own force to an extent such that it is never overtaken by another state. One can only effectively maintain the balance and equilibrium in Europe insofar as each state has a good police that allows it to develop its own forces. There will be imbalances if the development between each police is not relatively parallel. Each state must have a good police so as to prevent the relation of forces being turned to its disadvantage. One quickly arrives at the, in a way, paradoxical and opposite consequence, which consists in saying: In the end, there will be imbalance if within the European equilibrium there is a state, not my state, with bad police. . . . Consequently one must see to it that there is good police, even in other states. European equilibrium begins to function as a sort of inter-state police or as right. European equilibrium gives the set of states the right to see to it that there is good police in each state. This is the conclusion drawn explicitly and systematically in 1815 with the Vienna treaty and the policy of the Holy Alliance.[32]

During this second historical stage cameralism, police science, and *oekonomie* all emerge together as positive, interventionist, techniques for the general management of good order and equilibrium. Equilibrium is sought after by the elastic kinetic force of police power—specifically realized in the police patrol. In an international world of unpredictable oscillations, the police must strive for an equilibrium of social motion to avoid collapse. For example, the police must directly seize and stockpile enough grain and other goods so that if there are unpredictable economic contractions, there will still be enough food. When there is a surplus population of unemployed workers (beggars, vagabonds, proletariat, and so on) the police must also be called on to ventilate the streets, diffuse their riots, and facilitate commerce according to the just price. Police of this time made society into a kind of convent through a million tiny regulations (in contrast to laws), as Montesquieu writes, "continually employed about minute particulars."[33] As Mladek notes, policing "adheres much more to its economic—and especially cameral—dimension: the state is present in all relationships, *it keeps an eye on the business of the people while keeping it in motion*, and it constantly discovers new means and techniques to insure the comfort of all."[34]

The third historical stage of the police patrol is a more preventative one, beginning around the mid-eighteenth century and continuing up to the present. Rather than a band of informal watchmen or patrolmen paid to confine or bind deviant social motion back to its feudal enclosure, or an expansive army of enclosing and intervening patrol groups, police become increasingly organized as a mobile deterrent force. The theory of preventative policing emerges in the so-called reformist tradition: in the works of Italian criminal lawyer Cesare Beccaria, English and Scottish theorists Jeremy Bentham, Edwin Chadwick, and Patrick Colquhoun, German philosopher Johann Gottlieb Fichte, and French theorist Nicolas de la Mare. All of these theorists share a suspicion and criticism of an overreaching police force whose continual interventions in the details of social motion do more harm than good. For example, by restricting the sale of grain to ensure equilibrium, the police were artificially raising prices.[35] By acting on their own executive regulations, police were failing to enforce the law and protect the liberty of people's right to free movement.

The solution to this problem of the interventionist economic police state is a threefold liberal program. First, the police should be made to adhere directly to the law and not to their own executive regulations of good order. The people have the ability to reason and decide on their collective laws themselves.[36] Second, the economy and the private management of financial affairs should not be the object of interventions. Economic activity should be allowed free circulation, just as the people themselves should be allowed free movement according to their own self-interest—*Laissez faire et laissez passer*.[37] Finally, the government that is to govern best should govern least. Its primary aim should not be intervention but the security of an environment or atmosphere such that the private management of affairs and commerce should find its maximum freedom. "Political liberty," as Montesquieu writes, "consists in security."[38]

All three of these liberal reforms were achieved primarily through the concrete kinetic technology of the police patrol in three ways. First, the purpose of the preventative police patrol was to render visible the borders of the law throughout the town and country and force the potential criminal to rationalize the punitive consequences of legal violations. In this way the patrol does not need to directly coerce or enclose but can simply deter crime by its oscillating presence to and fro. The police patrol now functions more elastically—appearing in greater frequency and number according to the shifting crime potentials to produce an equilibrium. Second, the goal of the preventative police patrol was not to intervene in economic exchange, but rather to break up riots, remove beggars, deter theft, and disperse other obstructions to the free movement of commerce and persons. Third, the preventative patrol secured certain environmental borders—roadways, customs houses, watchhouses, streetlights, sewer systems, and so on—that were the conditions under which liberal movement could take place. "Future evils," as von Berg writes, "are in the last account only the object of police, for its principal goal is avoidance and prevention. Past evils, insofar as they are submitted to the judgment of law, belong to the justice system."[39]

However, preventative policing also produces a kinetic paradox. Although the aim of liberal police reform was to create fixed borders of legality and limit police motion, the practice of prevention actually destroys fixed borders and all limits to police motion. If the goal of deterrence is to prevent crime before it occurs by policing potentially criminal acts—the wearing of masks, begging, idleness, and so on—then the border between legal and illegal loses its fixed points and is stretched elastically to any activity whatever in any place whatever that may possibly lead to a crime. As Marx observes, "A preventive law, therefore, has within it no measure, no rational rule, for a rational rule can only result from the nature of a thing, in this instance of freedom. It is without measure, for if prevention of freedom is to be effective, it must be as all-embracing as its object, i.e., unlimited. A preventive law is therefore the contradiction of an unlimited limitation."[40]

This phenomenon is precisely what defines modern borders as checkpoints. The so-called contradiction of the unlimited limitation does not imply that modern borders have been abolished. On the contrary, since criminality is potentially anywhere, so is the border: unlimited in the sense in which it can take place at any point whatsoever, but limited in the sense in which it does take place in the form of an inspection or check. The inspection does not presume guilt, but only the potentiality of guilt. Thus the police are infinitely justified in their continual inspection of the populace via the patrol. "The boundary where it ceases is fixed not by necessity, but by the fortuitousness of arbitrariness," as Marx writes.[41]

The second function of the police patrol checkpoint is kinoptic. The police border is not only an optical border, it is above all a mobile optical border, an "ambulating lighthouse," as Chadwick calls it, whose movement allows it to appear at any point whatever.[42] The kinopticism of the police patrol has a dual function. On the one hand, it is a kinoptics that makes visible the patrol itself as a moving image of perfection and order.

> It is the "watchman" who is emblematic of the conception first developed in England by the police reformers. The watch is synoptic: the watchman is actually on display and it is precisely through his conspicuousness that he deters the potential offender; the watch is therefore a fully overt exercise . . . the visible watch is intimidating for offenders, but it is a factor of reassurance for potential victims. Hence, in contrast with the spy, whom no one follows, the watchman is a dual figure, threatening for those he guards against and friendly for those he protects and for whom he sets an example that may be imitated.[43]

The aim of the police patrol is to make itself visible in order to deter crime and to reassure the innocent that the police border is on the move and can appear at any point whatever. The power of the patrol is precisely in its constant visibility and mobility. Everyone knows that the border of criminality is not only visible in the fixed location of the watchhouse, but that the border is actively on the move. Foreigners, migrants, vagabonds, and beggars have crossed fences, walls, and cells, but the checkpoint is mobile and can reappear where it is least expected. They know this precisely because its appearance is visibly mobile in the patrol.[44]

The police patrol also renders itself visible as a moving image of civil propriety and masculine authority.[45] "The posture and regulated gait of the constable were complemented by the system of beat patrol, which envisaged individual constables moving at a regular pace through space. The regularity and uniformity of the constable on the beat would be projected out onto the space through which he moved, police authorities hoped, bringing about control over public space through steady surveillance and physical example."[46]

The bodily motion of the patrol officer rendered visible his control over social motion and its limits. "The regularity of spatial division was to complement the regulated body of the constable. Beats were revised in 1859 including detailed maps of individual beats compiled by Superintendent Freeman, which he claimed 'relate with minuteness the manner in which they should be worked.' Individual beats were timed, the superintendent having noted where every constable would be at ten-minute intervals. By 1888 two miles per hour was assessed as the correct walking pace to observe 'people and places.'"[47]

The kinoptic function of the police patrol was thus in part aimed at displaying a perfect moving image of controlled motion through the city. The regularity of its circulation, the rhythm of its "beat," the gait of its walk, the predictability of its most minute gestures, and the speed of its walk were put on display before the public as the ideal image of the city: "a massive vision-machine in motion constructed from a multitude of human moving parts."[48] In rendering itself visible, the modern police force also made possible an increasingly hierarchical and bureaucratic structure of police organization in which the beat system with its uniforms, numbers, and checkpoints allowed the patrol to be monitored and regulated.[49] However, one of the effects of this visible regularity, as Chadwick notes, was that criminals began to anticipate the patrol circuits in order to evade them.[50] The visibility of the patrol thus also makes possible its evasion.

On the other hand, the kinopticism of the police patrol also renders visible the mobility of the population itself. "Those who administer public power," as Fichte writes, "must have the power and the right to keep watch over the citizens' conduct; they have police power and police legislation."[51] In this way the preventative police patrol is more like a pair of eyes than a pair of arms. The more it watches, the less it needs to act.[52] Kinoptic surveillance makes the target feel that he or she is a suspect of a mobile investigation and in this way deters deviance. The purpose of this kinoptic investigation is, as eighteenth-century French theorist Antoine Servan observes, to "repress criminal conceits as soon as they spring to mind, and still they fear that the magistrate will see through them by surprise."[53] Even when one is not being watched, one still feels the eyes of the patrol's optical scrutiny. This type of surveillance is far from being able to literally oversee everything. This is precisely why we cannot understand police surveillance independently of the mobile optics of the patrol and the requirement of a variety of technical and architectural mechanisms for facilitating its moving view of the city. In particular, the removal of various fences, walls, and enclosures and their replacement by wider orthogonal streets and boulevards allow a police officer to "command a greater view of his portion of his beat, so he may make his presence necessary."[54] Additionally, the construction of a vast network of watchhouses allows an around-the-clock patrol to report to and be dispatched from a series of decentered checkpoints throughout the city,[55] forming a system of relays in a wider circulatory pattern of visibility.[56] A correspondence can then be established between the watchhouses, as Colquhoun advocates, "so as to be able more effectually to *watch the motions* of all suspected persons; with a view to quick and immediate detection."[57] Finally, surveillance cannot be understood independently of its dromology: the need to "walk slowly enough to observe everything."[58] If one is innocent, as Fichte concludes, "how could rectitude possibly fear and hate the eye of such watchfulness?"[59]

Therefore the kinopticism of the police patrol should be distinguished from panopticism on five points.[60] First, panopticism is the view from an immobile central tower, whereas kinopticism is the view from a mobile and decentered network of ambulating lighthouses. In this way we should look to Chadwick and not Bentham for our model of police power. Panopticism is immobile and centric, whereas kinopticism is oscillatory and elastic. Second, pantopticism takes place within an enclosed and cellular space, whereas kinopticism takes place in an open and punctuated space of circulating checkpoints. Third, the aim of panopticism is to render the watcher invisible so that the target never knows if he or she is being watched. Kinopticism functions differently by rendering the mobile watchman visible precisely in order to display and model its kinopower and possibility of rapid elastic mobility to any point whatever when needed. Finally, the aim of panopticism is to see everything at a single glance, but the kinoptic view is limited by its mobility and dromology.

Therefore the term "surveillance" (to oversee) does not fully capture the function of kinopticism as well as its more popular terminological counterpart during eighteenth-century policing in France and England: "superintendence." Superintendence is not merely an optical activity and does not presume the enclosed, immobile, and centric perspective of Bentham's prison model. According to the OED, superintendence refers more specifically to "the management or arrangement of (an activity or organization)" and comes from the Latin word *intendere*, meaning to spread out, direct one's steps, extend, and focus the mind or attention. The police patrol is thus much more related to the kinetic meaning indicated by the word *intendere* in its management of mobile activity, walking, and extension of focused visibility/knowledge of the conduct of the population than a simple overseeing.

Kinographic Function

The third function of the police patrol checkpoint is kinographic. Not only does the police patrol render itself and the population visible in the form of a mobile inspection that can appear at any point whatever, but it also functions as a recording apparatus: "This unceasing observation had to be accumulated in a series of reports and registers; throughout the eighteenth century, an immense police text increasingly covered society by means of a complex documentary organization . . . what was registered in this way were forms of behavior, attitudes, possibilities, suspicions—a permanent account of individuals' behavior."[61]

Just like its kinoptic function, this graphic or recording function has a dual role. On the one hand, police borders record their own movement with various mnemokinetic techniques. The citywide around-the-clock police patrol would not have been possible without a kinographic record of the city, the precinct borders, the routes to be patrolled, by whom, and at what time.[62] Patrols were often expected to complete their circuit in a certain time at a certain speed (two to three miles per hour). All these routes were synchronized and recorded by the constable or superior in a booklet or map of movements. This presupposes a vast graphism and division of the city and territory as a mobile arena of circulation. All police motion is recorded in miniature in the form of an elastic timetable whose orchestrated motions could be interrupted at any point by a criminal event, requiring patrols to be redirected to the scene. The increasingly bureaucratized police apparatus kept careful count of movements to show their efficiency and catalog its activities. The French police "listed the numbers entered in the registers of the *maisons garnies* as well as all of those apprehended by different patrols, all carefully categorized by offense—vagabond, prostitute, night-time prowler or known prowler (*rodeur de nuit or rodeur connu*), and so forth. The reports from the *Gendarmerie* companies were similar and during the Restoration they began carefully categorizing all of their patrols as ordinary circuits of their districts, as service at fairs or at markets, as physical support for the civil power, as the serving of warrants, and so on."[63]

Patrol officers not only cataloged and classified their activities, they also marked and mapped their own bodily movements with identifiable uniforms, numbers, and letters that made them visibly traceable and able to be monitored by superior officers.[64] Additionally, patrol officers often kept mobile booklets to record their practical duties, such as "checking doors and bolts, cellar doors and fan lights."[65] What is left behind is a perfect image of their movement. All these mnemokinetic technologies "where everything is registered"[66] were then compiled and made known to the police magistrate, who Lenoir claims was "aware of all details, whatever their nature . . . he knows every dossier in all of its extent . . . he alone makes all the decisions and gives all the orders that are issued in his name."[67] In this way all the kinographic recordings are ultimately inscribed in the memory of the magistrate.

On the other hand, police patrol borders record the movement of others throughout the city. Police patrols not only superintended the people's movements but also recorded them faithfully for their own use as well as the use of others. Police patrols recorded "any suspicious characters either arriving or leaving any parts of the city within the constable's beat," something historically reserved for fixed border guards.[68] They memorized or recorded any loiterers they saw[69] and actively "collected information from those willing to volunteer it, from those who were paid for it, and from those who could be pressurized into providing it."[70] To trace the movements of criminals, over the course of the nineteenth century French police increasingly recorded the details of all defendants and criminals in the *compte general* according to age, sex, civil status, place of birth, residence, level of education, occupation, urban or rural, status as wage earner, self-employed, unemployed, and so on. This format then spread across Europe to Austria, Belgium, Sweden, and several German states.[71] As Emsley reports:

> The Prefect of Police in Paris collected and listed daily statistics of the numbers of individuals entering the city, the numbers of crimes committed, the numbers of individuals arrested, the numbers of interrogations and of persons held in the various prisons. Particularly shocking and major incidents were noted in some detail in his daily reports under the heading *événements*. Initially the reports were all handwritten, but towards the end of the empire all of the information was entered in the appropriate spaces on specially printed forms. The Gendarmerie companies prepared monthly reports listing similar information, as well as the agricultural situation in their department, the state of public opinion, and the number of patrols that each company's brigades had made. The collection of this information long outlived the fall of the empire.[72]

The kinographic circuit can thus be formulated in the following way: watch, record, report, collect, distribute, repeat. The final distributed information was then returned through the gazette or bulletin back to the patrols so they would be prepared to make better observations and repeat the kinographic circuit. Chadwick develops an entire recording system to track social motion:

> At each police station of a subdivision, i.e., at each watch-house, a book should be kept for entering all information of the offenses committed within the district to which such watch-house may belong. That every such information should comprise the most material circumstances relative to the offense inserted by the injured party ... the time when, the place where ... the description of the person charged, names of informant.... the keeper of the watch-house or the

proper officer in attendance there should make copies of all such entries and forward them on the day they are made to the chief public office of the department to which such watch-house may belong. . . . the whole of the copies of these informations be transmitted on the night of the same day from the offices of the respective departments to the chief office; there arranged under the heads of the several departments, methodized, with an index to the descriptions of stolen goods, and printed with all the dispatch of that far more complicated publication—a newspaper. 4) That printed copies of these informations, i.e., copies of the Gazette, be returned on the morning of the next day to each department for further distribution within it: one to be given to each police-officer, one to every publican, and one to each pawnbroker within the district.[73]

A very similar kinographic system was set up in Germany and Austria with the *Fahndungsblatt,* a journal containing the names and descriptions of wanted men to aid police watches.[74] In Germany a vast apparatus of index cards recording all criminal motion and stolen property was developed.[75] "The prime requisite in the office equipment of a detective bureau is a criminal record file," as police historian Raymond Fosdick writes. "The police must be acquainted with the criminal propensities of specific individuals; they must be armed with accurate knowledge of the past records of those whom they arrest or suspect. Such knowledge is not only essential to successful detective work in providing a basis for action, but it furnishes a guide to magistrates in pronouncing sentence."[76] Accordingly, the detective bureau of Berlin kept a catalog of photographs, fingerprints, an alphabetic register of missing and dead persons, a register of persons wanted (*steckbrief*), a catalog of saloons and dance halls, newspaper clippings, and handwriting files.[77]

This massive kinographic apparatus was made possible at the lowest level by the police patrol that circulated the streets and collected the raw kinoptic data of social movement, but the assembly and interpretation of this data also contributed to the larger governmental project of maintaining a national self-knowledge and equilibrium with other nation-states through the invention of statistics, the science of the state. It is worth quoting Foucault at length on this point:

This instrument common to European equilibrium and the organization of police is statistics. The effective preservation of European equilibrium requires that each state is in a position, first, to know its own forces, and second, to know and evaluate the forces of the others, thus permitting a comparison that makes it possible to uphold and maintain the equilibrium. Thus a principle is needed for deciphering a state's constitutive forces. For each state, one's own and the others, one needs to know the population, the army, the natural resources, the production, the commerce, and the monetary circulation—all the elements that are in fact provided by the science, or domain of knowledge, statistics, which is founded and developed at this time. How can one establish statistics? It can be established precisely by police, for police itself, as the art of developing forces, presupposes that each state exactly identifies its possibilities, its virtualities. Police makes statistics necessary, but police also makes statistics possible. For it is precisely the whole set of procedures set up to increase, combine, and develop forces, it is this whole administrative assemblage that makes it possible to identify what each state's forces comprise and their possibilities of development. Police and statistics mutually condition each other, and statistics is a common instrument between police and the European equilibrium. Statistics is the state's knowledge of the state, understood as the state's knowledge both of itself and also of other states. As such, statistics is the hinge of the two technological assemblages.[78]

The border as checkpoint is no longer fixed in a single location, and the new enemy can longer be known in advance. What is known first is the massive collection of fragmented bits of information; these bits of information are then assembled and connected by the police and magistrate into a picture of the emergent or possible suspect. Finally, the police act on their interpretation of this mobile data. In this way the potential criminal subject reaches the border before any actual subject does. Kinographics and statistics are thus required to follow the vectors of social motion, where new potential divisions are required, and where old actual ones should be removed. In the modern world of unpredictable oscillations and social divisions, statistics provide probabilities for governmental action, and the police patrol is the source of these new kinographic borders.[79]

Circulatory Function

The fourth function of the police patrol checkpoint is circulatory. The aim of the police patrol as a border checkpoint is not only to stop and inspect, but to make move. The police patrol manages social circulation in three ways: (1) it functions as a conductor of traffic to secure the optimum conditions of safe transportation, (2) it functions as the dromological support for *speedy and efficient* circulation and quick response time to criminality, (3) it functions as a "move-on" power of mass mobilization against idleness, vagabondage, and riots. Circulation is the fourth privileged object of police power.[80] "In short, [policing] concerns the whole problem of the exchange, circulation, manufacture, and marketing of goods. Coexistence of men and circulation of goods: we should finish also by saying, the circulation of men and goods in relation to each other. It is the whole problem, precisely, of these vagrants, of people moving around. Let's say, in short, that police is essentially urban and market based, or to put things more brutally, it is an institution of the market, in the very broad sense."[81]

The practice of police patrols as a circulatory border force emerges precisely around a common understanding of modern government as an organic body whose health depends on the proper circulation of blood throughout, without obstruction. This is clearly attested to in both Hobbes's and Rousseau's philosophy of the political body. In *Leviathan*, Hobbes equates the circulation of money with the blood of the sovereign since it "passeth from Man to Man, within the Common-wealth; and goes round about, Nourishing (as it passeth) every part thereof."[82] Rousseau follows this point explicitly in *The Social Contract*, stating that "public income is the blood, [of] a prudent economy."[83] In this analogy, the police are the force of social division that ensures the proper circulation of blood/money through the commonwealth, preventing social motion from "flowing out of its due course," Hobbes writes, "in the same manner as the Blood in a Pleurisie, getting into the Membrane of the breast, breedeth there an Inflammation, accompanied with a Fever, and painfull stitches."[84] The police block some motions and facilitate others, keeping money and people moving in all the right ways through a network of coordinated social divisions—effectively fighting social disease.

The first circulatory function of the police border is that it conducts traffic. Up until around the eighteenth century most city traffic regulated itself. However, with the increase of transportation, population, and city blocks, street accidents became a common occurrence. As Chadwick writes, "The cry arose for police; coachmen were stopped, drivers directed, foot-passengers assisted, and freedom of passage ceased."[85] Traffic was controlled, cab and omnibus drivers were forbidden from loitering and drunk driving, and driving horse drawn carriages without reins were all subject to police action.[86] In France artisans were prevented from working in the middle of the street, and street stalls and buildings were reduced in size to accommodate wider streets and intersections.[87] New social borders of motion had to be invented for an increasingly mobile population. This took the form of the traffic cop and his commands to stop and move, following the vector divisions of the city block.

As early as 1332 in England constables were appointed to ensure the security of merchants traveling on the highways and look into dangerous wanderers.[88] In France ex-military cavalrymen performed a similar early police function on highways.[89] The policing of highways is an old function, but the emergence of police checkpoints on every corner directing traffic is a modern function that reveals a new social kinetic border condition. In his *Traite de droit public* (1697), French theorist Jean Domat even devotes an entire chapter to this natural relationship titled "Of Police for the Use of Seas, Rivers, Bridges, Roads, Public Squares, Major Routes and Other Public Places."[90] The same preoccupations reappear in 1749 in the works of police officer Guillaute: "No more revolts, no more seizures, no more tumults," he writes. "Public order will reign if we are careful to distribute our human time and space between the city and the country by a severe regulation of transit; if we are attentive to schedules as well as to alignments and signal systems; if by environmental standardization the entire city is made transparent, that is, familiar to the policeman's eye."[91] Thus by 1828 we find authorities like French *commissaire* Thouret making clear this essential connection between police and traffic management. "The essential object of our municipal police is the safety of the inhabitants of Paris ... free traffic movement, clean streets, the supervision of and precautions against accident, [and] the maintenance of public order in public places."[92] This modern connection between freedom, movement, and police-controlled circulation via a network of border checkpoints is rendered explicit by German philosopher Johann Gottlieb Fichte in his *Foundations of Natural Right*:

> Each citizen must be able to travel throughout the state's entire territory freely and secure from all accidents, as part of his right to cultivate the land, to acquire goods, to engage in trade and commerce, etc. . . . Thus armed guards and patrols are needed, even on the highways, if they happen to be unsafe. . . . Ensuring the safety of the citizens' lives and property requires that police superintendence extend to the roads and streets. The citizen has a right to demand good roads and streets, for the state has guaranteed him the ability to carry on his business in the quickest and most convenient manner possible, or—even if his travel is only for pleasure—to enjoy his rightfully acquired property in the manner most pleasing to him.[93]

The modern border is not merely a blockage, it is an elastic redirection, a mobile armed patrol or checkpoint that roams and secures the conditions by which freedom can be stretched now here, now there. It is no longer centric or even linked, but oscillates along a series in order to contract and expand where and when social division is needed.

Throughout the eighteenth and nineteenth centuries roadways were widened, made visible with lights, and patrolled in order to increase the elastic deployment of this new border technique, the checkpoint. The secure city had to be built so that its social flows could circulate freely under the kinoptic and kinographic march of the police patrol. In the eighteenth century a French architect by the name of Pierre Vigné de Vigny developed a renovation plan for Paris that "involved cutting routes through the town, and streets wide enough to ensure four functions," as Foucault writes.

First, hygiene, ventilation, opening up all kinds of pockets where morbid miasmas accumulated in crowded quarters, where dwellings were too densely packed. . . . Second, ensuring trade within the town. Third, connecting up this network of streets to external roads in such a way that goods from outside can arrive or be dispatched, but without giving up the requirements of customs control. And finally, an important problem for towns in the eighteenth century was allowing for surveillance, since the suppression of city walls made necessary by economic development meant that one could no longer close towns in the evening or closely supervise daily comings and goings, so that the insecurity of the towns was increased by the influx of the floating population of beggars, vagrants, delinquents, criminals, thieves, murderers, and so on, who might come, as everyone knows, from the country. In other words, it was a matter of organizing circulation, eliminating its dangerous elements, making a division between good and bad circulation, and maximizing the good circulation by diminishing the bad. An axis of circulation with Paris was organized.[94]

The key to controlling social circulation is the patrol of street traffic. Traffic, like blood through veins, must be circulated through the proper width and always kept moving against all the miasmas that would slow it down or block it. However, at any point whatever, the patrol can make a division between a good and bad circulation and redirect it.

In 1853 Baron Haussmann was commissioned by Emperor Napoléon III to widen the streets of Paris, increasing the elasticity of police and military deployments against the poor. Haussmann increased blood flow and broke up social pleurisies by turning "trouble neighborhoods" into boulevards, the terrain of police circulation. Haussmann describes these neighborhoods as homes to a "nomadic population without any real ties to the land [property] and without any effective surveillance [they] grow at a prodigious speed."[95] By turning their homes into streets, they could be effectively patrolled, circulated, and surveilled.

The second circulatory function of the police border is that it increases the speed or dromological power of the border. The social divisions produced by police patrols are not only at any point whatever, they are also at any time whatever. As Montesquieu writes, "The actions of the police are quick."[96] They must be quick enough to occur as close to any time as possible in order to function as deterrents. Potential criminals must know that they have no time to escape. In this way, modern checkpoint borders are time sensitive. If one moves fast enough, it is as if the border does not exist. Thus the police border is only as strong as it is fast. Police are not effective, as Chadwick notes, "because *every* furlong of the public road is protected by a horse patrol, or a police officer, but because an officer may appear on any furlong from every point ... within such short portions of time as must preclude the opportunity of committing a burglary in the intervals."[97] Chadwick was one of the first police theorists to emphasize the need for police vehicles that would increase their patrol speed and reaction time. In his book *The Health of Nations*, Chadwick proposes

> a patrol by a tricycle worked by two men abreast, armed with revolvers. The patrol with the tricycle would be regulated to be worked at eight miles an hour instead of three. There would be no footfall to be heard, and the patrol would be silent for all suburban districts. If there are any men perceived at night with a trap that takes to flight, the tricycle patrol may put on extra speed which will keep them in sight or overtake them, for the tricycle has now attained a possible speed of eighteen miles an hour. ... Another great advantage which would spring from this method of following and detecting crime and criminals would be the greater rapidity and certainty of detection.[98]

The emphasis here is not that the tricycle can chase down fast criminals since criminals could easily enter a narrow alleyway or other difficult terrain to avoid capture by tricycle; the important kinetic and dromological idea here is the potential speed of the police—that they could appear at any space-time whatever. When the police radio was invented in 1923, it condensed border space-time even further. "[The radio's] main usefulness will be as a deterrent. Many thieves and house-breakers will be afraid to operate when there is the possibility of the sudden arrival of a car load of police, bound to no particular beat, but likely to appear at any-time in any street in the suburbs."[99] Even without radios, modern police power has always relied on speed, even if it means the suspension of law. Speed is then of the essence, as Lenoir notes, and police operations must proceed unhindered by formal rules that would slow them down.[100]

The third circulatory function of the police border is its "move-on" power of mass mobilization against idleness, vagabondage, and riots. Interestingly enough, police patrols rarely apprehended criminals; most of their time was occupied with minor street offenses.[101] Police patrols largely used what were called "move-on" powers against idle populations. What seems like a minor kinetic power—to force someone to move—was actually one of the single most important police powers for managing the circulation and social division of the modern city.[102] In London the passing of the 1879 regulation for "keeping order upon and preventing obstruction of the carriage and footways of the City" offered enormous discretionary powers to remove people from streets and shift "nuisances" from one part of the city to another.[103] The law pertained to selling goods in the street but also to loitering, stating that no person "should loiter in a manner calculated to obstruct or hinder members of the public in the free and proper use of such street or footway and every such person shall move on upon being so required by any officer of the Council or any member of the police force."[104] In particular, such move-on powers were used to free up the flow of trade and commerce. Police would "sweep off the streets with an equable hand street traders, beggars, prostitutes, street-entertainers, pickets, children playing football and freethinking and socialist speakers alike." As E. P. Thompson writes, "The pretext very often was that a complaint of interruption of trade had been received from a shopkeeper."[105]

By the nineteenth century almost every police force in Europe had some equivalent amorphous law that allowed police patrols to mobilize people into circulation. The circulatory function of the police is thus to make sure that bad circulations are divided from good ones and that good circulations run smoothly. As police historian Klaus Mladek writes, "'Move along! There is nothing to see here' will always be the motto of the police. The police quells any disruption of its order; it refigures and transforms the space within the confines of what can be done, said and perceived."[106] As Jacques Rancière puts it, "The police is that which says that here, on this street, there's nothing to see and so nothing to do but move along. It asserts that the space for circulating is nothing but the space of circulation."[107]

Idleness was by far the prime concern of modern police. From 1667 to 1789 the idle poor were their obsession. In France Servan, a member of the Parliament of Grenoble, writes that an "idle man has begun to surrender to evil."[108] In Paris Lenoir writes that "the vilest of occupation is that of beggars; the worst plague for a nation is begging."[109] In England Bentham writes that "if idleness is to be discouraged, it is not because it is the non-acquisition of wealth, but because it is the source of crimes."[110] Idleness became associated with evil and crime not only because of what it does, but because of what it might do. Good circulation and good movement beget good order. Without movement, there is no order. Movement keeps everyone within view and subject to continual and multiple inspections throughout their traversal across various checkpoints. By remaining idle the vagrant resists the border patrol. As a senior constable Byrnes complains, "As soon as they [the men and women] see a Constable coming they move past him, and when he gets to the end of his beat, and looks back he sees that they have settled on again."[111]

Riots were another primary concern for police. Riots, or what we could call "collective idleness," block the flow of commerce and the ordered circulation between mobile border points. As police historian Jean-Paul Brodeur notes, "The absolute rulers of continental Europe did not fear individual crime as much as collective violence. Riots were a constant threat taken with utmost seriousness by absolute monarchs. Riots were often generated by external conditions such as the lack of food supplies that resulted in famine."[112] Riots and collective social action pose a threat because they have the possibility of blocking movement or redirecting it. They are more powerful than individual idlers. They are like the tumors in healthy police circulation. Again Fichte makes their danger entirely clear:

> Citizens cannot assemble inside a house without the police knowing about it; and the police have the power, as well as the right (since the street is subject to their authority), to prevent such an assembly, if it arouses their suspicion. If so many people assemble that public security is threatened—and any assembly can pose such a threat if it is strong enough to resist the armed power of local authorities—then the police shall demand an explanation of their intentions, and watch to make sure that they actually do what they claim to be doing. In such a situation, a person's right over his house ceases to exist; or, if the owner of the house does not want that to happen, then the group must assemble in a public building. . . . The situation is the same when people gather in the streets, in marketplaces, and so on: the police have the right to prevent, or to oversee, such gatherings.[113]

The danger is that any such assembly might be resistant to the police. Since the police are a preventative force, this possible congelation of motion must be dispersed like a blood clot before it gets out of control. The social kinetic effect of this border function is the shutting down of political movements and free association, which Marx bemoans at length.[114]

The Police Spy

The second type of police checkpoint is the spy. The spy is the shadow side of the patrol and thus follows the inverse of the three social kinetic functions found in the patrol: kinoptics, kinography, and circulation. The police spy functions as a border in the same sense as the patrol does: he establishes a mobile social division between good and bad circulation, legality and illegality, citizen and foreigner, patriot and traitor, idler and mover, and so on. But police spies also divide social movement and define a new system of specifically invisible checkpoints: autonomous inspections that occur at any point whatever. Anyone may be a spy, and anyone may be spied on at any point. The police spy is thus the continuation of the patrol by other inverted means. While the aim of the police patrol is to be able to appear at any point and any time, the aim of the police spy is precisely to be able to disappear at any point and time. "The thief cannot know where the spy is . . . a spy may pop up at any moment."[115] In this way the police spy makes explicit what was already implicit in the patrol: that the conditions of free movement and liberty are precisely the absolute and illiberal invisible control over the entire environment or milieu itself. Free movement, like the patrol, is only appearance. Constrained movement, like the spy, is the reality of bordered social mobility.

The first border function of the police spy is an inverted kinoptics. While the kinoptics of the patrol creates a visible model of the kinetic b(order), the spy renders invisible, but no less effective, that same b(order) since anyone may potentially be a police spy. The visible border and invisible border are simply two sides of the same border. Spying was an essential part of every modern police force in Europe and Britain. "One French lieutenant of police, Sartines, boasted to Louis XV that where three men were talking on the street, at least one of them worked for him, while in late-eighteenth-century Russia it was widely assumed that everybody's words and actions were watched to such an extent that there may have been no social circle without a spy."[116]

An officer in uniform would simply cause criminals to wait until he was not around. As English superintendent Andrew McLean pointed out, "A man in uniform will hardly ever take a thief." The main idea of the plainclothes police spies was to conceal their identity and thus apprehend criminals. In fact, three-quarters of the "beggars and felons" apprehended were taken by officers 'in plain clothes.'"[117] In France this was also similarly the case. According to Lenoir, three inspectors employing a network of spies and criminals arrested more criminals in Paris than the Guard and all other uniformed companies devoted to security taken together.[118] "There was first a score of "observers" (*observateurs*) acting in the traditional capacity of informants. However, these observers also ran an array of subobservers (*sous-mouches*—"flies," the French equivalent for snitches) for themselves; this network of informants encompassed prostitutes, those who had an obligation to inform the police, innkeepers, and persons running all kinds of gambling houses."[119] Through a vast network of anonymous informants and snitches, criminals began to police each other, but police also became criminals. In particular, English "thief-takers" (hired police) and other officers were convicted of setting up individuals to commit offenses and then claiming the reward money for their arrest and conviction.[120] Thus the detective in English literature is often depicted as a renegade: autonomous, plainclothes wearing, and dangerously close to a criminal himself. "The boundaries between whether the detective was a formal law enforcer or law unto himself seemed far from clear."[121]

This is the paradox of the spy: that the spy is trusted to deceive. The spy is invisible to criminals as a spy, but also remains invisible to the police insofar as the spy may actually be in collusion with criminals and spying on the police themselves. The social border between legal and criminal now comes down to the caprice of paid informants. Thus what occurs in the inverted kinoptics of the police spy is not only that the checkpoint is rendered simply invisible, but that it is no longer clear when, where, or if an inspection has taken place. The border becomes everywhere and nowhere at the same time.

The second border function of the police spy is an inverted kinography. While the kinography of the patrol records the outward or external movement of the population, the spy instead records the inward expression of the population that they themselves will voluntarily reveal. As Fichte writes, "Why should the state want to observe its citizens secretly? So that the citizens will not realize that they are being observed. And why should they not realize that they are being observed? Either, so that they will reveal without inhibition what they think about the government and what they are planning against it, and thus become their own traitors; or, so that they will reveal what they know of other secret, illegal activities."[122]

The spy simply records the words of the traitor's self-betrayal. When it comes to preventative policing, no utterance or secret is beyond suspicion. Thus the task of the spy is to record it all, the dust of daily events: "to observe everything that happened in Paris and report crimes, misdemeanors, and all disorders to the commissioners."[123] However, observation is never without (mis)interpretation. During the French Revolution in particular, an entire system of traceable kinetic signs was created to help the spy decipher the border between the true patriot and the traitor. "A panoply of exterior signs was invoked to identify conspirators, including their private friendships, suspicious gestures . . . overacting," and even "self-indulgent overeating."[124] The comings and goings of suspects were traced. Even the most minute gestures and affects were used to identify the border between foreigner and national.

The third border function of the police spy is an inverted circulation. While the circulation conducted by the patrol moves according to a regular and ordered rhythm, the circulation of the spy moves irregularly. The spy is not the model of good circulation, directing traffic and moving idlers along. The spy is the countermodel or shadow whose motions mimic those of the wandering vagrant. The regularity of the patrol is precisely what allows criminals to predict it like a clock and avoid it. If crime takes place in intervals between well-ordered circulation, then the spy must move within the "irregular" intervals of the patrol as its double.[125] In England in the 1750s, these privately hired "thief-takers" were appropriately called "runners" because their irregular appearance, patrol times (evening until midnight), and movements contrasted with the regular slow-paced walk of the police patrol.[126] The spy checkpoint is not only an invisible point that, out of nowhere, can lead to deportation, incarceration, or exile, but is also an irregular countercirculation that creates a social division precisely where it was not expected.

In this way, Thomas Hobbes compares the kinopower of spies to the invisible threads of a spider's web. The spider's web appears precisely where it was not expected, in some idle nook off the main boulevard. But this is precisely where bugs like to crawl. The invisible web catches the bug and alerts the spider through the kinographic signs of its shaking web. The spider can then devour its prey. "They who bear Rule," Hobbes writes, "can no more know what is necessary to be commanded for the defence of their Subjects without Spies, than those Spiders can when they shall goe forth, and whether they shall repair, without the motion of those threds."[127]

CONCLUSION

The police checkpoint and its preventative form of kinopower remains with us today. For example, the police still patrol neighborhoods kinoptically (now with video cameras), still gather and produce data on social mobility kinographically (fingerprints, mug shots, video surveillance), and still deploy various discretionary powers to facilitate good circulation (stop and frisk, profiling, and antihomeless or "loitering" laws). Today liberal governments still deploy paid spies (the FBI, CIA, and others) to track social motion. High-tech wiretapping, Internet browsing and consumption habits, and all kinds of surveillance programs at the National Security Agency are actively monitoring the patterns of mobile social life in secrecy. Contemporary life remains full of police encounters and secret surveillance technologies. Accordingly, contemporary social mobility cannot be understood without a careful analysis of the elastic kinopower of the checkpoints that watch, record, and secretly monitor human movement. But the offensive border is only the first of three checkpoints that require analysis: security and informational checkpoints remain to be analyzed in the next chapter.

CHAPTER 6
The Checkpoint II

THE SECURITY CHECKPOINT

The second major type of modern border is the security checkpoint. The security checkpoint is the defensive limit border that emerged in the modern period. While the police checkpoint offensively marches out into the streets to mark a division in the population between citizens and criminals, the security checkpoint protects, defends, and enforces the institutions that are defined and ordered by this border march. The security border ensures the stability and maintenance of this march border through two major kinetic institutions: private property and the nation. The police function offensively to carve out a route of social circulation, while private property and the nation preserve the circulation of what has been carved out. For example, the very existence of privately owned factories, workhouses, shopfronts, and markets must be legally and culturally defended so that enough commerce will be generated to pay for continued police borders. Modern policing presupposes private property to be defended. In this way there is a border circuit or feedback loop between police and the security institutions of private property and the nation: the latter guarantees a place for the former, which in turn guarantees the place of the latter's free flow of commerce and wealth.

Private Property

The first type of security checkpoint is that of private property. The invention of private property in the modern period was given legal definition in England in the seventeenth century.[1] It is defined by the two primary functions of the checkpoint border: the isolation of a point in a continuous social flow and an inspection of this point, which can occur at any point whatever. First and foremost, private property is defined by its mobility in a continuous social flow. Feudal property is bound by a vertically linked tension to the sovereign, who juridically decides on the territorial limits and borders of the land he grants to his vassals in fee and by a horizontally linked tension to the serfs bound to that land as customary property. This does not mean that feudal property is immobile, but simply that its movement is defined by a linked rotation of bound juridical relationships. Private property, however, is kinetically different. The motion of private property is oscillatory in the sense that ownership and deeds simply move to and fro to any person whatever who can pay for it. As Fichte writes, "There is no reason *a priori* why this meadow ought to be mine rather than my neighbors."[2] Furthermore, the owner of the property is free to oscillate here and there without any fixed requirement of territorial residence. Private property is an expression of the will of individuals to move as they please. This kinetic aspect is made clear in the original and etymological usage of the moral word "propriety" as interchangeable with the word "property" in John Locke's *Two Treatises*. "In the eighteenth century property-as-propriety was taken for granted.... Locke's comment that every man has a property in his own person should be read alongside his suggestion that man is 'Proprietor of his own Person.'"[3] Property and propriety were so closely connected because they both refer to the social kinetic freedom to move as one wishes. Good ownership begets good moral order and movement. The institution of private property frees up the mobility of the proper or well-moving owner, outside the links of vassalage.

Property ownership is in this way broken free from its territorial and juridical linkages and circulated across a fluctuating economic market. Private property enters into a whole new social kinetic regime of unpredictable expansions and contractions of value. One never knows where property will go, what it will do, or who will own it. This insecurity results in an elasticity of its value and an entire economic concern over the potential productivity of property. With the birth of market-valued private property in sixteenth- and seventeenth-century England came a radical transformation of "competitive rent" prices, now valued according to what a piece of land or property could possibly produce.[4] In order for private property to be secured, its value must be elastically adjusted. It must oscillate to and fro to whoever will pay the highest price for it. The value and possible productivity of property is itself a form of economic security and defense border of economic value. Given the social structure of unpredictable contractions and expansions, the ownership of potentially productive property offers the owner some security—the security of subsistence or future productivity. At the minimum, the private ownership of property guarantees one a piece of land from which one cannot be expelled into vagabondage and poverty. With the invention of private property, property was freed from feudal rotation and transformed into a continuous oscillation to and fro between owners whose ownership isolates any point whatever in the social flow as property.

Second, private property is defined by an inspection and division at any point whatever. In particular, private property introduces two major kinds of social division into the social flow: between owners and workers, and between poor workers and the indigent. Private property as a border or social division is fundamentally a class division subject to inspection at any point of trespass, encroachment, identification, deed, or title. Private property comes with a mobile and circulating record of ownership (title) that is subject to inspection at any point. Thus at any point whatever it becomes possible to classify any person whoever into an owner or worker. This is possible not because of police enforcement alone, but because the definition of private property itself guarantees the lack of any a priori right to property. Private property becomes "private" precisely in the sense that its ownership is restricted and contingent—not necessarily inherited, public, or customary. The ownership of property, like the market itself, is not given in advance of its acquisition; it is owned only by a series of mobile owner-individuals. This lack of a priori right is the basic condition for the emergence of a group of people who own no property at all. Kinetically, private property acts as a limit junction within an oscillating social flow to secure a social division between those who can circulate freely via ownership and those who cannot.

This basic kinetic division has several consequences. The first consequence is that it makes possible an asymmetrical kinetic circuit between the active movement of the workers and the passive movement of the owner. In order for private property to remain secure in its value, it must be made to produce at the level of its greatest possible productivity. Should it produce less, then it is worth less—and the mobility of its exchange and the mobility of its owner are contracted or slowed. To achieve its maximum mobility it must secure the active movement of labor through the wage relation. As Colquhoun writes, "It is the source of *wealth*, since without *labour* there would be *no riches*, no *refinement*, no *comfort*, and no *benefit* to those who may be possessed of wealth."[5] In other words, private property, like any other circuit, creates the social division it requires in order to secure itself. Private property and wealth requires the deprivation of such property from a laboring class of nonowners who have nothing left to sell but their labor power. As a social vehicle it has a motor and a driver—the proletariat and the bourgeoisie. Thus private property is only secondarily the condition for an accumulation of profit; it is first and foremost an accumulation of human movement in the form of the waged laborer.

The second consequence of the social division between owners and workers is it creates an asymmetrical freedom of individual motion. The ownership of private property is not simply a social inequality but also a kinetic inequality. By virtue of ownership the owner's own individual freedom of social mobility is increased. While the property owner is allowed to travel freely from property to property, from property to market, and to buy and sell property freely, the worker is not. Workers must frequently justify why they are moving and with what right. Since workers do not move from or to their property or in exchange of property, their individual freedom is always potential criminality and thus restricted or inspected constantly. In other words, private property, according to Fichte, "constitutes the first part of the civil contract, [and] grounds the relation of right between each individual and all other individuals in the state. It is therefore the foundation of what we call civil legislation, civil right, and so forth."[6] The liberal notion of individual civic freedom thus historically merges with the ownership of property and the freedom of human mobility outside the bonds of labor. If one owns property, one must be free to move between properties and exchange them freely (commerce). If one wants to freely participate in public affairs, one must be a free person. Jürgen Habermas argues this point at length: "While the wage laborers were forced to exchange their labor power as their sole commodity, the property-owning private people related to each other as owners of commodities through an exchange of goods. Only the latter were their own masters; only they should be enfranchised to vote—admitted to the public use of reason in the exemplary sense."[7]

Private property is thus not only the possession of a thing, but the kinetic condition of geographical, economic, and political mobility. From Hume to Hegel, the mobility of property becomes tied to the definition of the human being as a political and rational animal.[8] Private property thus performs a fascinating kinetic inversion: the active movement of the worker results in a limitation of its free mobility, divided by the social border of private property. On the other hand, the passive movement of the owner inversely results in an increase of free mobility. Private property thus functions as a security checkpoint insofar as it secures or defends the social division (class division) necessary for the free mobility (passive movement) of the owner, the reproduction of private property itself, and the further accumulation of active labor. In this way "the question of class," as Colin Gordon writes, "the problem of making an industrial market economy socially possible, becomes, from the bourgeois point of view, an essential part of the politics of security."[9]

The second social division introduced by private property is between the poor and the indigent. Within the class of workers who do not own any property there are those whose active labor has been accumulated by the wage relation to reproduce the private property division, and there are those whose unemployment makes it so that they cannot even sell their labor. This second-class division is also the result of the property border. The private property border is kinetically insecure because of the unpredictable oscillations of the market. Since one never knows the value of property, what it will do, or who will own it, property can only function as an isolated point in a continuously oscillating flow. The kinetic consequence of this is that the active movement of the working class is fundamentally unstable. One moment it is employed, the next it is unemployed. One moment it is accumulated and bound to private property and an owner, the next it is launched into vagabondage and wandering. Private property is both the condition for the security of class division and the condition of its own destruction through the creation of an indigent or rabble class of unemployed workers forced into theft for survival. This is not at all a contradiction and certainly not a synthesis; it is a matter of circulation.

Even Hegel understands that poverty is a necessary outcome of private property and class division. "The emergence of poverty is in general a consequence of civil society, and on the whole it arises necessarily out of it."[10] For Hegel there is no solution to it; the real problem lies elsewhere. The border that needs to be secured above all is the border between the working poor and the dangerous class that emerges from it: the rabble. "Poverty," Hegel writes, "in itself does not reduce people to a rabble; a rabble is created only by the disposition associated with poverty, by inward rebellion against the rich, against society, the government, etc."[11] The modern checkpoint border (private property and its offensive function, the police) must secure the division between the working poor and the rabble such that the rabble do not infect the workers or threaten the stability of the private property that secures the oscillation of commerce and the passive movements of the bourgeoisie. In the nineteenth century the word "rabble," according to the OED, would have indicated both a disorganized movement and excessive "mob/ility" surplus to the requirements of property. This idea of a border between the working and rabble or criminal class was not Hegel's idea alone. As police theorist Mark Neocleous writes, "The myth of a 'criminal class' gained currency in the nineteenth century, conveniently serving a bourgeois state increasingly interested in demarcating boundaries within the working class, to both fragment and police it accordingly."[12] The divisions of property were thus mobile social divisions that would oscillate and change according to the relative property and employment status of the population. Private property thus functions as a checkpoint insofar as it can appear or disappear at any point or time according to the changing social flows.

Where Hegel can only recommend a policing of the property border, Colquhoun, not surprisingly, develops a much more preventative approach: waged labor. Instead of actively putting down the rabble that continues to proliferate under the conditions of social oscillation, Colquhoun argues that "security [of property] does not proceed from severe punishments. . . . It is to be attributed . . . to an early and general attention to the education and morals of the lower orders of the people; aided by a system of industry and sobriety."[13] By educating the morals of the working class, keeping them sober, and putting them to work through waged labor, they will develop a work ethic and be more resistant to the evil of indigence. In this way the property borders and social mobilities between owners, workers, and rabble will be secured.

The Nation

The second type of security checkpoint is the national security checkpoint. National security functions as a defensive limit border that protects and preserves a specifically national division within modern social flows. While private property secures the social division between owning and working individuals, the nation secures the social division between nationals and nonnationals through the security of the people themselves as nationals. Cultural, linguistic, ethnic, and geographical divisions not only partition, they also define and preserve that which they have divided.

National security borders are distinct from feudal borders. During the Middle Ages, territory was attached directly to individual persons through vassalage and adscription and thus continually shifted based on juridical allegiances. The people who lived in these territories did not constitute a single ethnic, linguistic, or cultural identity, and the state was strictly equated with the aristocracy or ruling class. Thus most people did not identify with the state. From the fourteenth through the seventeenth century, European monarchs slowly began to define states according to increasingly clear territorial borders.[14] By 1648 European powers had agreed to the basic principles of a territorial-political order in the Peace of Westphalia. After decades of conflict, the modern state system was established in order to settle territorial conflicts and mutually recognize a system of sovereign states' rights to govern specifically defined territories, populations, and resources. While the linked juridical borders of the feudal period were overlapping and ambiguous, modern state borders were more clearly marked out.[15] This process of more accurately marking out these borders was also made possible by certain advances in surveying and cartography.

National borders emerged out of this modern state system of territorially defined borders. With the emergence of the nation, the territory became the place where the people belong and where the administrative boundaries of a single state lie. The territory was no longer constantly shifting according to the alliances of competing lords. Diverse peoples were defined as a single nation with identifiable characteristics and rights based on this identity, and the state was defined as the rule of the people who live in the territory and identify with its national features. "In short, the state ruled over a territorially defined 'people' and did so as the supreme 'national' agency of rule over its territory, its agents increasingly reaching down to the humblest inhabitant of the least of its villages."[16] A full account of the causes of this historical-political transformation is available elsewhere,[17] but what concerns us here is the emergence of a new kinetic border regime that made possible a whole new bordering technique: the nation. "The rise of modern nationalism transformed ideas about state sovereignty. If a nation is defined as a group of people who believe they constitute a unique grouping based on shared culture, language, history, and the like, then nationalism is a political ideology that assumes the nation commands the primary allegiance of its members and possesses an intrinsic right to self-determination within its own sovereign state."[18]

By the end of the nineteenth century the idea of a territorially delimited state determined by the sovereignty of its members—the territorial nation-state—became the ideal, although not the norm.[19] National borders, like other checkpoint borders, were no longer located exclusively at privileged territorial, political, or juridical sites (customs houses, tollways, the perimeter of the territory, and so on) but began to appear at any point whatever throughout society. Although the nation emerged out of the territorial state, it was much more mobile and diffuse. "As this new idea of state sovereignty gained acceptance, it became increasingly common to argue that borders should correspond to ethnic and linguistic divisions, instead of focusing on natural landmarks. So the borders of the state of France, for example, should be drawn to include all French populations and lands."[20] The nation thus poses a uniquely kinopolitical problem: that people, languages, and cultures are mobile and tend to migrate. The mobility of national borders thus continually transforms any fixed territorial-state borderline that would seek to contain it. This problem remains unresolved today, even in the charter of the United Nations—which paradoxically recognizes only states and not nations (Kurdish, Tibetan, and others). The invention of the nation is thus the invention of a new type of border: a checkpoint border whose social division secures a mobile population, but not always a territorial, political, or juridical order.

National security borders are therefore defined according to the two key features of the checkpoint: the isolation of a point in an oscillating and mobile social flow and an inspection of this point, which can occur at any point whatever. The following two sections explore each of these kinetic features in more depth.

First, national borders introduce a division between national and nonnational individuals at a certain point within a mobile and shifting population. National borders do not exist solely at the perimeter of a territory; they also suffuse the social body and can pop up at any point where a linguistic, ethnic, or cultural division occurs. The enemy or foreigner is no longer simply on the other side of a fence or wall, but circulates among the people. Accordingly, national security borders must be potentially everywhere.

This was originally made possible in France, for example, by the elimination of internal borders formed by separate provinces in favor of a uniform administration in which all national citizens were individually equal before the state and able to move freely.[21] According to Georges Lefebvre, this freedom of movement was one of the most important results of the French Revolution, and sparked the first public debate over passport controls in European history.[22] The French provinces were replaced with eighty-three *départements* because, according to the National Assembly, "France is and ought to be a single whole, uniformly subordinated in all its parts to a single legislation and one common [system of] administration."[23] As France was unified/departmentalized, the National Assembly gradually pushed toll barriers for goods and people as well as the attendant border patrol barracks to the frontier of the territorial border. However, like the destruction of the walls of Paris by Louis XIV, this only paved the way for a "new wall": the nation. French nationalism thus unified the population by dividing it along an entirely new vector: national versus nonnational.

Feudalism defined "foreigners" as everyone who resided outside a given juridical domain. With nationalization, "the French" were not only unified; they were at the same time newly divided from one another as individual citizens within a nation. Nationalization is thus both the unification of the people and a multiplication of individual persons, citizen or noncitizen. The political territory is filled with the constant oscillation of bodies, but the national border introduces into this flow an individuation or isolation of a strictly national body: the citizen. The citizen is the one who is allowed free movement through the nation. In order for this to be possible other forms of mobility—vagabondage, beggars, criminals, and so on—must be restricted to secure ordered national movement. Thus the nation-state, as John Torpey argues, can be defined kinopolitically as the monopolization of the "legitimate means of movement."[24] The free movement of citizens is therefore not a right at all, but a reward for a privileged group of citizens: the nation.[25]

The nation also functions as a checkpoint insofar as it isolates and divides national and nonnational individuals within an oscillating flow of international and economic mobility. From the eighteenth century onward, territorial states increasingly opened their external territorial borders to the international movements of capital and labor. Territorial borders began to allow the large-scale circulation of people into and out of the territory. By the eighteenth century there was an increasingly large and mobile population to cross those borders. Throughout the eighteenth and nineteenth centuries serfs and peasants across Europe were gradually freed from their hereditary ties to the land. In Prussia the October Edict of 1807 emancipated the peasants and allowed them to travel freely. Peasants could no longer be arbitrarily taxed by lords and did not have to ask permission to marry, thus increasing the population. However, just like commutation in thirteenth-century France, the October Edict also expelled huge numbers of masterless men and women whose lords no longer had an obligation to provide housing for them. These men and women were thus launched into the search for urban work across Europe. Upon entry they were regarded as individual noncitizens. Migrants were admitted not as Prussians but as freely moving individual noncitizens wishing to sell their labor.

In Germany liberal industrialists demanded the freedom of international movement for owners and workers to establish trade and industry throughout Europe. In particular, German capitalists worried that if native workers ever took control of the labor supply via strike it would be important for them to bring in workers from outside the country.[26] The demands of industrial capitalist economy thus led to a dramatic slackening of movement restrictions throughout the nineteenth century and the transformation of migrants into freely moving individuals. The territorial-political border thus became less a site of military defense than a site for the economic management of large movements of labor and capital. Meanwhile, the national border emerged within the territory to socially disenfranchise noncitizen individuals through the denial of property ownership, voting, collective assembly, begging, and all manner of social mobilities.

The national isolation of individual points within international mobility flows was also made possible through the invention of a centralized national administration and standardization of universal passport laws. In this way the nation is able to isolate identifiable points with determinate characteristics within larger population flows. But since a purely national border cannot verify a foreign passport, there must be national officials located in foreign countries to issue the passports. Hence an international visa system was developed in the nineteenth century to accomplish precisely this.[27] Although the passport is historically a medieval border technique aimed at marking out a legally defined cellular individual, by the eighteenth and nineteenth centuries this individuality increasingly became a universal requisite for social membership. Accordingly, the passport took on a new function, this time as a mandatory security tool to isolate and track freely circulating data points in an immense flow of national and international mobility.

In particular, the isolation of a unique social point was secured through the invention of the photo passport. The photo passport first emerged in France in 1854,[28] and afterward spread across Europe, becoming mandatory for all passports by the early twentieth century. Kinetically, the photo passport is not simply a mark or individualization meant to represent the unchanging features of the individual for the purpose of legal recognition (eye color, height, sex, name, and so on), it is a slice or snapshot, at a unique point in time, of the continuum of light composing the image of the individual itself. Photography is the writing or graphism of light reflected from the body. The photograph thus isolates a single point in a continuous oscillation of light waves. It literally makes possible the capture—not representation—of the body's light at a single point. The goal of the national border as a security point is no longer simply to wall up and centralize the mass of motions, or bind them to the earth through legal contracts, but to free up their movements while still being able to control them and snap an image of them at any given point. National security can thus be defined by the following twin phenomena: an increased freedom of oscillation as well as an increased punctual control of it.

In contrast to the written descriptions of physiological appearance previously included in passports that attempted to represent or describe an image but did not "look" like what they described since they were letters, the photo *is* the punctual inscription of the body on the photo plate. Furthermore, in contrast to painted portraiture that aimed to stockpile or synthesize a large mass of light flows over time—the motions of the object as well as the motions of the painter—the photograph instead captures a point in an indefinite series of points. The light paints itself on the plate or film. While the painter tries to synthesize a totality of motion over a long duration, the photographer simply wants a slice of it in a moment, a point extracted from a continual series. Thus it is no coincidence that as early as 1854, less than thirty years after the invention of the daguerreotype camera, the photographic image was incorporated into passport documents to create a literal anthropometric image of the people's body.[29] The national border is not at any single point, but is capable of introducing a division between national and nonnational individuals at any possible point or kinetic slice of mobility.

Once the social flow has been divided up into isolated individual points, the second function of the national border is to introduce a division between national and nonnational individuals through an inspection of any point whatever. It is precisely this mobility and mutability of the security checkpoint that gives it its vast and definitively punctual power of inspection. At no previous point in history was such a quantity of biometric data available for as many unique individuals as it was from the late eighteenth century forward. However, this capacity posed a new kinopolitical problem: where to intervene into the continuous flow of potentially isolatable points? With larger flows of mobile bodies and data came an increasing uncertainty as to where to draw the line.

National security borders thus increasingly come to require and rely on a demographic apparatus to record and determine where to intervene and inspect. Interestingly, modern demography and nationalism share the same kinopolitical border regime. Nationalism not only isolates a point or individual within the constant flow of people and things made possible by modern revolutions in economic mobility, transportation, and communication; it also isolates the points of the natural and biological body of the individual. The individual point is composed of biological points—hair color, eye color, skin color, language, and so on—that mark the national limits of the body. National borders are written on the body and can thus be inspected. For example, the Belgian statistician Adolphe Quetelet became famous for his invention of the "average man": "Just as astronomers considered the average of many measurements to represent the closest approximation to a theoretically exact measurement, so Quetelet concluded that the average of many measurements of humans represented not only the 'average man' but also an ideal type free from both excess and defect."[30] "The man whom I considered is the analog in society of the center of gravity in bodies; he is a fictional being for whom everything happens according to the average results obtained for society. If the average man were determined for a nation, he would represent the type of that nation; if he could be determined for all men, he would represent the type for the entire human race."[31] The "average man" is made possible by the social division of human life into binational data points. The idea is that one's natural and national life can be inspected and assessed according to a socially standard measurement.

The nation, as its etymology suggests, is something one is born into or with. One cannot choose to be French or German—one's blood must come from the soil of the territory; one's tongue must be one's binational mother tongue; one's land must be one's motherland, *Vaterland*, or patria, and so on.[32] National borders are natural borders. This is attested to in the eighteenth- and nineteenth-century determination of natural river and mountain formations as the pregiven "natural" borders of territorial-political-national bodies. Thus at birth (*natio*), one's body is already marked and bordered by the color of one's skin, the tongue in one's mouth, and the blood in one's body. The fluency of language is tied to the fluency and flow of nationalized social mobility.

Modern demography and biometry emerge as the twin kinometrics of nationalism: the inspection of the people and their living bodies. Above all, this becomes important because territorial-political unification allows freer movement within the territory, and economic liberalization allows freer movement between political territories. With such enormous populations moving around more than ever, governments became increasingly attentive to keeping track of the kinetic information that defined these bodies in motion in order to secure the nation. Beginning in the eighteenth century, the "health of the nation" was understood to be causally connected to a strong and large population. Thus the control of the movement of populations across the territory became a central part of the art of government and, according to Foucault, "in the wider sense of what we now call 'the economy.'"[33] Demography and biometry record the images of the people and their living bodies precisely because these are where the borders of the nation occur; their bodies literally make up the body of the nation. If one wants a strong nation, one can select for it through border enforcement. Hair color, eye color, skin color, language, and other biometrical markers all reveal something about the body's nationality and thus are points where a border can emerge. For example, the International Statistical Congress of 1873 recommended that all census data include "spoken language" because of its "national significance."[34] Thus the borders of the nation are not only territorial, they are linguistic.

Demography in particular collects huge databases and identifies trends in biometrical data in order to determine how many nonnationals are in the country and how many nationals are leaving in order to preserve a certain racial identity.[35] When these numbers reach a certain threshold, the checkpoint pops up across the administrative spectrum: police patrols, secret spies, highway patrols, guards of all kinds, ticket takers, census surveyors, conscription officers, inspectors, charity and philanthropic committees, bosses, and administrators of public access at every level. Any public figure can intervene to perform an inspection and secure the health of the nation.

The challenge of enforcing national security borders is, thus, assessing the current situation, interpreting the individual case, and making a judgment. When should documents be requested and by whom? Is there any reason to suspect that the individual may endanger public security? Is there currently social unrest or other events that should trump an otherwise legitimate document? For example, in France and Prussia at times of social turmoil requiring security during the eighteenth and nineteenth centuries all travelers had to have their passports checked in every district along a predetermined route. If they failed to register their visa at the appropriate checkpoint and at the appropriate place, including alehouses and hostels, they could be arrested by any of the gendarmes or national guardsmen (in the case of France) who had been given the universal power to check documents and arrest anyone across the districts.[36]

Another example of the punctual power of the national security point is the laws in France passed by the Legislative Assembly in December 1791 that required anyone receiving public money, social services, or alms to show a certificate attesting that he or she currently lived in the French Empire and had done so continuously for the past six months.[37] The hungry mass of the poor are thus individualized and given access to state funds only as identifiable data sets with a given kinometric status. If one fails at any point to present the correct documents or fails to report for one's duties in school, in the military, in the hospital, in the court of law, and so on, these same kinometric inspections make possible an increasingly powerful tracking apparatus by which the police, teachers, bosses, or hospitals are able to hunt down specific deviant individuals. By the eighteenth century such security checkpoints for manhunting had been institutionalized all over Europe.[38] In one very dramatic example, the French National Convention, concerned with internal enemies, passed the Law on Suspects of 1793 that created all-powerful *comités de surveillance*, charged with tracking down military deserters, "foreigners," and other enemies to the national revolution.[39] The *comités* roamed villages, forests, and mountains demanding papers, passports, or *certificats de civis*, and capturing anyone without them. While the offensive march of the police attests to a visible and constantly active kinopticism, national security attests to the defense of a series of natural kinometric markers on the body that tell where one is from.

Demography defines and borders the nation. At the frontiers, data is collected on the population's movements in and out, and inside the territory data is collected on the internal movements and features of the population via mobile security points. In addition to the transformation of existing institutions such as churches, schools, hospitals, and police departments into sites of data collection on marriages, births, deaths, and so on, the eighteenth and nineteenth centuries also gave birth to a whole new professional class of census "enumerators" across Europe. The census was perhaps one of the most important national security technologies of this age because it increased the efficiency and centralization of three important aspects of the modern state: taxation, conscription, and economic production.[40] As nineteenth-century English statistician John Rickman writes, "The human understanding cannot reason without proper data."[41] Demography is thus relevant for every aspect of national-political knowledge. "The execution of the proposed measure [Census Act of 1800]," Rickman writes, "would much facilitate many other useful enquiries," about property, taxes, and life insurance.[42] With accurate information, Rickman argues, "Legislation and politics must make proportional steps towards perfection."[43] For Rickman, the census is the technological form that self-knowledge takes in the nation-state: it is the people's knowledge of themselves. Patriotism and political economy are thus bound together in securitization. For example, if the state knew how many people were in a household, how much land they owned, and so on, taxes could be fairly individualized according to these factors. The British census also made possible the first accurate assessments of the country's possible military strength by discovering the ages and locations of all the young men in the population; thus facilitating conscription and military self-knowledge. Finally, the census was also used to assess the productive and consumptive capacity of its people and land. As Rickman explains, "No society can confidently pretend to provide the requisite quantity of food, till they know the number of consumers."[44] Similar ideas were expressed in Germany by Leibniz and in France by Jean-Baptiste Moheau. All "brought to full consciousness the idea that the nation-state is essentially characterized by its statistics, and therefore demands a statistical office in order to define itself and its power."[45]

The most important innovation in census enumeration was the shift from collecting data from communities in the eighteenth century to collecting data from individuals in the nineteenth century. As Kathrin Levitan explains in her book *Cultural History of the British Census*, "One individual would belong to multiple and overlapping groups, including an occupational group, an age group, and a gender group, as well as various local and regional groups. By deemphasizing geographic communities, the census essentially defined the nation as the primary locus of identification and analysis, and weighted each individual within that nation equally and anonymously. This meant that most of the aggregates to which individuals belonged were not located anywhere other than the nation, an abstract rather than a geographical location."[46] In order for this individuation in the census to take place, a whole new technology of security points is required: more enumerators are needed, and door-to-door inquiries must be conducted, individually collected, verified, synthesized, and sent to the central administration. Further, given the quantity of individuals involved and the increased possibility of error with more units over longer durations such as double counting or changing data, the census had to be faster and more mobile than the changing data. Previous censuses took several weeks or months to complete, but the 1841 British census was to be conducted in a single night. Speed and mobility is thus the key to successful kinometry. This was accomplished by allotting to each enumerator no more houses than could be collected from in a day, made possible by the expanding railways of the 1830s and 1840s. As a writer for the *Westminster Review* explained in 1854, "Our national portraiture must be taken by daguerreotype [photograph] process, and not by gradual finishing [painting]. Formerly, John Bull sat still, day after day, till the picture was finished; but now he must be caught in the attitude of the moment."[47]

Demography and photography thus share a historical as well as a kinopolitical affinity. Demography is the portrait of the people taken in a photographic snapshot: a point in a continuously oscillating flow. Demography treats the nation as a pulmonary circulation of oscillations to and fro. Thus the goal of the national border as a security checkpoint is to be able to inspect this demographic flow at any point whatever. Accordingly, there are two security images of the nation; the photographic and the demographic appear as its two poles—identity and anonymity. With the dominance of the national security checkpoint, the individual is a specific set of biometric markers governable at any point by passports, IDs, police surveillance, records, and so forth, but at the same time the individual is also the most anonymous demographic figure, since everyone is an individual. The passport makes possible the former and the census makes possible the latter as the enumeration of the anonymous biometric data that defines the people of the nation. Identity and anonymity, punctual control and free movement—these are the dyads of the national security point.

Finally, the national security checkpoint is secured by the invention of a completely unique kinetic border technology: barbed wire. In 1865 Louis François Janin first patented a unique double-wire design holding a series of sharp diamond-shaped spikes. The kinetics of barbed wire are fittingly the same kinetics of the checkpoint: a continuous series of smooth, flexible wires punctuated by sharp spikes of control. Barbed wire and the checkpoint share four major kinetic functions. First, contrary to the naked single wire, barbed wire has a structural elasticity by virtue of the twisted or torsional connection between the two intertwined wires.[48] When a single metal wire is exposed to heat, it expands and thus slackens or dilates. However, the elasticity of barbed wire allows it to maintain an equilibrium throughout contractions and expansions of temperature. Furthermore, unlike the single wire, this elasticity made possible by kinetic torsion makes barbed wire stronger and able to bend without breaking. Second, barbed wire is lightweight, compact, and thus extremely mobile and transportable. Barbed wire can be transported and installed faster than any other fence, wall, or cell in history. Just as the checkpoint is defined by its punctual control in a continuous oscillation of movement, so barbed wire can appear quickly and be transported to any point whatever. Third, barbed wire is highly flexible and adaptable to almost any spatial situation. It can be added to a series of fence posts (the barbed-wire fence), it can be added on any surface of a wall (the barbed-wire security wall), or it can be quickly be shaped into the cells of an institution (the iconic barbed-wire concentration camps or holding cells). Not only can it be transported quickly to any point whatever, it can be unrolled and installed at any point whatever. Fourth, barbed wire is thin. At a distance it is barely visible, under gunfire it is practically invincible, and in production it is inexpensive to make. Like the checkpoint, it is like a spider's web, fishnet, or sieve that lets light, air, and bullets pass through but captures the bodies of animals and humans in its barbs. Like the checkpoint, the thin, quasi invisibility of barbed wire "inverts the game of visibility. Whereas before one could make oneself hidden in order to attack a visible barrier, now it is the barrier itself that is hidden to the person who would attempt to breach it. Surprised, he is caught fully exposed to the reply that awaits him."[49]

Barbed wire functions as a specifically national security checkpoint technology in several historically important ways. This is first attested to in the national securitization of the American West. With the patenting of barbed wire in America by an Illinois farmer named J. F. Glidden, settlers, pioneers, and prairie farmers had access to large quantities of cheap barbed wire. Under pressure from poor, landless farmers, the 1862 Homestead Act had given any American citizen free ownership of 160 acres of public land on the condition that it be cultivated. Armed with barbed wire from the 1870s on, American citizens expanded westward into Indian territories, sectioning off their plots of land as they went. The open West became subdivided into a thousand tiny individual plots. In this way barbed wire functioned as a securitization of both private property and American nationalism at the same time. Thus, "It was neither the railroads nor land settlement laws which enabled the farmer to advance beyond the Missouri; it was barbed wire."[50] One never knew where a new barbed wire fence would appear, disappear, or move further west. Barbed-wire expansion cut Natives off from their hunting grounds, from migratory patterns, and from each other. By "granting land" to Native Americans, the American government even explicitly tried to force "Indians [to] assimilate and become citizens" or move further west, as Thomas Jefferson writes.[51] By granting land only to individual Native Americans and not to tribes, the government hoped to fragment them into immobilized and atomized points: into a national security checkpoint regime under government inspection.[52]

The national security function of barbed wire was next attested to historically in the trenches of World War I. Here too barbed wire played a strategic role that secured a defensive position between nationally organized armies. While previous wars had focused largely on dromological concerns (how quickly troops could be deployed), World War I and barbed wire marked a new warfare defined by temporary defensive checkpoints—trenches surrounded with wire—until the invention of the tank. Barbed wire was easy to repair, quick to install and transport, and most importantly resisted artillery fire. The fact that barbed wire was so thin (and trenches hidden behind brush) made it so that enemy soldiers did not realize they had crossed the border until they hit the barbed wire with their bodies, at which time it was too late.

Finally, barbed wire secured national borders in the camps of World War II. The first basic core of the concentration camp was made up of two vertical rows of electrified barbed wire, or what has been called the "burning frontier."[53] Many concentration camps in Germany were built to be temporary, invisible, or out of the way, and when many were deconstructed, almost no trace was left behind. At Sobibor, "as at Belzec, the terrain was plowed and planted with trees in order to hide the traces of extermination."[54] Barbed wire made this possible. Camps with more substantial architecture—big fences, walls, or cells—took longer to build and were more visible, more costly, and harder to repair. Barbed wire could also be deployed within urban areas to quickly section off a Jewish ghetto and create an instant network of security checkpoints around the perimeter and throughout. Barbed wire in the camps and ghettos also secured a specifically national type of division. One of the first things the Nazis did to people before sending them to the camps was to denationalize them.[55]

The camp was the barbed-wire border that secured and purified the nation from nonnationals. The national body was the living biological body and barbed wire was a specifically antiflesh type of border. Its effective target was the living body on which it left its traces or marks. Its barbs opened the flesh to inspect the nationalized blood within. We can even call the years of (1867–1967) "the century of barbed wire."[56] Because of these three major functions, barbed wire has become an almost universal symbol of political violence, nationalism, and oppression.[57] Despite this, however, one can still find barbed wire used at borders and checkpoints around the world.[58] In many instances those using barbed wire may even intend for the wire to summon this historical and violent meaning.

INFORMATION CHECKPOINT

The third major type of modern border is the information checkpoint. In contrast to offensive police borders and defensive security borders, information borders have a unique boundary or binding function: they compel or bind social flows together as assemblages of data points. A data point is an isolated bit of social flow—a location, a name, a color, a date—that is used to divide and arrange the passage of social flows. For modern boundaries these data points become the keys or codes required for social circulation. The informational checkpoint aims less at stopping, enclosing, or blocking than at collecting and redirecting flows of data. While medieval boundaries were defined by the time-space-activity matrix or grid of the timetable, modern boundaries are instead defined by the oscillation and redirection of collections of data.[59] Instead of enclosing the individual into spatial temporal activity cells—"Now here do this, now there do that"—modern boundaries are much more open and fluid. The aim is not to physically bind individuals into and between enclosed times and spaces, but to produce a kinetic environment such that data groupings (individuals) regulate themselves according to the boundaries of their informational complex: traffic will follow the path of least resistance on its own; trade will move to the most profitable areas on its own, water, food, waste, and all social flows will move just like water flowing downhill toward natural basins. Thus the question of modern boundaries is how to manage a kinetic milieu such that data flows and pools in the most desirable places. In other words, modern limology is a question of social landscaping based on an informational topography—no longer simply a coordinate matrix or cartography, but a topological surface with trajectories, slopes, and curves.

The creation of information and its binding together into social bodies in motion is a form of social division or bordering. First, points of information are extracted from the continuous flow of social movement. These points can be geographical, political, biological, educational, and so on. They can be any point whatever. Second, these points are attached to or bound to one another to create a unit or individual in motion. The mobile individual does not preexist the binding process but is a product of it: the person is bound by it. The person is an "in(fo)dividual." Informational boundaries define individuality but are also the codes that allow the individual to move and pass. As we have seen in the previous sections, the police record, trace, and bind social motion according to these points. Property deeds, national identity cards, photo portraits, passports, and so on are all composed of informational points—assembled and bound to a mobile body. Although precursors to data borders exist in previous historical periods, such as ancient writs or medieval identification cells, information is not the same as identification. Identification produces a cellular, individual person, and links the person to centers of juridical power. Information, on the other hand, is punctual, deindividualized, and oscillatory across national and international administrations. The period beginning in eighteenth-century Europe is accordingly defined by Daniel Headrick as a "cultural revolution in information systems,"[60] and by Ian Hacking as an "avalanche of numbers."[61] The medieval technologies of letters and passports do not disappear but are simply absorbed or transformed into informational points, one among many others bound into a file, folder, or document collecting, managing, and predicting this data. In this way informational social divisions function according to the two kinetic functions of the checkpoint.

The first kinetic function of the information checkpoint is that it isolates a data point in a continuous social flow. From the continuity of living movement, waves of sound, light, and matter, information isolates a series of single, discontinuous points. The life of a body is fluid and continually mobile, but an information checkpoint does not attempt to capture the totality of this living flow under a single political power or even within a network of linked juridical letters, especially when European life was more mobile than ever. Information simply isolates discrete aspects of social life in order to conjoin and manage their circulation more economically. In this way, an "individual" is nothing but a collection of these points: a population of points. These points were increasingly collected in documents of all kinds throughout this period: passports, health records, libraries, encyclopedias, photographs, fingerprints, identification cards, licenses, train tickets, laboratory reports, birth certificates, school records, military papers, voting documents, and so on.[62] Information checkpoints are not only biometric. Biometry is only a subset of a larger kinometry that records and categorizes all forms of mobile data points: how many trains arrive and leave the country, how many and what types of people use the trains, how much money a country makes in a year, how much labor is required, the ratio of imports to exports, and so on. All modern social flows become groupings of data bound together and apart from one another according to their informational boundaries within classification systems: scientific taxonomies, cartographies, lexicographies, statistics (political arithmetic), postal services.[63]

The transformation of life into information points is the division of social continuity into discrete and separate points. Information, more than physical walls, separates modern individuals from one another and from themselves. While police, property, and the nation all act directly on individuals, the informational checkpoint is what binds those individuals together as data collections to be recorded, tracked, and managed in the first place. The information checkpoint is a border process of binding and bounding data sets together into discrete assemblages for criminal, private, and national management. The first information point establishes the original point of reference—date of birth, number, and so on. Every subsequent punctual identification, such as licenses, passports, or train tickets, makes another point in the series, which is then referred back to and attributed to the first information point. Individuality, subjectivity, agency, and causality are thus retroactively woven into a kinometric assemblage of informational boundaries. The individual is no longer a thinking thing, but a mobile informational assembly: a mass of kinometric data whose movements can now be tracked, modulated, and circulated accordingly.[64]

The second kinetic function of the information checkpoint is that it makes possible an inspection at any data point whatever. Data is assembled into collections or documents and increasingly accumulated and divided according to certain relevant criteria or classification systems. As social flows are increasingly bounded as information, the point at which one may undergo a possible given inspection becomes increasingly uncertain. For example, large-scale trends only appear at higher levels of accumulated data. Certain geographical locations only appear as "hot spots" for crime, traffic accidents, or riots at a certain informational boundary level—city population, regional population, national population, and so on. As Headrick writes, "In order to do something about vagrants or licentious persons or children without schooling, reformers first had to know how many there were and then count how many were saved or cured."[65] Problems and progress had to be measured at the right level. Certain times of day, certain activities, or certain assemblies of biometric data only appear as more or less likely to produce certain outcomes according to the perimeter or scope of the data sample. Informational boundaries make these kinds of mac-rolevel statistical observations possible. They render visible the invisible at another level. At a certain threshold or probability all these potential information points become boundaries that indicate a social-kinetic division between desired circulation and undesirable circulation. Nation-states created extremely accurate informational maps in order to keep track of increasingly multiple social divisions of all kinds: between rich and poor, between cold- and hot-climate dwellers, between living and dead, native and nonnative language speakers, young and old, married and unmarried, and so on. Thus inspection becomes possible at any data point whatever and can be verified by a system of recorded documents matched to the identification documents of an individual at any time whatever.

An excellent and prescient theoretical example of informational boundaries as social divisions and possible points of inspection comes from Fichte's political theory. The central problem with which Fichte grapples is the kinetic problem of circulation: given the relatively free movement of liberal social flows (transport, commerce, internationalism, and so on) how is it possible to produce the correct mobile informational assemblages and to inspect them at the right place and time? In the medieval period this problem is solved with the invention of the *horarium* or timetable matrix: everyone in the right place at the right time doing the right activity; in other words, cellular boundaries. But modern social motion calls for a new kind of *laisser-passer* boundary that lets pass. Although many new technological innovations have occurred since Fichte's 1796 *Foundations of Natural Right*, the form of modern boundaries has changed very little.[66]

For Fichte, "The principal maxim of every well-constituted" form of bordered social motion "must be the following: every citizen must be readily identifiable, wherever necessary, as this or that particular person."[67] Thus, first and foremost, according to Fichte, "Everyone must always carry a passport with him, issued by the nearest authority and containing a precise description of his person; this applies to everyone, regardless of class or rank."[68] This passport is later more accurately described as an "identification card" since it is (1) mandatory at all times, (2) must completely render an individual identifiable according to as many data points as possible "including photo," and (3) must make possible the universal and constant knowledge of its owner's movement at all times. "In a state with the kind of constitution we have established here," Fichte continues, "every citizen has his own determinate status, and the police know fairly well where each one is at every hour of the day, and what he is doing. . . .

With the help of the identity cards described above, every citizen can be identified on the spot."[69]

This is accomplished by requiring that these mobile cards be inscribed at a vast network of checkpoints such as inns, sentry boxes, hospitals, schools, or places of residence.[70] All of society effectively becomes a system of informational checkpoints both inscribing data points onto mobile cards and creating a duplicate register kept at every checkpoint: a dual kinometric archive.[71] "No one is allowed to leave one locality (he can be stopped at the city gate) without specifying the place he intends to travel to, which will be noted in the register of the place and on his identity card. He will not be received anywhere other than the place noted on his identity card. And if he should leave that place, the very same rules would apply again, and so there will be a continuous record of his whereabouts."[72] At each checkpoint one must identify the next checkpoint to be crossed. In this way social flows can not only be controlled since they can be blocked at each point, but all movement can be perfectly tracked by authorities. Following this checkpoint system, social mobility is freed and borders disappear. But in this same system one simply chooses to constrain one's own movement, and borders emerge everywhere in the form of informational checkpoints that record all social motion.

For Fichte, even money itself becomes a kinographic recording technology for binding information and tracing data flows. In the eighteenth century, bills of exchange were documents that recorded the history of credits and debts of exchange. The bill was a promise to pay a determinate sum to a given party by a certain date. The problem, however, was that these notes and their signatures were often forged. By following Fichte's system of informational checkpoints and identification cards, forgery was exposed and the criminals could be tracked down.

> According to our suggestion, anyone who transfers a bill of exchange (assuming that the recipient does not already know exactly and personally who he is) would have to present his identity card in order to show that he is this particular person, where he can be found, etc. The recipient of the bill has a duty to look at the identity card and then recognize the transferor accordingly. On the back of the bill of exchange, next to the name of the transferor, he will simply add the words: with an identity card from such and such an authority. The recipient will have to write down only two more phrases, and it will take just a minute or two longer to look at the person and his identity card; but otherwise, the matter is just as simple as before.[73]

If an inspection revealed that the bill of exchange was counterfeit and that a certain person was suspected, he or she could now be tracked down because the identification card would have been recorded in duplicate through the network of informational checkpoints. All that remained was to alert these checkpoints, inspect all related mobility, and apprehend the suspect. Thus informational social divisions occur at every point of inscription, but only become active on the spot when needed. In contrast to the cellular boundaries of the *horarium*, the informational checkpoint appears everywhere and nowhere at the same time.

Fichte's kinometric system was not complete fantasy; over the next two centuries it increasingly became reality. In particular, with the invention of fingerprinting technology, kinographic information appeared on everything the mobile body touched. The body itself became the infographic record of its own mobility, like the slime trail of the snail. "The finger-print system is, therefore, available for two purposes," as police theorist, Raymond Fosdick writes, "first, after arrest to identify a prisoner with a previous criminal record; second, to discover the author of a particular crime before any arrest is made by comparison of finger-prints left behind him with finger-print cards on file at headquarters."[74] Biometric data is thus not only a recording process but a preventative process: to apprehend criminals by inspecting the boundaries of the information that composes their kinetic assemblage.

This new modern system of information checkpoints based on identification cards and documents of all kinds makes possible a new paradigm in kinometry: the a priori traceability of mobility. In contrast to simply finding the marks left behind by the mover, as Grégoire Chamayou writes, "The paradigm of traceability proceeds differently. In fact, it reverses the temporal logic. In place of these *a posteriori* material traces, we now organize in an *a priori* way the production of future traces. The spontaneous traces that served as the base of the evidential paradigm are replaced by prefabricated traces captured by means of automatic recording apparatuses integrated into activity itself, every material flow now being coupled with a production of a flow of data."[75] Informational boundaries are thus not based on surveillance but on control. Chamayou continues,

Etymologically, the "contre-rolle" referred to the copy of a document—of a list, an account book, a register of births, marriages and deaths—that is archived and used to verify other items. Control is defined first of all as an operation of verification by means of a system of written notation. As such it is *stricto sensu* distinct from surveillance, which as a process is originally much more optical than scriptural. At the limit, to survey it suffices that one have eyes, whereas control implies an ensemble of documents and archives. . . . If surveillance functions in the present—"I see you"—traceability functions in the future anterior: "I will know what you will have done."[76]

Information boundaries thus bind and divide individuals between two poles—data and the archive. On one side, the raw data of mobility is inscribed on the identification card, the biometric body (fingerprints, footsteps, and so on), or the physical environment; on the other side this information is duplicated in the database or archive and can be matched to the raw data flows. Between these two parallel flows an inspection is possible at any point whatever. The inspection leads both to the binding of kinometric data to a mobile body and the division of this body from other bodies. With data boundaries social flows are now recorded, deported, criminalized, redirected, restricted, slowed down, sped up, and modulated at any point within a network of oscillating flows punctuated with checkpoints.

CONCLUSION

The security and informational checkpoint border persists in hybrid formation alongside other contemporary border regimes. For example, national citizenship and the institution of private property continue to pose divisions between global elites and underclasses today. The distribution of power and property now occurs not only within nations but between them as well. Citizens of wealthy countries travel relatively freely across borders, while citizens in poorer countries end up migrating to wealthy countries under conditions of partial or criminal status as a source of exploitable labor. Today information or data power has grown to include new levels of biometry and kinometry, including iris scans, DNA testing, and enormous databases of bio- and kinometric information that can be summoned almost instantaneously by law and border enforcement. If we want to understand contemporary security and informational border technologies of social division, we have to understand the border regime that they came from and under what social conditions they emerged in the eighteenth and nineteenth centuries.

In this spirit, the final part of this book turns now to a close examination of the contemporary border phenomenon of the US-Mexico border, whose kinetic border regimes can all be found previously in history but now mix together in a new hybrid formation.

PART III
Contemporary Borders

United States–Mexico

CHAPTER 7

The US-Mexico Fence

Contemporary borders are complex hybrids of all previously existing border regimes. This does not mean that all the same material technologies persist in the exact same way, but that contemporary borders simultaneously deploy a mixture of all four kinetic border regimes: centripetal, centrifugal, tensional, and elastic. In these hybrid structures there is not always an equal mixture of kinetic regimes; sometimes and in some places one form of motion may be dominant, and at other times or places it may function to a lesser extent. Contemporary border technologies are thus materially hybrid insofar as they are composed of mixtures and fragments from fence structures, walls, cells, and checkpoints. Most contemporary borders deploy all of these technologies in some combination. For instance, at the US-Mexico border it is not uncommon to see a checkpoint built between a wall, wrapped in barbed wire, sandwiched by two lines of fence with cameras on top, and with a temporary detention to the side. Each of these historical border technologies is taken up and deployed according to several different forms of motion at once and can change regularly. Thus contemporary limology is never done once and for all. It begins again and again not only as a typology or diagnostic but as a kinetics, as the continual tracing of the mobile set of processes that define social division. Since the border is mobile, theory must be too.

The previous parts of this book have prepared the conceptual and historical tools required to conduct a kinopolitical analysis of the hybrid forms of social motion deployed by contemporary border regimes. Part I defined the border and identified three distinct border operations shared by all types of borders: their offensive mark, their defensive limit, and their binding boundary. Following this basic kinopolitical framework Part II then analyzed four major historical border regimes during the periods in which they rose to dominance and were associated with territorial, political, juridical, and economic types of power. These logical and historical categories are not ontological or universal but rather develop historically and enter into increasingly hybrid structures only afterward. Today's borders are their heirs.

In a globalized world defined by constant movement and mobility, there are more types of social borders today than ever before. The analysis of contemporary borders is an enormous task that cannot possibly be managed in the final part of this book, or even the entirety of a whole book. Given this constraint, I focus here on a single exemplary border sufficient to demonstrate the hybrid and kinetic composition of contemporary borders: the US-Mexico border. The aim of this study is not to exhaustively analyze the border, but to analyze it in a new way that has not been done before. This analysis offers three unique contributions to the theoretical limology of the border.

First, this study analyzes the US-Mexico border kinopolitically. That is, instead of interpreting the border as a fixed, spatial, or even temporal entity, this final part analyzes it as in motion, in between, and as a technology of social circulation.

Second, this study analyzes the US-Mexico border as a social kinetic technology. In other words, the method of analysis is not concerned with what various authorities, politicians, or engineers intended to accomplish with the construction of various border technologies, but with the actual kinetic functions of the material technologies themselves. For example, many border theorists and analysts have argued that the US-Mexico border is a failure, but such critiques presume that power must be somehow consistent or logical in order to function. The opposite is true: power functions primarily in and through its conflicts, mobilities, instabilities, and hybridity. It is not monological, it is kinological. Thus the question is not "Is this border a success or failure?" but "How does it move?"

Finally, this study analyzes the US-Mexico border as a social kinetic hybrid. Borders have multiple coexisting and heterogeneous forms of motion. They exert all the forces of centripetal attraction, centrifugal repulsion, linked tension, and elastic oscillations without contradiction. Motion has no contradiction. However, not all contemporary borders are exactly like the US-Mexico border. It is not meant to be an ideal form of limological analysis. Every border exerts a different mixture of kinetic forces and to different degrees, but every contemporary border is a hybrid of the same four kinetic regimes and their corresponding territorial, political, juridical, and economic dimensions. By analyzing the US-Mexico border according to this framework, Part III of this book demonstrates the strength and usefulness of these three novel approaches made possible by the conceptual-historical work of the previous chapters.

This final part focuses on the US-Mexico border for several reasons. This border is 1,989 miles long, cost over $100 billion over the last fifteen years to construct and maintain,[1] is composed of dozens of different materials and technologies,[2] and remains the most frequently crossed international boundary in the world.[3] Mexico has more of its population living abroad than any other country in the world (11 percent of Mexican citizens live in the United States).[4] The United States has the largest population of immigrants in the world, 58 percent of whom come from Mexico alone. Furthermore, the status of US-Mexico border security has been a particularly controversial political issue both nationally and internationally for the past twenty years, and continues to be. For all of these reasons the US-Mexico border poses a robust and high-profile microcosm of contemporary kinopower. Thus Part III is organized as a microcosm of the whole book.

The next four chapters analyze the contemporary redeployment of the historical border regimes developed in Part II of this book—the fence, the wall, the cell, and the checkpoint. The empirical technologies of contemporary borders differ in many ways from their historical antecedents. Today we have drones, night-vision sensors, surveillance cameras, and so on. For all this, however, the regimes of social kinetic motion remain strikingly similar, despite their innovative hybridity. As Octavio Paz writes, "In Mexico, the past reappears because it is a hidden present."

THE BORDER IN MOTION

The US-Mexico border is in constant motion. The border does not stop motion, nor is it simply an act of political theater that merely functions symbolically to give the appearance of stopping movement. The border is both in motion and directs motion. Thus the definition of the border developed in the introduction can be used to understand the mobility of the US-Mexico border.

First, the US-Mexico border is in-between. The creation of this border cannot be reduced to the direct action of states on the territory. Historically, the US-Mexico border, like many borders, was defined by a continual process of often-violent contestation over the location of the border. Up until around the 1920s the border was largely a disputed in-between zone where Apaches, cattle thieves, American settlers, and indigenous Mexicans moved back and forth freely. As Joseph Nevins writes, "The region that was to become the US-Mexico borderlands was, in the 1800s, a dynamic, multinational zone of fluid identities and porous and flexible social boundaries."[5] Over a century this in-between zone has increasingly shrunk into a more-limited area through violent confrontation between various territorial groups, but it has not disappeared. While these groups sometimes acted in favor of the national or state interests of the United States or Mexico, their motivations were not the direct actions of states. In fact, some of the most important events in shaping the border occurred entirely outside the rule of law, such as the illegal entry of slave-owning American settlers into Mexico (modern-day Texas), where slavery was outlawed; the social/racial tension among settlers and Mexicans; the indeterminate nature of the North American border agreement between imperial France, England, and Spain; and finally, the illegal capture and overthrow of Mexican territory in the Mexican-American War.[6] But the state has not concretized the border; it has only complicated it.

Despite hundreds of years of increasing state involvement in determining the border, it remains in between. For example, the border wall/fence does not follow the exact geographical line that separates the two states; it weaves back and forth across the line where there are rivers, mountains, gulches, or expensive golf courses that are not suitable to build on. In places where the national border is miles away from the fence, is the border at the fence, at the line, or in between? Where the Rio Grande / Río Bravo runs between the two states, the river itself is neither in the United States nor in Mexico, yet the water in the river is used by both US and Mexican farmers. Again, the border remains neither/nor/both/and—it is in between. Where drones fly above the line and underground sensors and tunnels exist below it, is the border above the line or below the line, or both, or in between the three? Where the wall moves around gulches, Indian graveyards, golf courses, and other places in which the US and Mexican states must negotiate with natural, tribal, and financial interests, who defines the border? Surely we cannot say in these cases that the border is solely reducible to definition by a single state; rather, the border is the result of a negotiation between states and even between states and nonstate forces. Like the cut that divides two pieces of paper, the US-Mexico border remains an open and disputed nexus between territorial, state, legal, and economic forces, irreducible to one side or the other. Borders should not be studied as geographical lines between sovereign territories; rather, they must be studied as open vectors of diverse and contentious kinetic phenomena. Rather than a sharp divide, the border functions as a bifurcation point where continuities between natural and social groups are simply channeled off or bifurcated like the irrigation ditches siphoning off water from the Rio Grande / Río

Bravo. Movement, like the border, like the river, is not blocked but flows in between and around.

The second kinetic consequence of the theory of the border developed in this book is that the US-Mexico border must be understood as in motion. The border is always made and remade according to a host of shifting variables. First, the border literally and actually moves itself. For example, where the border fence stretches out into the San Diego beach, the sands and tides move the metal posts in various directions, creating openings in the fence that are easily traversed. Further inland, seasonal desert streams and rains in the Sonora overflow and erode the hillsides, fence posts, and concrete foundations of the border fence, creating openings in the fences. The geomorphological changes caused by desert streams, wetlands, canyons, floods, and dramatic temperature changes of up to fifty degrees in one day rapidly decompose, erode, and topple desert fence structures. The border must literally be moved to accommodate these forces or repaired to endure them. Either way, there is a continual mobility.

Second, the US-Mexico border is moved by others. This is especially apparent in the continual negotiation and renegotiation required to determine where to build or rebuild the border fence. For example, the border is moved and rerouted by American Indians demanding that the wall not traverse sacred burial grounds, by politicians demanding that their city or district needs a larger or stronger wall, by property owners who refuse to allow the US government to requisition their property, by civilian militias like the Minutemen who start building their own fences on the border and demanding more, and by environmentalists demanding that the wall be only a certain height or not cross through a certain park because it will endanger the plants and wildlife. In fact, after the US government had waived numerous federal environmental protection laws and built the border fence in 2007, it had to go back in 2009 with $50 million to "assess, restore, and mitigate" the environmental damages the construction had caused.[7] This required the fence, foundation, roads, and valleys to be moved and reconstructed again in order to mitigate erosion, flooding, and other damage.

The movement of the border is also apparent in the literal movement and transport of the border as dirt, repurposed military materials, railroad ties and track, and so on.[8] The US-Mexico border is literally made possible by the mobilization of dirt and steel. In order to build seven hundred miles of new fencing along the border, as mandated by the 2006 Secure Fence Act, engineers required that all the ditches, gulches, and valleys be filled in with dirt to in order to create a smooth and stable foundation for the border and free mobility of the border patrol. "This is done to prevent migrants from utilizing irregularities in the local terrain to bypass the fence. Vales, gorges, dells, hollows and other so-called 'irregular' geological formations are subject to redesign according to the operational needs of the border patrol. Both of these operational aims require the massive movement of dirt."[9] In order to do this the United States cut two million cubic yards of earth off of tops of nearby mountains to fill in the canyons.[10] The result of this environmental disaster is not only that the bare mountain tops have been moved elsewhere by erosion, destroying plants and wildlife, but that the bare embankments that have replaced the living canyons of Smuggler's Gulch are eroding into the Tijuana estuary, destroying the ecological habitat and inhibiting the mobility of the border patrol along washed-out roadways.[11] The border as dirt, water, and roadway is in a constant circuit of erosion and mitigation. Furthermore, the border fence itself is a mobile assemblage of repurposed military materials transported from all over the world. The wires, posts, and fences that imprisoned Japanese Americans during World War II were dug up from the deserts of Crystal City, California, and driven into the sands of the US-Mexico border along with other materials brought in from around the world.[12] The border is a material assemblage of various mobile war machines—transported from around the world—into a single war machine. It is perhaps revealing that the old technologies of military mobility have now become the tools of restricted and forced mobility at the border, since the flip side of free state-centered mobility is the forced motion of the territorial periphery. At the border railroad ties are turned into vehicle barriers, crushed cars into walls—mobility into constraint.[13]

The border is also moved by migrants and *coyotajes* as they cut and dig through the border infrastructure. In March 2001, the US Customs and Border Protection agency (CBP) reported 4,037 breaches in 2010 alone. The agency estimated that "it would cost $6.5 billion 'to deploy, operate and maintain' the existing border fencing over an expected maximum lifetime of 20 years."[14] Migrants have been cutting holes in the US-Mexico borders for years. Even in 1951 one government document reports that four days after all the holes in the Calexico fence had been repaired fourteen new holes were cut, eleven new panels were torn out, and seven new cuts had been made in the barbed wire.[15] In many cases coyotes and migrants will even replace their holes with similar materials to give the appearance that the wall has not been damaged. In one case coyotes replaced a Normandy-style vehicle barrier with a cardboard facsimile.[16]

The third kinetic consequence of the theory of the border developed in this book is that the US-Mexico border must be understood as a form of circulation. The border is a division, but division is not blockage—it is bifurcation. The border has never succeeded in keeping people in or out absolutely, but only in redirecting them through detention, deportation, customs, high-surveillance areas, and so on. The US-Mexico border is thus poorly understood as a technique of inclusion and exclusion. Since border technologies always respond kinetically to a mixture of forces—territorial, political, juridical, economic—they are constantly changing vectors through redirection. For example, after 9/11 the US-Mexico border was transformed into a national security outpost against terrorism. Suddenly who was allowed in and out, and the criteria for determining passage, changed. New techniques of bifurcation emerged. New holding cells, interrogation techniques, and new laws suspending habeas corpus and others went into effect. As the National Terrorism Advisory System (NTAS) level rises from yellow to orange, so the border recirculates accordingly: increasing wait times at the border redirect traffic, increasingly invasive searches redirect people to "security zones" and "interrogation areas," increasing fortifications along the border redirect migrants into the scorching desert. As security conditions change, new interior Border Patrol checkpoints emerge fifty miles away from the border, and others disappear or close down. As these temporary interior checkpoints move (every fourteen days), so traffic is rerouted or delayed. Since the border is never done once and for all with its divisions, people who are expelled come back again from inside as undocumented workers and others from the outside recirculate again after deportation. After detained migrants have spent their maximum time in a for-profit detention facility, costing taxpayers $200 a day per bed, they are deported back into Mexico, where they attempt reentry.[17] This cottage industry is not a logical exclusion, it is a social kinetic circulation made possible by the circuits of the border.

THE FENCE

The fence is the oldest of all border regimes and has had innumerable incarnations and hybridizations throughout history. The fence regime is a specific type of kinopower that delimits an area of the earth as socially distinct: as territory. It captures the wild flows of water, soil, rock, and organic life, and folds them into junctions for stable storage and accumulation. The kinopolitical function of the fence is thus centripetal. It brings the periphery into the center. The fence opens a pit and centripetally contains a pile.

Historically, humans used this border regime to establish fenced-in social circuits, such as corrals, gardens, pens, houses, villages, and graveyards. Three types of fences were invented to accomplish this: an offensive corral, a defensive palisade, and a binding megalith. Today the concrete technologies are quite different and even differ geographically, but their social kinetic function remains the same. Fencing remains a centripetal technology for bringing the outside in, marking a territory, and binding wild flows into vessel junctions. Historically, the US-Mexico border was first marked by border monuments and sections of fencing to designate a territorial limit, and added solid steel walls in and near cities only in 2006. This is because fencing is largely, although not exclusively, a rural bordering technique. It does not completely restrict cross-border movement but functions more as a physically distinctive and visually imposing territorial landmark.[18] It allows some natural flows to pass, like wind, water, and pollinating insects, but keeps in larger more agriculturally desirable mammals and plants. The size of the holes in fencing can even be adjusted to let in and filter out different kinds of beings. It is more like a porous net than a solid barrier. Its construction is typically cheaper, faster, and easier to build and repair than solid walls, making it a preferred border technique for larger areas of land.[19]

Furthermore, it is a preferred border regime for the purposes of centripetal accumulation—where peripheral movement is directed inward toward a center-—because it allows for a visibility and surveillance between posts that allow the hunter to follow the flows. As a 2009 congressional report states, "Concrete panels, for example, are among the more cost-effective solutions but USBP agents cannot see through this type of fencing; the USBP testified about their preference for fencing that can be seen through, so as to identify the activity occurring on the Mexican side of the border and thus preserve their tactical advantage over potential border crossers, and to better avoid potential rockings [the hurling of stones or other items] or other violent incidents."[20] One builds a fence facing the direction of the movements it wants to capture. Today fences compose the vast majority of the largely rural and wild US-Mexico borderland. As the fence approaches the cities of San Diego, Nogales, and El Paso, a wall has been added to the border that changes its function, as we will see in the next section. In the case of the US-Mexico border we see the centripetal function of the fence in three distinct kinetic technologies: the offensive funnel effect, the defensive security fence, and the binding monument.

The Funnel Effect

The first type of fence at the US-Mexico border is the funnel fence or "funnel effect," as it is popularly called. This funnel effect is a fundamentally offensive border technique that brings a diverse periphery toward a central point for capture. The historical technique of corralling has probably been around as long as humans, and border funneling is only a contemporary manifestation of this technique. At the US-Mexico border we can identify at least four major types of funnel fences or funnel effects.

First, the US-Mexico border centripetally funnels or corrals undocumented migrants from the periphery in Mexico to certain privileged central points along the border where they have a higher risk of dying or being more easily captured: between eastern Arizona and western Texas. Architecturally, the border is largely composed of hundreds of miles of fence structures. Pits are dug by machines, and metal posts, railroad ties, and all kinds of materials are placed into these holes to create a verticality that rises above the earth. These fences are by no means uncrossable, but pose a deterrent or appearance of deterrence to mobility. Just like the desert kites of history, these fences both mark out a territory and create a social division between the wild outside and the fenced-in interior.[21] Like historical hunting corrals, an offensive group (United States) marches out into the periphery (Mexico) and through various strategies (the North American Free Trade Agreement) forces them into migration.[22] In the middle of the Mexican desert there are no significant fences and almost no border patrol, but there is also no water. There are triple-digit temperatures in the day and freezing temperatures at night, poisonous snakes, and scorpions. By constructing a fence that is wide at the periphery and narrow with an opening toward the center, the US-Mexico border becomes an enormous two-thousand-mile desert kite. Migrants are expelled from their homes and centripetally funneled by a fence structure into a chosen pit for extermination (by dehydration or hypothermia), capture (by the Border Patrol Search, Trauma, and Rescue Unit, BORSTAR), or accumulation (into the United States). Although it seems counterintuitive, the border fence actually makes possible an increased centripetal accumulation of migrants:[23] "During the 1980's, the probably that an undocumented migrant would be apprehend while crossing stood at around 33 percent; by 2000 it was at 10 percent, despite increases in federal spending on border enforcement."[24] In this case, building increasingly secure border fences actually decreased the number apprehensions and increased the number of migrants who were able to go around unfenced, unpatrolled areas. In other words, the fence functions centripetally to increase the accumulation of migrants just as the corrals of history have done, despite so-called intentions to keep migrants out.

By forcing migration from Mexico and creating a funnel-shaped fence, the US-Mexico border effectively becomes the world's largest centripetal manhunting apparatus. According to federal records, more than six thousand immigrants have died crossing the southern border since 1998.[25]

A 2013 report by the Binational Migration Institute argues that these deaths are the result of the US policy of "prevention through deterrence" that was initially implemented in the mid to late 1990s to militarize and secure the border.[26] However, this funnel effect has been occurring since 1945, when the government first starting erecting substantial fencing on the border.[27] Immigration and Naturalization Services was completely aware of what it was doing. The INS explicitly stated that, by not erecting a continuous line of fence along the border, but relying instead on strategic placement, it would "compel persons seeking to enter the United States illegally to attempt to go around the ends of the fence."[28] Because only some parts of the border are secured, migrants are centripetally funneled into a few major corridors. This funnel effect has more recently turned Tucson into "the single most traversed crossing corridor for migrants along the entire U.S.-Mexico border."[29] Even the phrase "migration corridor," from the Latin word *currere* (to run, gallop, or trot), refers to the running of animals into the corral.

Second, the US-Mexico border centripetally funnels all authorized border crossing into a few specific ports of entry. This function dates back to the some of the earliest border fences.[30] By building an enormous fence across the territory, including off-road vehicle barriers (large metal posts stuck in the ground), all authorized border traffic is funneled into a few single points, where it is bottlednecked for hours. These points are so overwhelmed by traffic that rigorous ID checks are not possible. The result is that these funnels actually end up admitting more unauthorized migrants than before.[31] In other words, the border fence creates two centripetal funnel effects, each the inversion of the other. Each social flow is funneled toward the path of least resistance. In the first, unauthorized migrants are funneled toward the desert where there is a gap in the fence that is easy to cross. In the second, authorized or unauthorized migrants are funneled toward the city and bridges where there is an easier gap to cross (customs) than driving through a vehicle barrier. "Rather than a secure and closed border, cross-border movements are funneled to the bridges, which lack the capacity to inspect even a small fraction of the traffic that crosses, and to more isolated locations that have less effective types of barriers or no barrier at all."[32] Thus the fence functions as an apparatus of capture.

Third, on the US side of the border, authorized migrants are funneled along the fences of property owners and by migrant-hunting groups. After unauthorized migrants are funneled down the corridor of harsh desert terrain, they are again funneled by rural property fences built by Arizona and Texas farmers. In many cases these fences are made of barbed wire or are electrified. One Texas farmer, Michael Vickers, enclosed nearly one thousand acres with a 220-volt fence. "It won't kill them," he says "but it will make them wet their pants."[33] In addition to these fences some residents engage in direct centripetal manhunting, funneling migrants into their traps. "It's a cat-and-mouse game," says one of these hunters. "Her Heckler & Koch P2000 pistol rests in the cup holder next to her right knee. She starts by looking for footprints—they are most noticeable on the sand tracks she has set up next to the trails that she smooths by dragging tires. When she sees a fresh set, she speeds through the trails, finds the migrants, chases after them until they tire out, corners them and then yells, 'Pa'bajo!'—Spanish for down."[34] In Texas many of the properties around border checkpoints are monitored with sensors. To avoid these technologies migrants move further into harsh brush areas filled with burrs, tiny seeds, irritating thorns, and venomous snakes. A group called the Texas Border Volunteers, made up of some three hundred recruits who dress in fatigues and patrol private ranches in south Texas, then use night-vision goggles, hunting dogs, and thermal imaging to track people in the dark and funnel them into the hands of the Border Patrol.[35] Another vigilante border patrol group, the Minutemen, "by their placement along the darkened border, would create a 'funnel' through which all human traffic would have to pass." At the end of the funnel one of the Minutemen reports there would be a "turkey shoot"—a hunting reference meaning an easy kill.[36] One Border Patrol officer remarked to the press that he "appreciated the help."[37]

Fourth, the US-Mexico border fence not only centripetally funnels human migrants into basins of accumulation, but also funnels nonhuman flows into basins of accumulation. For example: "Water from desert rains typically drain[s] across the border—yet in areas such as the port of entry at Sonoyta, Mexico and Organ Pipe Cactus National Monument and in the Ambos Nogales (Arizona and Sonoma) the fence acts as a dam. It not only attempts to block northern flows of immigrants, the wall diverts water flows on both sides of the border into nearby cities, causing flooding and enormous environmental damage."[38] The centripetal effect of the fence is not only urban; it also occurs in the middle of the desert. The US-Mexico border fence runs across rivers, estuaries, and other waterways. The construction of the fence fills in the estuaries and dams up the rivers centripetally, accumulating flows of water, plant species, and animals on one side. However, these accumulations also destroy watersheds on the other side of the fence. The fence blocks corridors for animal migration or redirects it elsewhere. Creating an ecology without a diversified gene pool and fresh water, the fence is killing thousands of animals and plants. Wild animal flows are funneled into residential areas in search of food, where they are more likely to be injured by cars and die. According to the Mexican government's report, there are more than four thousand affected plant species across the border area, and the fence negatively affects eighty-five endangered species of plants and animals.[39] In this way the fence also functions as a corral for environmental flows, cutting off movement and pooling it into destructive pits.

The Security Fence

The second type of fence at the US-Mexico border is the security fence. As its name suggests, this security fence is a fundamentally defensive border technique that protects the captured flows accumulated by the border. There are at least two major ways that security fences function to detain, limit, or "cage" accumulated social flows at the border.

First, the US-Mexico border fence functions centripetally to capture migrants from Mexico and keep them in the United States. This may sound like a contradiction since the stated intention of the 2006 Secure Fence Act is to "stop all unwanted migration," not to retain it. But kinopolitics has no contradictions, only bifurcations and vectors. Multiple different social motions can coexist as hybrid formations. The United States benefits immensely from the accumulation of migrant labor, specifically undocumented migrant labor. Migrants in the United States work disproportionately at less desirable jobs, under less desirable conditions, and for lower wages than other workers in America.[40] Undocumented migrants are particularly underpaid, poorly treated, regularly threatened by their employers with deportation,[41] are unable to unionize, vote, or legally drive, and yet still must pay taxes to the US government.[42] In many sectors of the US economy migrant workers are the only workers willing to do low-paying construction labor, seasonal agricultural work, and janitorial work. Without these workers, some of these sectors would collapse. Thus it is absolutely in the best interests of the US economy to accumulate cheap migrant labor and retain it. This is precisely the defensive centripetal function of the border fence: to make it more difficult for migrants to leave. This is what the US government now officially and appropriately calls "the caging effect" of the border,[43] but it has this effect in an interesting way. The fence makes it more difficult for unauthorized migrants to leave precisely by making it more difficult for them to return (if they left).[44] By fortifying the border, reentry becomes more difficult for migrants already in the United States (not less probable, in the end) but more unpleasant to endure (desert travel) or expensive to pay for (coyotes). Migrants already in the United States would rather stay in the United States without status than return to Mexico, knowing that the conditions of reentry keep getting more oppressive. In this way the fence keeps migrants in the United States.

Second, border security fencing functions defensively in order to retain migrants in detention centers for extended periods of time. By retaining migrants in holding facilities for as long as possible, private prison corporations like the Corrections Corporation of America aim to make as much profit as possible, charging $200 a bed per night.[45] For-profit prisons are interested in centripetally accumulating migrants. Among other border technologies deployed in detention centers, holding facilities, and other migrant detainment camps is the near universal usage of "security fencing." Fenced-in detention and refugee camps are not a new phenomenon at the US-Mexico border; they have been in existence for over one hundred years, dating back to the fenced refugee camps during the Battle of Agua Prieta in 1915.[46] Despite the recent attention given to the modern proliferation of camps (refugee, migrant, military) and its theoretical/ juridical consequences, insufficient attention has been given to the material and kinetic technologies that make the camp possible.[47] The security fence provides the material and kinetic conditions for the actuality of the detention camp. In particular, the kinetic structure of the fence makes possible a uniquely temporary, visible, and modular border regime.

Fencing is used at detention centers, particular temporary detention centers, because their mobility needs are constantly changing, depending on how many bodies they can accumulate and what kinds of movement they are allowed. When the flow of migrant detainees rises, the fence posts are simply uprooted and moved further out; when the flow of detainees wanes, the posts are moved back in.[48] When a flow of migrants is conjoined in one area. a new detention center can appear in a very short period of time and at very low cost because of the material kinetics of the fence. The fence regime gathers disjoined flows into a single, central point faster than any other border regime. It also has the benefit of directly acting on large numbers of bodies in motion, while simultaneously rendering them visible as a group. As it has for thousands of years, the visibility of the fence makes possible a social surveillance over the detention of captured flows. This is another advantage it has over other border regimes.

As the movement of the detained group changes, the fence can physically adapt quickly by modulating its shape, size, and subdivisions. Many temporary camps and detention centers could not function successfully without this modular ability, made possible by the kinetic structure of the fence. Take, for example, almost any emergency center aiming to centripetally gather and detain a disjoined human flow. The recent "invasion" of the United States by 47,000 child refugees from Central America is one such case.[49] The rapid spike in refugees was handled by transforming various warehouse spaces into "human cattle pens," like the one in Nogales, Arizona.[50] In many of these temporary shelters thousands of children were socially subdivided from their families by age and sex, using chain-link fence. Reverend John Torres of New Life Community Church described the conditions as "squalid": the children were filthy, curled up on thin foam mats, covered in plastic bags, with access to only a few portable toilets, and surrounded by modular fencing.[51] It is not kinetically inaccurate to describe these fence regimes as human cattle pens since this is precisely the historical legacy and kinetic function of fencing: to centripetally accumulate and detain human and animal flows into temporary, visible, and modular fence structures.

The Monument

The third type of fence at the US-Mexico border is the monument. The monument fence is distinct from the offensive funneling function and from the defensive security function of the fence; it has a binding or boundary function instead. The monuments of the US-Mexico border wall create points of centripetal social attraction that draw in and bind people into their surrounding area. These monuments are defined by the same basic motions of the fence: to strike or cut a pit into the earth and to erect a vertical junction so large that it will exert a social force of attraction and accumulation for generations to come. Border monuments mark important boundary points to which people return again and again. They serve as material reminders in the form of pits or wounds dug in the earth and filled with a vertical structure that will resist the chaos of forgetting. Border monuments, from the Latin word *monere* (to remind, advise, or warn), cut a material memory into the earth. Nietzsche famously describes human memory as the process of "mnemotechnics," or the creation of human memory through the pain of physical punishment and mutilation of the body.[52] We could thus similarly describe human social structure as the process of "kinotechnics," or the creation of social division through the material cuts made into the earth's flows to establish a territorial and kinetic memory. Borders are the social scars left by these wounds. There are at least two major monumental fence technologies that bind people to these scars at the US-Mexico border.

The first monumental fence structure of the border is the territorial boundary monument. These are the first and earliest boundary monuments on the border, cut into the earth to serve as reminders of where the earth's flows were centripetally bound into a single unified territory.

On February 2, 1848, in Mexico City, representatives from the Republic of Mexico and the United States signed the Treaty of Guadalupe Hidalgo. In the treaty Mexico ceded over half its territory to the United States for $15 million, ending the Mexican-American War and increasing the US land mass by one-third.[53] But these signatories had never seen the territory they were deciding on. When they verbally described the border in the treaty they simply relied on an 1847 map, published by the New York mapmaker John Disturnell. Article V of the treaty thus reads: "In order to preclude all difficulty in tracing upon the ground the limit separating Upper from Lower California, it is agreed that the said limit shall consist of a straight line drawn from the middle of the Rio Gila, where it unites with the Colorado, to a point on the coast of the Pacific Ocean, distant one marine league due south of the southernmost point of the port of San Diego."[54] These statesmen and their treaty simply drew an abstract and arbitrary political border with their words—a straight line across a map. The territorial border was materially put in place by a binational survey team sent to out to walk the two-thousand-mile border and install boundary monuments into the earth. This Boundary Survey Commission, composed of astronomers, cartographers, scientists, and artists, was sent to the border for six years, beginning in July 1849. Along the way they built rock cairns pegged with a flag, but these were often moved or destroyed by Native tribes that rejected such territorial land grabs.[55] However, in the 1890s these cairns were replaced with 276 boundary monuments made of stone and cast iron, generally spaced between two and four miles apart in order to be visible by line of sight, from El Paso / Juarez to Tijuana / San Diego.[56]

The centripetal function of these boundary monuments persists today. In many places along the border these monuments continue to be the only physical or territorial boundaries in existence. In fact, in many cases these boundaries were the limological and territorial condition for the more recent (post-1994) construction of new fencing, wall, and surveillance points along the border. These monuments were not destroyed but simply built over, around, and combined with other border regimes, producing new hybrids.

The second monumental fence structure at the US-Mexico border is the tomb monument. Tombs and graves were some of the first social boundaries. They centripetally bound a community of dead ancestors in common graves or gravesites (pits and piles), and bound these dead ancestors to a living social group that would regularly return centripetally to the territorial site. Today this border function has not disappeared but is simply added to others. The US-Mexico border functions as a tomb monument in several ways. At the Tijuana–San Diego border, ten painted coffins have been placed against the fence, each marked with a year (1995–2004) and the number of migrants that died crossing the border that year. The peak year for deaths was 2000, with approximately 499 deaths. Every year after 1998 has recorded over 300 deaths. This border deaths monument centripetally binds all the migrant dead together in a single location for the living community to return to and mourn. The verticality of the monument is important. The coffins are not buried horizontally under the ground, nor are they marked with any other structure such as a cross or obelisk. The coffins themselves protrude from the earth, themselves becoming territorial monuments. The deaths of the migrant dead in this monument have been unearthed, disinterred, and exposed to the sun in their raw form without proper burial and in many cases even without identification. Just as the bodies of dead migrants mark the territorial boundary with their blood and bleached bones, so this coffin monument marks a boundary between life and death, exposure and concealment, below and above the earth.

Border death monuments line the US-Mexico border. Crosses of all varieties are placed by mourners all along the border.[57] In 1998 migrant activists in Tijuana hung a cross on the border for each migrant who died as a result of Operation Gatekeeper.[58] In 2009 the Defense Coalition, a promigrant group, hung 5,100 white crosses on the Tijuana border, listing names, ages, hometowns, and dates of dead migrants. For anonymous deaths the crosses and coffins read, "No identificado."[59] Monuments of all kinds have been built along the border, from collective monuments composed of vertical piles of discarded clothing, animal bones, named crosses, and votive candles to the Virgin Mary (at the No More Deaths camp in Arivaca, Arizona),[60] to individual monuments dedicated to a single person (like the monument to Mexican teenager José Antonio Elena Rodriguez, who was shot and killed by the US Border Patrol).[61] These deaths are not epiphenomenal or so-called side effects of the functioning of the border. In kinopolitics there are no side effects, only different kinetic effects. Throughout history graves have lined the boundaries of territorial peripheries, from Neolithic roadways, to Greek cemeteries on the edge of town, to the "death strip" of the Berlin wall. They create a territorial division in the earth and bind a territorial community of the dead to a territorial community of the living. Just as mnemotechnics burns a memory into the human body through punishment, so kinotechnics burns a kinetic memory (where and how one is allowed to move) into the human body through punishment and scarification, and ultimately the burial of bodies into a scarified and territorialized earth to remember the boundaries of movement: the tomb monument.

There is a social kinetic reason that almost all of these monuments are on the Mexico side of the wall. They are there to burn a memory of warning and death into the Mexican people. The historical function of tomb monuments has always been a centripetal and binding one that ties the bodies of the dead to a specific territory and to a specific community. Only certain bodies can be buried in certain places. The message is clear: Mexican bodies and their tombs belong on their side of the territorial divide. Since the migrant deaths have largely been Mexican and largely mourned by Mexicans who return to the monument again and again both as border crossers and as mourners for their ancestors, for them the monuments are social kinetic attractors and memorials: "Every November 2 over the last decade, the faithful from Ciudad Juárez led by their bishop join with their counterparts from El Paso and Las Cruces, New Mexico, and their bishops, to celebrate the Eucharist on the "Day of the Dead." . . . The site of the celebration is divided right at the altar by the fence . . . the prayers for the dead are offered especially for those who have perished in the New Mexican desert after crossing this international boundary into the imagined promised land without documents."[62] When many Mexicans see the fence, they see a tomb monument, a colorful memorial for the dead, a warning of death in a shrine, and a community of fellow migrants in mourning.

On the northern side of the border, anonymous paupers graves are the predominant tomb monuments. Border towns like Tucson and Holtville have paupers' cemeteries filled with the bodies of unidentified migrants. The cemeteries are clearly divided between migrant and nonmigrant grave monuments. The migrant side of the cemetery is marked by small, unfinished-pine crosses sticking out of the rough desert sand, while the nonmigrant side is furnished with tombstones and covered in grass. As soon as a body is identified it is exhumed, and shipped back to Mexico to be buried in the family grave. The territoriality of the border grave is crucial. Migrants are socially divided even in their anonymous deaths, centripetally accumulated on their side of the cemetery and shipped back to their side of the territorial divide. Their graves mark the border not only between life and death but between anonymity and identity, status and alienage, and between American and Mexican territories.

Despite their anonymity, these migrant tomb monuments still effect a centripetal social movement north of the border. Each month the San Diego promigrant group Border Angels makes a pilgrimage to the county cemetery in Holtville to bring small wooden crosses and flowers to the graves. The verticality of the cross creates a kinomnemonic preservation of life's movement beyond death. The tomb junction allows for the centripetal return of the memorial. By denying anonymous migrants monumental verticality, the county is effectively denying them the right of movement, to be forgotten and decomposed into the earth's disjoined flows. In Tucson the groups Derechos Humanos, No More Deaths, and Inter-faith Immigrant Coalition meet for a weekly vigil at the monument to the *tiraditos* (the discarded) to remember the "migrants who have died in the desert on their way to find work in the US."[63] The group Humane Borders documents the location of nearly half of these deaths on a southern Arizona map.[64] They monumentalize the anonymous. But how can one remember those whom one did not know and who are still unknown? Again, in kinopolitics there are no contradictions. The tomb binds the centripetal motions of a community, whether Mexican mourners of specific family members or American mourners of anonymous migrants. The border monument binds a community and divides a territory.

The fence is only the first border regime in the hybrid structure of the US-Mexico border. In the next chapter we can see how centrifugal wall structures are added to this fence regime to create a new limological hybrid that preserves the motion of both without completely synthesizing the two.

CHAPTER 8

The US-Mexico Wall

The wall is the second major border regime of the US-Mexico border. Although the usage of walls as social borders first emerged as the dominant form of bordered motion during the urban revolution of the ancient period, its centrifugal kinetic function persists today. The wall regime adds to the territorial conjunction of the earth's flows a central point of political force: the city. Once a centripetal accumulation of flows has been achieved, a central point begins to centrifugally redirect the organization of the territory. Kinetically, the wall regime is defined by two functions: the creation of homogenized parts (blocks) based on a central model, and their ordered stacking around a central point of force or power. The kinetic structure of walls, unlike fences, tends to be much more urban, military, permanent, expensive, and centrally organized.

Unlike the fence regime, the wall regime at the US-Mexico border functions to centrifugally expel migrants outward, away from the center. Although the US-Mexico border has always been militarized and under the political power of a centralized government to some degree, it was not until the 1990s that we saw a massive expansion of centrifugal wall power at the border and in the "war on immigration."[1] In particular, the militarization of the border in the 1990s began as a largely urban force and expanded outward toward the periphery. This militarized wall regime is defined by three major kinds of political walls: offensive walls (federal enforcement operations), defensive walls (landing mats), and binding walls (transportation controls).

The first type of wall at the US-Mexico border is the offensive wall, defined by the marking and marching function of the border. The federal enforcement wall is expressed in three major border technologies: the Border Patrol, Immigrations and Customs Enforcement, and the National Guard. Each functions according to a centrifugal and offensive social force that creates bricks of homogenized matter, stacks them in a compact formation, and marches them outward to control social kinetic power at the periphery. Each of these three border technologies is federal (centrally directed), is a show or exertion of centrally sovereign political force, and is defined according to a series of military-style operations. The OED defines "operation" as "a strategic movement of troops, ships, etc., for military action; a planned and coordinated activity involving a number people." Border operations are operations involving the mobilization of a centrally organized body of people, not just materials. As in ancient history, the human wall of the military body precedes the brick wall of the architectural body. The latter is modeled on the former, not the other way around.

The first federal enforcement wall is the Border Patrol. The US Border Patrol (USBP) was founded on May 28, 1924, as an agency of the Department of Labor to prevent unauthorized entries on the US-Mexico border in the aftermath of the Mexican-American War. Before the USBP, the border was patrolled directly by US Army soldiers. Today the USBP uniform retains the same green-colored uniforms as the army—making clear its offensive military function and contrasting it with the blue uniforms of civil police officers. The creation of Border Patrol agents followed the typical historical and military kinetic structure of transforming human beings into standardized and homogenous units with uniform regulations, grooming regulations, and other physical and ideological regulations—grouped according to larger and larger military-style blocks or rank-and-file columns under central and hierarchical command. The standardized body of the agent is "hardened" with armor and then stacked into an ordered configuration by a central, federal power. Border Patrol agents' bodies are made into "human walls," as Shawn Moran, vice president of the National Border Patrol Council, describes them.[2] The border wall extends only to where political power can enforce it through the body of the patrol agent. Thus during the 1990s, when the "militarization of the border" began,[3] Congress began to centrifugally shift the Border Patrol away from the interior of the country and focus agents on the peripheral borders. Once at the border, the Border Patrol wall was stacked and expanded: from 4,139 patrol agents in 1992 to over 21,370 in 2011.[4] In particular, Border Patrol agents on the southwest border have been increasingly steadily since the early 1990s: from 3,555 agents in 1992 to 20,119 in 2009.[5]

The model for this militarized human border wall is Operation Blockade. Operation Blockade was invented by El Paso Border Patrol chief Silvestre Reyes on September 19, 1993, in order to stop unauthorized border crossings through the city. Operation Blockade consisted of 400 Border Patrol agents lined up for twenty miles in fixed positions within eyesight of each other along the banks of the Rio Grande and through the middle of the city. "The human wall of hundreds of highly visible Border Patrol agents had the effect of quickly halting the unauthorized migrant flow within twenty miles of the El Paso area."[6] Instead of roaming around the interior of the country and border cities looking to apprehend authorized border crossers, Operation Blockade stacked its human bricks into fixed locations at the urban periphery. They do not move to chase people down; instead, they relied on other agents who were not posted at the border to do so. In addition, a second line of agents was stationed slightly further interior as a second line of defense.[7] The human blockade wall kept its eyes on the border as a "line watch" and left only when a replacement arrived.

The English word "blockade" is of specifically military origin and means "to seal off as an act of war."[8] Operation Blockade was specifically theorized to be a "massive show of force"[9] that made visible the sovereign centrifugal power of federal enforcement. Three weeks later, however, Operation Blockade was renamed Operation Hold the Line because local business leaders disliked the idea of an absolute blockade. The phrase "hold the line" means "to remain steadfast under pressure," but also has a historical military meaning since soldiers have been organized into offensive line structures like rows and columns. "Hold the line" means "fight to hold your military position." We could also add to these meanings the kinetic meaning used in the ancient art of walling: the geometric line and level of reason according to which a good wall should be built.[10] The wall, in contrast to the pile, is built according to a geometrical model centrifugally applied outward to homologous material pieces and brought into resonance around the line and level of the central idea. All lines are forced into the resonance of a model level line: the borderline. This centrifugal motion is described by the USBP as a "forward deployment" of "constant vigilance" and "high profile presence."[11]

Operation Hold the Line in El Paso soon became the model for militarized human wall power along the border. Operation Gatekeeper was launched in San Diego in October 1994, using the same model of highly visible, fixed border agents along key sections. Around this same time Operation Safeguard was launched in the Tucson sector using the same tactics and focusing on eliminating unauthorized traffic through the urban Nogales port of entry.¹² The last of the four, Operation Rio Grande, was launched in summer 1997, in the McAllen, Brownsville, and Laredo urban Border Patrol sectors in south Texas. As a result, the numbers of Border Patrol agents in these sectors nearly doubled from 1996 to 2000, reaching 2,160 agents.¹³

The second federal enforcement wall is Immigration and Customs Enforcement (ICE). After the attacks of September 11, 2001, the Department of Homeland Security disbanded the Immigration and Naturalization Services and created two new immigration enforcement agencies: ICE and Customs and Border Protection (CBP). While the USBP focuses on expelling unauthorized migrants from the periphery (air, land, and sea ports), ICE focuses on expelling unauthorized migrants from the interior. If the USBP is the exterior human wall, ICE is the interior human border wall. In particular, Enforcement and Removal Operations (ERO) functions as an agency within ICE to centrifugally expel unauthorized migrants from the territory through raids.

The social kinetics of ICE raids follow the model of the human wall of centrifugal extraction. First, ICE agents surround the home or workplace and block all exits, effectively creating a human wall around the building. Next, the agents use the element of "surprise, intimidation, and shock" to catch residents and companies off guard.¹⁴ Heavily armed ICE agents in uniform and in combat formation bang on the door, ordering occupants, whom they refer to as "targets," to open up. If not, they break down the door and barge into the building. ICE agents can then begin questioning anyone in the building, regardless of their initial "target," and make arrests based on the information provided by residents and employees. Those who admit to being unauthorized migrants are detained and deported within a few days. Those willing to be deported voluntarily are put on a bus back to Mexico within a few hours. The extraction is fast, offensive, and centrifugal. Fugitive Operations claims to focus on the "most threatening criminals and terrorist suspects," but nearly 75 percent of the targets have no criminal convictions.¹⁵

ICE has a centralized and federal organization similar to the Border Patrol, but also focuses on the process of stacking: transforming local law enforcement into homogeneously trained bricks and stacking them in a political resonance with central federal power. The first centrifugal strategy of federal expulsion is Operation Secure Communities. This operation fosters cooperation between local law enforcement and federal immigration officials. Kinopolitically, it uses central (federal) authority to bring its peripheral (local) authorities into a shared resonance around a center point of enforcement. In particular, this operation requires local law enforcement to turn over to federal agents the fingerprints of anyone with whom they come into contact.[16] By centralizing these fingerprint databases and searching them for immigrants, Operation Secure Communities led to the detention of hundreds of thousands of migrants with no criminal record who were apprehended simply because they were undocumented. In this unique action of directing central immigration enforcement over its radial localities, the Obama administration deported over a million people in the operation's first two years.[17]

The second centrifugal strategy of expulsion in the United States is Operation Wagon Train. This national operation used federal immigration enforcement agents to raid local workplaces, looking for undocumented immigrants. Kinetically, it directly deploys centralized (federal) force to control the subordinate movements of peripheral workplaces through raids. Operation Wagon Train culminated in the largest workplace raid in US history in December 2006, when ICE officers raided six Swift & Company packinghouses: "Some 1,282 workers were detained by hundreds of heavily armed I.C.E. agents in military garb. Afterward, Homeland Security secretary Michael Chertoff openly linked the raid to the administration's reform proposals. At a Washington, DC press conference he told reporters that raids would show Congress the need for 'stronger border security, effective interior enforcement and a temporary-worker program.'"[18]

In 1999 Operation Vanguard conducted similar raids using Social Security databases in order to find discrepancies among the 24,310 workers in forty Nebraska meatpacking plants. Seventeen percent quit, were fired, or arrested. In 2001, raids dubbed Operation Tarmac targeted airports around the country, leading to the firing and deportation of hundreds of mostly food-service workers.[19] In 2010 Operation Stonegarden even provided federal reimbursement to local law enforcement agencies to compensate them for immigration and border enforcement work, something local law enforcement is not required to do.[20] ICE also constitutes an offensive border wall that divides migrants from nationals and divides families from one another through centrifugal deportation, or "removal." Between 1998 and 2007 ICE "extracted" 108,434 people and 204,810 more from 2010 to 2012, resulting in the separation of thousands of families in the United States.[21]

The third federal enforcement wall is the National Guard. President Bush deployed six thousand National Guard troops to the US-Mexico border as part of Operation Jump Start between 2006 and 2008.[22] The primary aim of these troops was to demonstrate a sudden show of armed offensive sovereign military force to build roads, fences, and stack more bodies into the human border wall. Operation Jump Start more or less followed the human wall model developed by Operation Blockade by placing soldiers at fixed locations along the wall. Although the National Guard did not have arrest powers in their occupation of the border, they worked with the USBP to alert it to unauthorized crossers. If the historical legacy of the military border wall is not yet explicit enough, consider President Obama's deployment of the National Guard to the US-Mexico border in 2010 under the name Operation Phalanx. The historical military border reference is crystal clear. The border has an offensive military formation. The kinetic function of Obama's phalanx of twelve hundred troops was to create a human line blockade of troops in fixed positions along the southwest border, adding another row of human bricks to the US-Mexico border wall.

THE CORRUGATED WALL

The second type of wall at the US-Mexico border is the defensive corrugated wall, defined by the limiting function of the border. Following its historical precursor, the rampart wall, the corrugated walls of the border function as both urban inner walls running through cities and outer territorial walls radiating outward from the cities. As defensive walls they function as a resource and supply line for the offensive march of federal enforcement agents. It is the march of the federal agents that first marks the borders. The walls emerge only later, showing a territorial limit of political power.

The corrugated-steel walls of the US-Mexico border should be distinguished in content and kinetic function from the numerous types of fencing deployed along the border: picket-style fencing, bollard fencing, wire-mesh fencing, decorative fencing, chain-link fencing, and Normandy-style vehicle fencing. While fencing on the border has a largely centripetal function, funneling and caging migrants with cheap, fast, easily repairable, and transparent kinetic features, the corrugated-steel walls have a largely centrifugal function that make possible direct expulsions from central urban areas. Instead of simply digging pits and placing vertical piles or stakes in them, engineers use corrugated wall made of standardized opaque squares or bricks stacked on top of one another in staggered formation, each marked with a number.

Beginning in 1990, the USBP began building a barrier known as the "primary fence" at the US-Mexico border in San Diego.[23] This new fence structure formed part of the larger militarization of the border strategy known as "Prevention Through Deterrence," which called for "reducing unauthorized migration by placing agents and resources directly on the border along population centers in order to deter would-be migrants from entering the country."[24] The San Diego primary fence was completed in 1993 and cut across the main port of entry. The wall is made of corrugated-steel "panels 12 feet long, 20 inches wide, and 1/4 inch thick, which are welded to steel pipes buried 8 feet deep every 6 feet along the fence."[25] Each mile of wall requires the use of 3,080 panels; and each section of paneling is numbered. These standardized steel panels were welded together by the Army Corps of Engineers and California National Guard into a stacked and staggered wall formation ten feet high, starting at the Pacific Ocean and stretching four-teen miles inland. The corrugated-steel panel material itself is made from metal landing mats used by helicopters in Vietnam, fighter planes in the Gulf Wars,[26] and pontoon bridges and temporary bridges used by troops in World War II.[27] Today these mats can also be seen all over the Philippines and Papua New Guinea, sometimes stretching for miles.[28] Once San Diego built its steel wall, other major urban border areas followed this same model: Campo, California; Yuma, Nogales, Naco, and Douglas, Arizona; and El Paso, Texas.[29]

Several kinolimological consequences follow from the material con-struction of these walls. First, it is interesting to note that the construction of the corrugated wall on the US-Mexico border is modeled precisely on the road, just as it was in the first ancient urban societies. What used to be a horizontal roadway used to create a homogenous surface across various terrains (Marston mats) to increase military deployment and force became the model for a vertical structure used precisely to enforce the inverse on the enemy as a wall. Second, the construction of the corrugated wall has a distinctly centrifugal effect that supporters love to cite: that apprehensions in walled areas dropped significantly and immediately after the wall.[30] Unlike fencing, which merely slows migrants down by about three min-utes, the fortified primary steel wall directly expels unauthorized border crossers. However, like all walls, the steel wall does not stop movement; it simply creates a bifurcation point. In this case, the corrugated-steel wall along urban areas at the US-Mexico border simply redirects movement into the funnel structure of the fence apparatus, leading to increased mi-grant deaths, increased successful border crossings, and increased human smuggling costs.[31] Since national USBP apprehension rates remained ap-proximately the same in 1992 as they were in 2004, these walls have ob-jectively failed to reduce unauthorized crossings.[32] Third, the opacity of the corrugated wall decreases visibility for migrants and the Border Patrol. This has two effects. First, the opacity of the wall makes it more difficult for migrants to see Border Patrol agents on the other side, thus discour-aging entry and encouraging crossing elsewhere with better visibility and unsurveilled passage; alternatively, it allows migrants to use the wall as a shield.[33] Second, the opacity of the wall makes it more difficult for the Border Patrol to see migrants, thus requiring increased stadium floodlight systems, increased brush clearing, video surveillance systems, helicopter support, and an additional row of secondary fencing to increase visibility. Finally, it is important to note the kinopolitical connection between the repurposing of military technologies like landing mats for the construction of the border wall. This is not a coincidence; the two share the same kinetic border regime of centrifugal force.

THE PORT WALL

The third type of wall at the US-Mexico border is the port wall, defined by the binding function of the boundary. The port wall compels or binds flows into circulation by controlling the passage across the border. It is the road wall that makes possible imports, exports, deports, reports, and transports. If the US-Mexico wall has two sides—federal enforcement and corrugated steel—the port is between the two and ensures their communication. These roads function not only to divide the territory, as many roads have historically, but also to expedite the centrifugal removal of migrants. It draws on both federal power for enforcement and the steel wall for security. The wall supports a passage and regulates the circulation and mobility of various social flows at each concentric level. For most of history, the road has served a primarily military function directly related to state warfare: the rapid movement of troops and supply of construction materials. The US-Mexico wall is no exception.[34] At the US-Mexico border we can identify two major types of ports: transports and ports of entry/exit.

The first port wall is the transport wall, which regulates and binds the circulation across and along the border. Without an expanded system of roadways to, from, and along the US-Mexico border, the centrifugal system of expulsion would be almost impossible. The border road is the material and kinetic precondition for the effective operation of federal enforcement at the border and for the construction of any significant tactical infrastructure such as fences, walls, towers, and cameras. Before any of these could be built, a road had to be built to allow construction equipment and Border Patrol agents to move freely across rough desert terrain. The structure of both dirt and all-weather roads along the border basically does not differ from those invented by ancient Greeks and Romans: stacked layers of gravel, sand, dirt, and asphalt.[35] Not only does the border as a road require the massive movement of dirt to secure its transport, but these roads are also constantly moving on their own. As quickly as many border roads are built, monsoon rains relocate parts of them down the hillsides.[36] Border roads are thus in a constant state of movement and decay, and take up hundreds of hours of labor, and millions of dollars of public funds, and destroy hundreds of acres of wilderness.[37] In response to this, USBP has built hundreds of miles of new all-weather roads. These roads reduce erosion and flooding, but also end up killing wildlife as vehicle speeds are increased. The Border Patrol requires a border road extending from the urban center to the desert periphery to centrifugally apprehend, transport, and deport migrants along the transport wall. Border Patrol vehicles work in shifts along the wall; the road allows them to circulate from center to the periphery and back again as they expel migrants.

In addition to these construction roads, the Border Patrol also builds special "drag roads" that allow USBP to track and estimate how many migrants "got away." The drag road is a border transport road created by creating a smooth dirt surface in which the footprints of migrants can be captured. Border Patrol agents create these roads, often just to the north of an all-weather road,[38] by dragging a tire, scrap metal, chain-link fencing, or other heavy objects behind their vehicles every day as they move outward from urban centers, standardizing a centrifugally smooth space as they go. On their way back they "cut the signs" or hunt down migrants based on the traces left in the sand: a kinocynegetic technique.[39] Movement always leaves a trace. From these traces trained agents can determine the vector, speed, weight, and gait of the motion. Migrants have figured this out and now frequently wear pieces of carpet on their feet to disguise their tracks; these pieces of carpet can be found along the border.[40] When the drag road works, it turns the transport road into a record of motion, just as the border fences and walls bear the traces of the thousands of holes cut through them or dug under them. Both are material records of mobility. Thus the border road as a kinographic device or "drag road" functions as a border wall that deters migrants even in places where no fence or corrugated-steel structure exists.

The second major port wall is the entry/exit port. The entry ports at the US-Mexico border function not to stop or block movement, but to filter, screen, and regulate certain continuously mobile elements: the number of cargo trucks, visitor visas, commuters, foreign nationals, and so on. US-Mexico entry ports are the passageways or gaps in the urban walls along the border that regulate the movement between the center (inside the territorial state) and the periphery (the border zone). Just as the port has historically functioned, the US-Mexico ports of entry aim to keep track of how many people leave and how many return. They extract a kinetic tax from this mobility in the form of tolls, customs, application fees, and restrictions on the quantity and quality of goods and people transferred into the country.

The problem of the entry port is essentially dromological: how to centrifugally expel undesirable migrants and goods while increasing the speed of authorized travelers. In relation to the number of admitted migrants, the number of those expelled is relatively small. In 2009 360,967,962 migrants were admitted, 225,073 were denied admission, and 37,914 were subject to expedited removal.[41] These few expulsions slow everything down because of the unique kinetic inspection required at the port.

The port of entry is an interesting kind of border wall because of the profoundly individualizing and contingent structure of the interviews and inspections conducted by the border agents. Previously obtained visas do not guarantee admission, duration, or status of stay until approved at the port of entry. Mobility at the port of entry is subject to whether one's individual movements "arouse suspicion" through behavior, responses to questions, or suspicious documents.[42] If suspicion is aroused, migrants are subject to a secondary inspection in which they can be detained, searched, and closely interviewed for hours until the commanding border agent is no longer suspicious or finally determines that a migrant is suspicious enough to warrant removal. In other words, moving across the border is a performative and kinetic activity in which migrants must move in just the right way and say things in just the right way. Usually this means restricting all physical movements to only the minimal necessary and not moving in any "irregular" or "alien" way that would mark an affective border on the body of the migrant. What is under suspicion is not only the content of migrant documents, but the microkinetic affects—facial expressions, body language, posture, and general appearance—of the migrant body. The border thus appears on the body of the migrant: the wrong accent, the wrong tone, the wrong gesture, and so on. The port of entry inspection thus locates a social kinetic division directly on the body of the migrant in the form of a kinographic image of deportability.[43] Even if the migrant passes this port of entry inspection, it often continues to have a binding or boundary effect on the mobility of the migrant as he or she circulates through the United States. The postentry migrants often feel the gaze of the entry inspection on their movements and thus are always "performing" status, even when they have it. Will the police become suspicious? Will a neighbor or employer become suspicious and call federal immigration enforcement?

The wall regime adds a centrifugal force of expulsion to the fence border. Thus the US-Mexico border not only accumulates migrants through a centripetal funnel or attraction, but also expels them at the same time through other techniques. In the next chapter we see how a third border regime becomes mixed with the previous two to add yet another kinetic dimension to the US-Mexico border: a tensional or cellular border power.

CHAPTER 9
The US-Mexico Cell

The cell is the third major border regime of the US-Mexico border. The cell regime first rose to social dominance during the Middle Ages, but today its tensional kinetic function persists and mixes together with other border regimes to produce a hybrid structure at the border. Once the centrifugal forces of federal expulsion have created a resonance between central control (federal enforcement) and peripheral control (border enforcement), the possibility of a distance or gap between the center and periphery makes possible a specifically cellular border power at the US-Mexico border. In particular, with the federal funding for the expansion of an enormous immigration enforcement network of extraction industries and agencies like Customs and Border Patrol, Immigrations Enforcement and Customs, private detention centers, prisons, fence and road construction contractors, local law enforcement agencies, and numerous branches of the military, it has become increasingly difficult to maintain centralized control over their function and activity. The larger the interconnected network of anti-immigrant forces becomes, the harder it is to centrally control and the more likely it is that these various subagencies and industries will begin to take on a life of their own. This phenomenon is what many critics now call the immigrant military-prison-industrial-detention complex.[1]

Despite the US government's attempt to unify and centrifugally organize many of these heterogeneous agencies into a single Department of Homeland Security with a single executive secretary, this immigrant industrial complex continues to function as a system of linked centers of force—often in tension with one another and often resisting federal control. The Border Patrol, US employers, private detention centers, ICE, immigrant transportation agencies, and all kinds of local enforcement groups are now bound to one another in a social circulatory system of tensional kinetic linkages. One cannot move without affecting the movement of another. However, just like the feudal complexes of the Middle Ages, these juridical linkages are often overlapping and conflictual. For example, local law enforcement is not required (or paid) to enforce federal immigration law. If they do not, they make federal enforcement more difficult. If they do, they make migrants afraid to report crime to the police, thus undermining local law enforcement. Laws are added or changed to reflect the interests of private detention centers that now lobby politicians to legally mandate the detention of immigrants for longer periods of time solely because it increases their revenue.[2] Multiple centers are thus linked together by immigration laws, but differences in local, federal, and customary law are often in tension.

The border regime formed by this juridical immigration complex is the cell. The cell is defined by two kinetic functions: enclosure and linkage. While the wall regime produces bricks by formal and material uniformity, exclusive divisions, and orthogonal stacking, the cell encloses and links confined individuals together without unifying them. Rigid juridical links do not create immobility but move instead according to a linked rotational motion defined by the tension between two or more centers of kinopower. At the US-Mexico border we can identify three major kinds of cells: the identification cell, the detention cell, and the processing cell.

THE IDENTIFICATION CELL

The first type of cell at the US-Mexico border is the offensive identification cell. Just as the identification cell functioned during the Middle Ages to mark individuals with the mobile juridical borders of letters and passports, so the US-Mexico border today deploys kinetically similar technologies for achieving the same cellular and tensional regime. In particular, cellular borders are put in place through two main technologies: the visa and the passport. Both cellularize and individualize large social flows according to a system of rigid juridical linkages, tying individuals to multiple centers of legal power and controlling their mobility.

US visas are social kinetic technologies for bordering the mobility of migrants within the territorial United States. The visa has two cellular functions: identification and jurisdiction. Materially, the visa remains very similar to the original medieval letters on which its name is based—*charta visa* in Latin literally means "paper that has been seen." The visa is a document that itself has no power beyond its being seen and approved by a juridical authority. Legal right is not granted by the paper, but by the authority who sees the paper. Accordingly, the visa can be revoked at any time for any reason. It is entirely subject to the juridical power of its viewer. Thus its power may even vary depending on who sees the document at the port of entry or inside the United States. The visa is a lightweight, highly mobile, mechanically reproducible paper document or stamp usually folded into one's passport book. In this context the passport functions as the national-territorial basis on which the visa acts to authenticate and control the movement of foreign migrants. The passport is an individuation—cellularizing a foreign flow—while the visa links this foreign juridical center to a national network of controlled mobilities.

Following their medieval precursors, the markings and material structure of both visa and passport are made in such a way that their authenticity can be verified by the thickness of special paper, scripts, colored design, and so on. This unique paper triply authenticates itself, its issuer (US Customs), and the identity of the individual whose name appears on the document. The visa, by its material authenticity and duplicate record of is issue, defines and marks the individual who carries it. The visa does not individualize a space or time but a mobility or set of mobile individuated features (name, birthdate, nationality) and links them to the passport. Wherever the individual moves, the power of the visa-passport follows. It is a mobile border. The visa-passport system extracts from the flow of mobility a discreet, cellular individual whose identity is enclosed and marked by this paper cell and bound to a territorial limitation on individual mobility. The visa is an especially important kinolimological function for many Mexican migrants who are not authorized to receive any other formal identification from the US government such as driver's licenses, Social Security cards, and other state IDs. The visa is the border: with it one has a chance of staying in the United States; without it one is deported. With it one is a legalized individual; without it one is treated as an illegal being.[3] This social division occurs at each moment the letter is seen. This is the first border function of the visa-passport: it encloses a cellular individual from the anonymous flow of movement across the border.

The second kinetic function of the visa border is jurisdictional. The visa not only identifies and encloses individual bodies in motion, it also creates a provisional juridical border around individuals, restricting their mobility. With the visa migrants carry the border around with them. The visa is a mobile legal enclosure linked to multiple heterogeneous points of juridical authority. Workers' visas rigidly link migrants to one employer, to Customs, and to an address where they claim to reside. Student visas link migrants to universities, foreign bank accounts, and foreign universities sending transcripts and approvals. Every visa application weaves a complex web between heterogeneous centers of legal authentication and approval. The visa specifies the exact duration of stay, restrictions on where one may go, whom one may work for, where one may go to school, how often one may return, and so on. The visa is a juridical cell in which one may legally move. It also marks a juridical division between what one may do legally (study) and what one may not do (drive, vote, work, and so on). Visas are crucial dimension of the US-Mexico border. More than half of Mexican migrants enter the United States with legal visas.[4]

These legal visas are kinetic border technologies designed to create temporary cellular linkages, but they just as often facilitate the production of undocumented migrants. From the Bracero Program (1942–1964) to Bush's H-2A visa program, the United States has had a long history of using guest workers from Mexico.[5] Interestingly, in both of these cases the result has actually been an increase in criminalized motion: undocumented migration and labor.[6] This is the case because guest worker programs restrict migrant's mobility to employment with only one company and for a limited period (one to two years), after which they must return to their country of origin. Thus workers have no leverage to negotiate wages or conditions and can be deported at the discretion of their employers. Guest-worker visas do not lead to permanent residence and are limited to a certain number of people per year. These restrictions lead to an increase in migrants overstaying their visas, breaking these restrictive tensional links, or finding undocumented work elsewhere. Furthermore, a 2007 report by the Southern Poverty Law Center documents extensive abuses of workers under this visa program. No one gets overtime, the report says, regardless of the law. Companies charge for tools, food, and housing. Guest workers are routinely cheated.[7] In this way the visa functions as a kind of juridical bubble or border cell around migrants, linking them to heterogeneous centers of control, but also highly prone to "popping" and pushing them to the other side of the juridical border.

THE DETENTION CELL

The second type of cell at the US-Mexico border is the defensive detention cell. While the identification cell marks out a juridically linked network of controlled cellular mobility, the kinetic function of the detention cell is to protect this network from flows that have been disjoined from the system: unauthorized migrants. As its etymological origin indicates, the detention cell (from the Latin *tenere*, to hold + *de*, back: *detentus*) functions to hold back or hold down and recellularize or retain (also from *tenere*) a disjoined flow. The detention cell is a special form of social division or border that creates an interiority within existing territorial and political junctions. The detention cell functions as if a point along the border had bifurcated into the United States, folded over onto itself in a cellular interiority, and enclosed the detention center and each of its detainees.

Detention centers, including local jails and ICE processing centers, are even modeled on the same kinetic technologies that compose the border— fences, walls, barbed wire, and so on. The cell itself is a microcosm of the detention center, surrounded by fence bars and brick walls. The detention cell hollows out space and acts directly on the contents of the space to produce an individual interiority, but this confinement is neither static nor immobile. Individuals are not held forever; the cell is simply a temporary (but indeterminate) border enclosure through which the migrant circulates. Furthermore, the detention cell produces or trains a specific kind of restricted, individualized, and linked mobility among detainees. The cell (b)orders their mobility as enclosed, quiet, precarious, deportable, and docile. The detention cell does not confine "individuals" but, in confining, produces individuals—it connects names, numbers, locations, and dates and links them to various centers of juridical power (local, federal, and private) to confine and define the migrant.

These linked heterogeneous centers of juridical power form an immigrant industrial complex of interconnected detention cells. In the past twenty years these cells have become increasingly legally connected. Federal immigration enforcement agencies (INS, ICE) have always had the ability to detain suspects. However, beginning in 1996, when Section 287(g) was added to the Immigration and Nationality Act, the power to detain suspected unauthorized migrants was extended to state and local law enforcement officials, provided they were trained and monitored by ICE.[8] In 2005 Operation Streamline was created jointly by the Department of Homeland Security and the Department of Justice to federally prosecute unauthorized migrants in the southwest border states instead of simply deporting them.[9] As a result, detentions skyrocketed. In 2013 97,384 people were prosecuted for federal immigration offenses, an increase of 367 percent from 2003.[10] Expanding this initial idea, in 2007 ICE created a program specifically designed to help state and local law enforcement to identify, prosecute, detain, and deport unauthorized migrants, called Secure Communities. In 2008 the program was piloted by fourteen jurisdictions; by 2013 the program was nationwide. The detention system that housed 6,785 immigrants in 1994 now holds nearly five times that amount in 260 private detention facilities called "Criminal Alien Requirement"

(CAR) centers across the country.[11] Financially, since 2003 Congress has doubled the budget dedicated to incarcerating immigrants, now totaling over $1.7 billion.[12]

These three major detention cell border regimes—federal, local, and private—are all linked together through a system of tensional legal contracts. They compose an entire regime of social circulation. Migrants move from one bordered enclosure to the next until they are finally deported. Migrants are first picked up in local communities for routine traffic violations, minor crimes, or even just suspicion and police profiling. They are detained by police in holding cells and have their fingerprints scanned. Their information is then cross-listed in ICE's database. If the person's documents are out of status, ICE requests an "immigration detainer" that requires local officials to detain migrants (up to forty-eight hours) until ICE can pick them up. Once ICE takes them into custody, they are moved into another detention cell in a privately run CAR, built especially for noncitizens. Here detainees are held until they are deported. Since immigration violations are not criminal offenses in many states, migrants there do not have the right to an attorney or trial. Those being federally prosecuted may wait years for a trial because of the enormous immigrant prosecution backlog, but more than half do not even have criminal convictions.[13] In the first two years of the Obama administration over one million migrants were detained and deported using this system. Each year ICE is required to meet its deportation quota of four hundred thousand migrants.[14]

The architecture of the detention center and its cells also have border functions. First, most CAR detention centers are socially divided from populated urban areas. This marks a visible division between illegal and legal persons, and also discourages public and official oversight, creating conditions for rampant abuse and degraded living conditions.[15] The Willacy County Correctional Center in Texas is even nicknamed "Ritmo" (a combination of "Gitmo" and "Raymondville") because of its geographical isolation, record of physical abuse, and inhumane living conditions.[16] The very existence of the CAR as a special facility just for undocumented migrants already creates a division between citizen and migrant populations. Second, CAR detention centers divide individuals from others within the facility. This is made possible through the use of individual cells, denial of access to attorneys and visitors, retaliations for working with other detainees to file complaints or lawsuits, more solitary confinement cells, and longer durations of solitary than facilities managed by the Federal Bureau of Prisons.[17] Private CAR detention centers are almost all composed of a central walled building subdivided into numerous detention cells and surrounded by a ten- to fifteen-foot-tall chain-link fence topped with barbed wire, razor wire, and security cameras. Willacy has even built separate tent structures to subdivide groups of migrants. In this way the detention center quite literally moves the border inside the country and captures "dangerous criminal" migrant flows to protect society.

The detention cell also has a direct border effect on the mobility of the detainee. The detention cell does not immobilize the migrant; it structures a highly bordered bodily mobility within the confined circulation of detention centers. There are several dimensions of this cellular mobility. First, detainees are forced to wear uniforms that strip them of their previously individuating clothing. The uniform is an attempt to wipe clean and homogenize the body in order to work more effectively on the interiority of migrants: to make them reflect, repent, and transform themselves into law-abiding people. Monks and prisoners have historically dressed in similar fashion for similar reasons. In both cases, even lighting, both natural and artificial, is restricted and rooms are darkened.[18] Physical reality and mobility is diminished so that a memorial image may be etched. As former US attorney general Eric Holder said in a recent speech to the American Bar Association, "We need to ensure that incarceration is used to punish, deter, and rehabilitate—not merely to warehouse and forget."[19] The detention cell is a place where the migrant body is punished through physical, verbal, and sexual abuse, isolation, boredom, degraded food and water, lack of medical attention, and so on.[20]

It is a place that must not be forgotten. The border must be burned into the migrant body through punishment. It is a place where the migrant is deterred from re-entry by fear of further incarceration and future pain. Finally, the migrant is transformed through a process of interior reflection and circumspection. The body must be restricted, punished, homogenized in its cell so that the mind can bring itself into alignment with the law. Bodily mobility is excessively restricted by handcuffing, forcing detainees to walk along a narrow yellow line that runs along the grid at Willacy, even by intentionally overcrowding cells. As one detainee reports from the Big Spring detention center: "The men are released into an outdoor cage that is about eight to ten paces wide."[21] Even when they are let outside, it is only another small, enclosed cage. "Sometimes," he says, "I feel suffocated and trapped." In migrant detention centers the detainees are not even allowed to work. In particular, migrant detainees are subject to nearly double the rate of isolated confinement in other federal facilities. "Prisoners have reportedly been sent to isolation cells because they complained about

> food, complained about medical care, or helped others draft grievances and file
> lawsuits. As one prisoner put it, 'anything you do or say' can get a person locked

up in conditions of extreme isolation, spending 22 to 24 hours per day confined in a small cell where he must eat, sleep, use the toilet, and sometimes even shower.[22]

All of these border cell techniques produce and train a certain kind of bordered mobility. Migrants will not stop moving or crossing borders; they will only move elsewhere or differently. The effect of these cellular techniques is that they seek to produce a quiet, socially isolated, docile, hard-working, physically and verbally abusable, deportable migrant body. After the migrant leaves the detention center and completes the deportation circuit, these cellular borders follow him or her in the form of a bodily training: restricted, constrained, obedient, and docile. The detention cell simply prepares the migrant body to move differently: to work hard, endure abuse, fear authority, and keep to itself. This is the "model" migrant produced in the detention cell.

THE TIME CELL

The third type of cell at the US-Mexico border is the time cell, whose function is to bind and direct the movements of detainees through the system of cellular linkages. While the kinetic function of the detention cell is to protect a linked juridical network by confining migrants in bordered detention centers, the function of the time cell is to bind cellular mobility into a border-time matrix that orchestrates the tempo and rhythm of social circulation across and through the borders of detention. In this matrix, time itself becomes the boundary.

Once apprehended, migrants are moved from one cell to another. Each cell has its own unique space-time-activity boundary. First, the migrant is arrested and detained by local law enforcement and placed in the back seat of a police car for a relatively short duration. The migrant is detained in this cell in handcuffs and told to keep quiet and not to move around while being transported. The migrant then enters a local law enforcement building and is held in a temporary processing cell, often handcuffed to a wall, stripped of possessions, fingerprinted, and detained in this cell for up to forty-eight hours while under an "immigrant detainer" by ICE. This immigrant detainer binds a length of time (less than forty-eight hours) to a single place (local jail cell), and to a specific activity (being handcuffed to a wall or bound in a cell). If ICE does not transfer migrants within forty-eight hours and they were not arrested for a criminal charge, local law enforcement must release them. However, if they have committed a criminal offense, they can then be detained by local and state police up to the time of their court appearance and sentencing.

The cells are sparse. Any activity in addition to eating, bathing, and using the toilet is not encouraged. After local detention, migrants are sentenced, released, or transferred to a CAR. If sentenced, the migrant ends up in a county, state, or federal prison. The migrant not only "does time" but is "done *by time*." Time binds the mobility of the migrant. Individual mobility is bound by a very specific matrix of daily time-space-activities: the time the lights are on, the time for meals, the time to return to one's cell, the time for solitary confinement, the time for outdoor activity or work, the time for commissary and showers, the time for lights out, the time for sleep. The cellular timetable is materially forced onto the body through repetition, pain, and fear. The body of the migrant is forced not only into a spatial cell but into a temporal cell regime that regulates all of its kinetic functions. Every single minute of prison life is orchestrated and enforced along the lines of the medieval *horarium*. Prison schedules are boundary technologies that deploy a rhythmic control over the flows of social circulation and the periodicity of the movement between cellular circuits: prayer, work, meals, reading, sleep.[23] Even if migrants are transferred to a lower-security CAR, they are still subject to a similar prison *horarium*, despite the fact that more than half have no criminal convictions. The daily time cell repeats itself over and over again in the CAR, often without a known release date.[24] Detainees are thus kinetically forced into and bounded by a matrix of cellularized time in a Kafkaesque world of "indefinite postponement."

The cell regime thus creates a tensional border of interconnected detention points. Accordingly, the US-Mexico border not only accumulates and expels, but also confines and detains through a tensional network of identification, detention, and time cells. We turn now to the fourth border regime of the US-Mexico border hybrid: the checkpoint.

CHAPTER 10
The US-Mexico Checkpoint

The checkpoint is the fourth major border regime of the US-Mexico border. The checkpoint border regime first came to social dominance during the modern period, and arguably remains the dominant regime today across numerous geographical contexts. The US-Mexico border is no exception. In many ways the development of the US-Mexico border has followed a similar trajectory as the historical emergence of dominant border regimes: fences, walls, cells, and finally checkpoints.

In particular, the rise of the checkpoint as a border regime of the US-Mexico border responds to a similar problem posed historically by the proliferation of tensional juridical structures and systems of cellular confinement. Beginning in the 1990s, at the start of the US "war on immigrants" and the immigrant industrial complex, the dramatic increase in cellular juridical structures of migrant identification and detention revealed an excess of disjoined and juridically unlinked motion. Cellular borders confronted the twin problem of an overly complex and conflictual network of heterogeneous power centers (local, state, federal, private) all trying to enforce various borders, laws, and confronting record numbers of unauthorized Mexican migrants entering the United States.[1] Between 1990 and 2010 more than 7.5 million Mexican immigrants—many of whom were unauthorized—arrived in the United States.[2] In 2007 the number of undocumented migrants living in the United States peaked at 12.2 million and today hovers around 11 million.[3] Over the last twenty years it has become increasingly unrealistic and undesirable to permanently remove all unauthorized migrants from the United States.

The question of US-Mexico limology has thus shifted its emphasis by deploying a fourth border regime to the mixture of the previous three: the checkpoint. The function of the checkpoint is not to juridically enclose and link increasingly large and unpredictable oscillatory flows, but rather to establish a kind of functional economic equilibrium between rapidly expanding and contracting flows of migration. The checkpoint balances the desire for precarious labor with the reproduction of an atmosphere of perceived insecurity and danger. The historically privileged sites of immigration enforcement—fences, walls, ports of entry, detention cells, and so on—are no longer sufficient to ensure the continuous control and rapid redirection of migrant flows required under contemporary circumstances. The US-Mexico border must now be deployable at any point whatever throughout society.

The kinetic structure of the checkpoint is defined by two interrelated functions: the point and the inspection. Given the fundamentally unpredictable and nontotalizable nature of social flows across and along the US-Mexico border, the checkpoint simply tries to isolate a series of single points for inspection. Unlike the juridical dimensions of immigration law (duration of stay or detention, restrictions on work or study activities) that largely seek to identify cellular individuals as unauthorized crossers and detain them, the checkpoint is primarily occupied with the superintendence and circulation of migrants. The checkpoint regime is not interested in permanently accumulating, expelling, or detaining social flows but in keeping them in good circulation through constant and modulated monitoring, surveilling, and data collection on passing traffic. In particular, after the attacks of September 11, 2001, the threat of terrorism is believed to be able to manifest itself at any point whatever. After 2001 record numbers of undocumented migrants came to live in the United States. The threat of a so-called invasion can appear anywhere, no longer simply at the border. The US-Mexico border simply becomes one more point in a continuous series of security points diffused throughout every dimension of society. Accordingly, the border must be managed as a constantly oscillating series of indefinite security points. This is attested to in three major checkpoint borders: the police checkpoint, the security checkpoint, and the informational checkpoint.

THE POLICE CHECKPOINT

The first major type of checkpoint of the US-Mexico border is the police checkpoint. Just as it has functioned historically, the police patrol is the offensive checkpoint responsible for marching the streets and marking out the border. Police have almost always functioned as a kind of civil border patrol that partitions society into citizen and criminal elements. The present is no exception. Kinetically, the police patrol divides social movement and defines a system of inspections, which can emerge at any point within social circulation. Although immigration enforcement in the United States is typically understood to be the purview of the federal government, local law enforcement has played an increasingly active role in antiterrorism operations and immigration enforcement after 9/11. With over eighteen thousand state and local law enforcement agencies and over seven hundred thousand local and state police officers in the United States, this has effectively allowed the US-Mexico border to appear at any point whatever. In particular, the police patrol or "beat" constitutes several specific kinetic border functions: preventative and circulatory, kinoptic, and kinographic.

First, US police patrols function as a preventative force against any kinetic disruptions to existing social borders, including class and racial borders. If the Border Patrol functions according the national program of "prevention through deterrence" (preventing immigration into border cities through a deterring wall of bodies), US police patrols function according to the inverse. They deter through prevention (deter crime by preventing its very conditions). Despite popular opinion to the contrary, several major studies show that undocumented migrants do not increase crime levels at the national or local levels.[4] In fact, undocumented migrants are actually more likely to be victims of theft and robbery than citizens, and less likely to commit crimes than citizen groups.[5] Accordingly, the kinetic function of local law enforcement is not to arrest all undocumented migrants or build enormous walls to redirect immigrant movement elsewhere. Among other consequences, this would result in a negative effect on the local economy, both in costs of law enforcement (increased detention costs, paperwork, and so on) and in costs to the local businesses that exploit this migrant work force (agricultural, construction, janitorial, and food-service labor).[6]

The preventative kinopower of police patrol borders is to create an environment in which migrants are prevented from committing crimes and producing any blockages in the "good circulations" of the local economy. The aim of the police checkpoint is not only to prevent crime, but specifically to keep migrants quiet, off the streets, and in the shadows. As one officer says, "If you have people who are undocumented but are good, law-abiding, contributing citizens, I'm not sure all the negative impacts of this issue are worth removing a law-abiding person."[7] In other words, a good migrant stays within certain social borders: goes to work, consumes, and then goes home.

Unlike border patrols, police patrols respond to a milieu of unpredictable oscillations or events in which one cannot know in advance whether or not it is best to enforce immigration law. If migrants are quiet and law abiding, they actually facilitate good circulation, in which case it would be best to not report them to ICE. A recent national survey of law enforcement jurisdictions shows that the less disruptive and criminal individuals are, the less likely that local law enforcement across the United States is to ask people for immigration documents. For example, 90 percent of those arrested for violent crime are checked, 50 percent of those arrested for nonviolent crime are checked, and 15 percent of those who are victims of crimes are checked.[8] What this shows is that local law enforcement is primarily concerned with good circulation and continuous movement within a network of maximum potential checkpoints. Police prefer that the control over circulation remains up to their case-by-case judgment of the situation in an open and fluid milieu, not up to the mandate of centrifugal federal power.[9] Accordingly, the checkpoint border may appear at any point or not at all.

This preventative kinopower to stop and make move is attested to in several specific police patrol strategies. First, police prevent migrant crime by making themselves a visible and mobile presence in neighborhoods with large Latino and undocumented populations, which are inspected disproportionately to other areas.[10] The kinetic aim of heavily patrolling these neighborhoods is not to physically coerce (like a wall) or detain (like a cell) every undocumented migrant in the area, but simply to prevent criminal acts before they happen by creating a visible regular patrol power and a quick response time to crime (the checkpoint). The goal is not to eliminate all crime, but to reduce it to the most affordable or optimal levels in the right places without alienating the wrong parts of the law-abiding community.

Second, police do not intervene directly in economic affairs but simply remove obstructions to its laissez-faire process by making sure migrants are sufficiently scared of reporting their employers for abuse, low wages, or denial of collective bargaining activities for fear they will be deported by law enforcement. Even informal labor practices in which migrant day laborers gather at known locations are not crushed, but migrants are simply moved on. As in the nineteenth century, as police patrols approach these locations a lookout warns everyone to scatter. The migrants disperse, the patrol passes, and the migrants assemble again or move along to another spot. In this way the flow of migrant labor and capitalist profit continues without obstruction or local intervention. The police simply perform the possibility of criminalization in order to perpetuate the exploitation of migrants in the informal economy. In this case "Move along" kinetically means "Work, but do not be visibly unsightly or cause any other disturbance in social circulation."

Third, the preventative patrol secures certain environmental borders—well-lit, ventilated streets filled with cameras and businesses where commerce can occur without the threat of impoverished migrant beggars, loiterers, or unsightly day laborers. The police patrol does not rid the world of migrants, but simply keeps them moving in the right areas at the right times: out of sight and out of mind.

Furthermore, local police patrols can also redirect undocumented migrants from one city to another by strengthening anti-immigration laws like 287(g) and publicly advertising that local police are working with ICE to crack down on undocumented migrants. Police can thus crack down or ease up on immigrant flows as they choose. Police can even use immigration policy to deport certain individuals whom they would normally have to release on bail. In this way they can more effectually control the population flows of their cities. Immigration law thus allows police a more flexible and elastic control over social flows. Finally, the local police use of immigration law also allows them better control over "potential terrorists." Since anyone can be a potential terrorist threat, this allows local law enforcement an incredible elasticity of motion: anyone can now be removed from local circulation based on suspicion alone.

The second kinetic border function of the police patrol is kinoptic. Just as it has functioned historically, the police patrol today still functions as a kind of ambulatory lighthouse to superintend a mobile population. On the one hand, the police patrol deters crime and keeps undocumented migrants in line by making itself visible in their neighborhoods. On the other hand, the police patrol also seeks to render immigrant flows themselves visible to the police through the maintenance of systems of good circulation: wide roads, well-lit streets, open parks, transparent fences, authorized commercial activity. The more the police watch, the less they need to act. Kinoptic surveillance makes migrants feel that they are the target of a continuous and mobile investigation. The patrol is just around the corner. In this way kinoptics deters crime through a network of coordinated patrol patterns and strategies that allow targets to move freely within bordered spaces but always know they are being potentially watched.

The kinopticism of the police patrol is expressed in two significant strategies: electronic monitoring and community policing. In the 1960s American scientists first began using radio transmitters to monitor the movements of wild animals in their environment. This radio frequency information was then automatically transmitted to software programs that would create a visual map of their movements.[11] In 1964 two behavioral psychologists at Harvard developed a radio transmitter system for humans to be worn as a belt. Ralph Schwitzgebel and his twin brother, Robert, tested the belt on juvenile offenders with the aim of not only mapping their movements but "engineering" their behavior through a system of incentives tied to other physiological processes that the belt could monitor: pulse, brain waves, alcohol consumption. The brothers were aware of and excited about the use of their idea as an "electronic parole system" that could monitor movement (kinoptics) as well as "precursors to illegal behavior."[12]

Today electronic monitoring is used across the United States in thousands of criminal, parole, and now immigration cases. On December 1, 2014, ICE adopted this police technology to track migrants in the Rio Grande Valley. After migrants with families are apprehended, they are now given the option of wearing a GPS-enabled radio transmitter on their ankle. Immigrants who do not pose a threat to public safety and good circulation are selected for the program, named RGV 250. Thousands of immigrants from Mexico and Central America are enrolled in the program, and ICE plans to monitor about twenty-nine thousand in the coming year.[13] With these devices, private security companies can track migrant movements in real time. If migrants do not move within their virtual borders or they try to remove the device, ICE and local law enforcement are contacted and a local patrol is dispatched to enforce the border by apprehending the migrant.[14]

Instead of expelling migrants with walls or confining them in cells, electronic monitoring systems allow law-abiding migrants to circulate freely in an open environment of possible points of inspection. The exact location and movements of the migrant are known kinoptically at every moment through a series of oscillating radio waves. Continuous movement is transformed into a series of data signal points. At any point whatever these points can become the subject of an inspection or enforcement. These checkpoints allow for more elastic borders that can stretch within certain flexible and optimal parameters. With this device border enforcement also becomes more elastic: expanding where and when there are violations, and contracting where and where they are not, instead of simply hoping that migrants return for their trial, which can take up to ten years. Rather than police patrolling the migrants, the migrants patrol themselves under the kinoptic gaze of their mobile GPS device.

The second significant kinoptic strategy deployed by the police patrol is community policing. Community policing is a new name for an old strategy used by police patrols to solicit information from community members that will lead to the prevention of certain types of crime. In the nineteenth century it was well known that the police solicited information from "observers" and "subobservers" who kept their eyes open watching for crime and potential criminals within their community. Today the mobility of community members is used as a kinoptic device to keep an eye on the community in between the intervals of the police patrol. Community policing is not technically the same as spying since informants are not compensated for their work and communications are not centered around direct criminal apprehension. However, through community meetings, phone surveys, and town meetings, police obtain an image of social motion from the mobile eyes of the neighborhood watch. Police then respond to this moving image not by expelling or detaining criminal elements, but by improving the social environment such that the structure of the community itself prevents crime through a new milieu, optimized for good circulation (improved lighting, visible public parking areas, gated areas, friendly police interactions, modified patrol schedules, and so on). For example, building a children's playground is a way for police to ensure that families will keep watch over that public space and want crime to be prevented in that area.

But community policing also creates a system of social borders that serve to render visible the movements of "criminal" migrants. Police patrol migrant neighborhoods but do not aim to arrest every single undocumented migrant or even specific migrants who are undocumented. Police-community coordinations are not aimed at discovering undocumented migrants, but at creating a safe zone for general social circulation. Seeking out undocumented migrants, as evidenced by Operation Secure Communities, alienates the community and makes migrants unwilling to communicate with police and report crimes.[15] This degrades general public safety and preferred circulation. Rather, police patrols function as checkpoint borders in an open environment of freely circulating undocumented migrants, intervening only where there are blockages to acceptable social oscillations. Once a blockage or criminal miasma occurs, however, local police are able to use immigration law, ICE, and federal immigration phone support to aggressively remove migrants in ways that other criminals could not be removed. In this way community policing plus the elastic application of immigration law by local law enforcement makes possible a highly orchestrated social kinetic environment.

The third kinetic border function of the police patrol is kinographic. Police patrols are not only watching as they move, they are also recording. In-car police cameras were initially introduced in the mid-1980s, but it was not until widespread concerns over racial profiling were catalyzed by the 1991 police beating of Rodney King in Los Angeles that the Department of Justice funded a national installation of cameras. Prior to this program only 11 percent of state police and highway patrol vehicles had cameras. By 2015 72 percent of state police and highway patrols had been equipped with video systems.[16] Cameras inside patrol cars record an officer's movements, traffic stops, and the movements of those in front of the camera outside the vehicle. These videos are used as the basis for daily police reports, training videos, evidence in court cases, and for review by commanding officers.[17] Although the technology of the video camera is new, the basic form of police kinography remains the same as Chadwick's system for police recording. Police record as much relevant social motion as possible, assemble the data into patrol maps and patterns, and elastically direct their patrols to areas of high crime potential according to emergent and changing trends in the mobile data they collect.

As a function of the US-Mexico border, not only do police record the movement of Mexican migrants through the city, but migrants are also fingerprinted, photographed, and recorded in a file system if they are arrested. Since many undocumented migrants have no other form of identification, the police patrol is literally creating their identity as they enter it into local law enforcement databases and forward it to ICE's federal immigration database. This national database is then shared and can be cross-indexed by any other police department. Police patrols are the front lines for collecting the kinographic data of migrant motion. They are the recording apparatus by which Operation Secure Communities and other immigration databases function.

In addition to the police patrol, the second major police checkpoint technology is the police spy. Today everyone is a potential informant. Even if local law enforcement chooses not to work with ICE, which is currently the case in most US jurisdictions, ICE has created a hotline by which anyone can report an "illegal alien." Disgruntled police officers, racist neighbors, family members or friends seeking retribution, or anyone at all can anonymously report someone to ICE as an undocumented migrant. This has at least two kinetic consequences. First, undocumented migrants now have a reason to remain as reclusive and restricted in their social motion as possible in order to avoid detection by anyone. Undocumented migrants are afraid to use social services, report crimes, participate in political activity, or go to school. They live in constant fear of deportation. Second, by creating an immigration hotline, ICE has effectively transformed the entire country and everyone in it into a potential border spy. Anyone can become the border between the residence and deportation of a migrant. Just as ICE has given the power to invoke immigration law to local police officers, it has now given this power to everyone.

THE SECURITY CHECKPOINT

The second major type of checkpoint on the US-Mexico border is the security checkpoint. The security point is the defensive checkpoint responsible for limiting and protecting the borders marked out by the offensive police patrol. Once a patrol goes out and actively marks out a regular area, there will inevitably be gaps in its patrol circuit: places it cannot reach and times when it is not present. This kinoptic dilemma is thus the opposite of the panoptic dilemma. Panopticism sees everything within an enclosed space but sees nothing of the outside world; kinopticism, in contrast, sees in circulation the outside world and thus leaves gaps inside or in between its circuits. Since it is in constant motion it cannot be in two places at once, but only here *then* there—as process or circulation. The security checkpoint aims to secure the gaps left behind in these movements. At the US-Mexico border this is attested to in three major kinetic technologies: the virtual fence, interior checkpoints, and aerial monitoring.

The first major security checkpoint technology is the virtual fence. The virtual fence is a kinotechnic surveillance system for detecting, identifying, and tracking movement along the US-Mexico border, especially in open areas where there are no barriers. In the deployment of the virtual fence, the centrifugal force of the Border Patrol wall is augmented by the elastic force of a virtual checkpoint system, creating a border hybrid and secure border shield. The Border Patrol's use of virtual fencing, including cameras, ground sensors, night-vision radar, and so on, began in 1998 under the former Immigration and Naturalization Service (INS) and Integrated Surveillance Information System (ISIS), which was eventually folded into the larger national border surveillance program called America's Shield Initiative (ASI) in 2005. ASI was then folded into DHS's Secure Border Initiative (SBI) in 2006, contracted to Boeing Corporation, and renamed "SBInet."[18] The creation of a virtual security shield was meant to function defensively to fill in the kinetic gaps left between the sections of fencing and walls along the border.

Under all these different names, the virtual fence system was composed of a variety of remote video surveillance (RVS) systems (cameras, infrared systems) and sensors (seismic, magnetic, and thermal detectors), all connected to a central computer network known as the Integrated Computer Assisted Detection (ICAD) database. The aim of this remote surveillance system was to allow for continuous, real-time observation of movement at any point whatever along the border. Once a sensor was tripped or operators in a central control room observed movement, they could remotely reposition cameras and zoom in on the location, dispatch Border Patrol to the location, and coordinate their response. However, all these systems failed to meet deployment deadlines and make good on this kinotechnic dream of total mobile observation. DHS secretary Janet Napolitano ordered a department-wide assessment of SBInet in January 2010 and suspended the SBInet contract in March 2010, terminating it in January 2011.[19]

After termination, DHS immediately diverted previously allotted funds from SBInet to the Arizona Surveillance Technology Plan, which will cover the rest of the 323-mile Arizona border for $750 million. Arizona Border Patrol currently uses a vast array of different kinetic border technologies.

As of November 2012, deployed assets included 337 Remote Video Surveillance Systems (RVSS) consisting of fixed daylight and infrared cameras that transmit images to a central location (up from 269 in 2006), 198 short and medium range Mobile Vehicle Surveillance Systems (MVSS) mounted on trucks and monitored in the truck's passenger compartment (up from zero in 2005) and 41 long range Mobile Surveillance Systems (MSS, up from zero in 2005), 12 hand-held agent portable medium range surveillance systems (APSS, up from zero in 2005), 15 Integrated Fixed Towers that were developed as part of the SBInet system (up from zero in 2005), and 13,406 unattended ground sensors (up from about 11,200 in 2005). According to CBP [Customs and Border Protection] officials, the department's acquisitions strategy emphasizes flexible equipment and mobile technology that permits USBP to surge surveillance capacity in a particular region, and off-the-shelf technology in order to hold down costs and get resources on the ground more quickly.[20]

This border strategy is different from all the previous regimes—the fence, the wall, and the cell. Rather than accumulate, expel, or detain, the kinetic function of the virtual fence is to transform the open milieu of the desert environment into a system of kinetic data points. The ground is no longer a flow of dirt, but a series of seismic data points created by ground sensors. The body is no longer a flow of flesh and blood, but a series of thermal data points created by heat sensors and radar technologies. A migrant's metal pocketknife is no longer a tool or weapon but a homing beacon, a magnetic data point for the USBP. Migrants viewed with these remote surveillance devices become blurs of color on a screen, a fluctuation of pixels across the landscape.

With the addition of Mobile Vehicle Surveillance Systems and handheld devices, the Border Patrol transforms the open environment into a network of data points for possible inspection as they move. Mobile surveillance towers control systems named "Cerberus," after the three-headed hellhound border guard of Greek mythology, can even be attached to trucks or carried as trailers along the border and positioned at any point whatever—monitoring movement in real time using its three monitor heads—up to 7.5 miles away with obstructions up to 50 percent.[21] The mobility of these

Cerberus towers transforms the entire border into a series of potential surveillance points. As their mythological namesake suggests, these points keep migrants from escaping from the world of the dead: Mexico. The goals of the virtual fence are consistent with the kinetic function of the checkpoint: to predict, detect, deter, and track potential entrants in an open and mobile area before they enter: to create what the CBP calls "turn backs." The meaning of the "virtual" fence thus should not be understood as an unreal border but rather as a real network of kinoptical security points that allow the border to appear at any point whatever. In this case "virtual" also means remote. Since most of these monitoring devices are remotely viewed and controlled, the border becomes dislocated or bifurcated. Where is the border? In the control center miles away, or at the borderline? Both and neither; the border is potentially everywhere.

The second major security checkpoint technology is aerial monitoring. Since the border is always in motion, each kinetic regime produces a gap unique to its form of circulation. The centrifugal wall regime of the Border Patrol's Operation Blockade defends an urban area but creates a gap in the desert periphery. This gap is then filled by an elastic virtual fence regime that can move its towers and equipment back and forth in rapid response to changes in the environment. However, the virtual fence also produces a mobile gap as it oscillates back and forth along the border. Between moving towers and border vehicles, the mountains and valleys remain terrain that is difficult to surveil. Ground sensors and trip lasers are thwarted by using baby powder. Cameras and thermal sensors are thwarted by digging tunnels underneath the border and flying drug-filled drones above it.[22] Aerial monitoring fills this gap by turning the entire border into a matrix of stratospheric data points as it flies above.

The Border Patrol deploys manned and unmanned aircraft to places inaccessible to other surveillance technologies. In 2012 the Border Patrol deployed 269 aircraft and reported 81,045 flight hours.[23] Border Patrol also operated ten unmanned aerial vehicles, or "drones," and logged 5,737 flight hours, up from 4,406 hours in 2011.[24] A Border Patrol Air Mobile Unit, composed of fifty-four men, was created in 2003 to fly over remote parts of the Arizona and California mountains along the border.[25] Black Hawk and attack helicopters drop two-man teams—equipped with night scopes, infrared devices, and tracking dogs—onto steep mountain slopes and deep canyons to patrol them in shifts. This special air patrol unit now captures around thirty to one hundred migrants a day in these remote areas.[26]

The Border Patrol also uses unmanned aerial vehicles to patrol the skies. This includes the same large and small drones used in aerial combat strikes in Iraq and Afghanistan (Predator and Reaper drones) as well as remotely operated Aerostat surveillance blimps. Now that the United States has pulled out of Iraq and Afghanistan, surplus military technologies are now being moved to the US-Mexico border. Drones now regularly fly over the entire US southwest border—sweeping remote mountains, canyons, and rivers with a near 100 percent detection capability, according to a 2014 CBP report.[27] The purpose of this aerial surveillance is to identify tracks, clothing items, cut barbed wire, broken branches, and migrants themselves crossing the border so that the Border Patrol can be dispatched to high-traffic areas. "You want to deploy your resources to where you have a greater risk, a greater threat," says the commissioner of Customs and Border Protection, R. Gil Kerlikowske. This incredible detection rate is made possible by a new mobile aerial radar system called VADER, or Vehicle and Dismount Exploitation Radar, used to track Taliban fighters planting roadside bombs in Afghanistan. According to the CBP, "VADER data is streamed simultaneously . . . for strategic analysis, and . . . for actionable intelligence."[28] Drone pilots record border entrants or evidence of entrants and stream this to Border Patrol on the ground, who can use the information to track migrants through the desert in real time.

However, drone intelligence also reveals the "gotaways." "Between October and December 2013, records show, the remotely operated aircraft detected 7,333 border crossers during . . . Arizona missions. Border Patrol agents, however, reported 410 apprehensions during that time, according to an internal agency report. The drone sensor was credited with providing surveillance that led to 52 arrests."[29] Drones create an aerial zone of possible border points, but it is still up to the Border Patrol to intervene and make those points actual ones.

The names of these border technologies are not insignificant. Just as Darth Vader in *Star Wars* is the master pilot of the "death star" that watches and destroys from above, so the appropriately named Reaper drone is visually imagined as death himself parachuting from above, under the direction of its VADER radar equipment. This specialized radar system has now turned the skies and the earth of the US-Mexico border into a series of control points under a totally mobilized vertical power, just as the death star did in *Star Wars*. The uniforms of Reaper drone operators include an image of death holding a bloody blade with the slogan "That others may die."[30] The military death imagery used by border-war technologies creates a disturbing mythology that can be synthesized as follows: the "devil's highway" leads migrants through the middle of a desert hellscape where they are targeted by giant flying "predators," "death stars," and "reapers," and where they must ultimately confront the three-headed Cerberus that guards the gates of hell (Mexico) before they can pass over to the world of the living (United States).

This mythology also reflects a unique kinopolitical relation between what CBP calls the total "operational control" over bordered social motion and the kind of social death that results from hunting down, detaining, and deporting poor migrants back to Mexico. Although hunter-killer drones on the US-Mexico border are deprived of their claws, they remain hunters nonetheless. Drone pilots still observe the border through the sights of a crosshairs as a point of potential inspection and enforcement.[31] The "kill box" of military strategy is simply replaced with the "tracking box" of border strategy. The migrant is still treated as a "target" even if she or he is not assassinated.[32]

This same kinetic aerial border regime is at the heart of the popular fear over the domestic use of drones. In 2011 the FAA projected that thirty thousand drones could be in the nation's skies by 2020 after Congress passed the FAA Modernization and Reform Act (FMRA) that forces the FAA to devise a "comprehensive plan to safely accelerate the integration of civil unmanned aircraft systems into the national airspace" by September 2015.[33] Opponents from the left and the right are united around the concerns of violation of privacy, commercial data collection, and even weaponized assassination. The fear of domestic drones gives US residents a taste of life in the crosshairs that is already in effect in Iraq, Afghanistan, Syria, Yemen, Pakistan, and the US-Mexico border. The border is coming home as an invisible stratospheric power, continuously tracking social motion in order to make every data point a possible border point.

The third major security checkpoint technology is the deployment of interior checkpoints up to one hundred miles inland of the US-Mexico border. The US-Mexico border is not isolated at privileged geographical locations—the fence, its ports of entry, or even detention centers. A system of interior checkpoints aims to fill whatever kinetic gaps remain in the virtual fence and aerial monitoring. A 2009 Government Accountability Office report describes these interior Border Patrol checkpoints as "the third layer in the Border Patrol's three-tiered border enforcement strategy. The other two layers are located at or near the border, and consist of line watch and roving patrol."[34] Most of these interior checkpoints are located within one hundred miles of the US land or coastal border, but at least two federal circuit courts condone Border Patrol operations outside the one-hundred-mile zone.[35] Although the actual number of interior checkpoints has not been publicly released since 2008, based on more recent news reports the American Civil Liberties Union estimates that there are at least 170 currently in operation, mostly along the southwest border area, and have increased significantly since 9/11.[36] Since roughly two-thirds of the US population lives within this one-hundred-mile zone—about 200 million people—the border has effectively moved inward and transformed the majority of social circulation into a series of potential checkpoints.[37] A border may now appear almost anywhere according to fluctuating security needs and modulated threat levels.

The interior checkpoint is an elastic security border. There are two kinds of interior checkpoints in the United States: permanent and tactical. Both remain relatively fast, easy, and inexpensive to install or relocate based on changing patterns of migrant circulation. Permanent checkpoints consist of brick and mortar structures with regular patrol staff and a host of surveillance equipment. They have remote video surveillance, electronic sensors, and agent patrols in the vicinity of the checkpoints, which may also include horse patrols and all-terrain vehicles.[38] Permanent checkpoints are prohibited in the Tucson sector, and so CBP has created what it calls "tactical" interior checkpoints. These tactical checkpoints are composed of a few Border Patrol vehicles used by agents to drive to the location, orange cones to slow down and direct traffic, a portable water supply, a cage for canines (if deployed at the checkpoint), portable rest facilities, and warning signs. Tactical checkpoints are highly mobile and can even be set up or transported within hours. They open and close elastically based on "intelligence and changing patterns of smuggling and routes used by illegal aliens."[39] Within hours or within a day the checkpoint can move several times. Accordingly, no one ever knows where the checkpoint will appear next, not even the Border Patrol.

In principle these elastic security points are meant to enforce customs and border-related issues only, since crime control checkpoints have been ruled unconstitutional.[40] At these checkpoints the Border Patrol does not have the right to legally detain anyone or ask for identification, but does have the right to question suspects until they are no longer under suspicion. As the CBP clarifies, "Although motorists are not legally required to answer the questions 'Are you a U.S. citizen, and where are you headed?' they will not be allowed to proceed until the inspecting agent is satisfied that the occupants of vehicles traveling through the checkpoint are legally present in the U.S."[41] In practice, however, the ACLU has collected reports of motorists "being subjected to extended detentions, interrogations unrelated to citizenship, invasive searches, racial profiling, verbal harassment, and physical assault by agents, among other rights violations."[42] The US-Mexico border is now a mobile and temporary autonomous zone of inspection. Social circulation through these checkpoint zones is now slowed down, stopped, redirected, and regularly inspected according to the elastic demands of various security threats. These checkpoints also have the kinetic effect of continually rerouting those who intentionally avoid passing through: migrants, smugglers, irritated locals, and so on. Whether they move through the checkpoint or not, their movement is being bordered, controlled, and rerouted. Sometimes it is rerouted into traps along secondary roads where a surprise checkpoint awaits; at other times these byroads can be profiled for suspicious checkpoint avoiders. In either case, these elastic checkpoints are able to quickly respond to and manage regional circulations.

THE INFORMATION CHECKPOINT

The third major type of checkpoint on the US-Mexico border is the information checkpoint. While the offensive patrol marches out and around to mark the border and ensure good circulation, and the defensive security border aims to fill or limit the gaps left behind, the information border binds social flows together as assemblages of data points. Informational checkpoints aim less at stopping, enclosing, or blocking than at collecting and binding flows of data. This is accomplished by two kinetic functions: the extraction of data points from a continuous flow of social motion, and the binding of these points into collections or "in(fo)dividuals" that can be tracked in motion. At the US-Mexico border this is attested to in two major kinetic "smart border" technologies: immigrant databases and biometric Radio Frequency Identification (RFID) cards.

The first major information checkpoint technology is the use of immigrant databases for federal, state, and local border enforcement. As early as 1994 the INS developed an Automated Biometric Identification System (IDENT) that collected and processed biometric data, including digital fingerprints, photographs, iris scans, and facial images, and linked these biometrics with biographic information to establish and verify identities.[43] By 1999 the INS initiated Operation Vanguard, which used IDENT data to look for discrepancies and out-of-status workers.[44] In 2001 Operation Tarmac proceeded by similar means but targeted airports across the country instead. In 2003 INS functions were transferred to ICE, and IDENT was obtained by the Department of Homeland Security. Finally, in 2008 the largest coordinated data collection effort and database-sharing project put all this data in the hands of immigration enforcement. Operation Secure Communities was the single largest effort to maximize new data collection techniques, share databases between enforcement agencies, and develop new techniques for tracking migrant mobility across borders. Ordinarily the fingerprints of county and state arrestees are submitted to the FBI only. Under Secure Communities this biometric information goes to ICE as well, giving ICE direct access to the FBI's Integrated Automated Fingerprint Identification System database and to IDENT, now managed by the DHS Office of Biometric Identity Management (OBIM). These two enormous databases are now accessible by ICE's Law Enforcement Support Center (LESC). The LESC defines itself as "a single national point of contact that provides timely immigration status, identity information, and real-time assistance to local, state, and federal law enforcement agencies on aliens suspected, arrested, or convicted of criminal activity."[45] LESC is available by phone twenty-four hours a day, seven days a week. Although Operation Secure Communities is now defunct, as of November 2014, LESC remained available for use by local, state, and federal law enforcement.

The first kinetic function of this massive immigration database is that it isolates a series of data points from a continuous social flow of migrants. The body of the migrant is transformed into a series of biometric data points: fingerprints, mug shots, iris patterns, height, weight, eye color, and so on. This data is then bound into an individual with a name, nationality, and certain mobility behavior. This data bundle or data boundary, as Fichte fantasized, can then be identified and tracked by law enforcement anywhere and at any point. The biometric body is the mobile identity card that cannot be lost or stolen. This traceable data bounty can then be used to do a "pattern-of-life analysis," assessing migrants' mobility patterns and life habits to determine their threat potential: where they have been, where they are going, how often they come through here, and so on. Risky individuals, such as those with violent criminal records, may be deported, while others—first-time offenders or those with families—may be set free and monitored continuously using GPS ankle bracelets.[46] According to DHS, this process of retaining kinometric data is called "enrollment." It quite literally tracks rolling data flows in discrete conjoined data points.

The second kinetic function of this immigration database is related to the first. Each time an individual's biometrics are enrolled in IDENT, it is called an "encounter."[47] If enrollment is the isolation of a series of data junctions in a continuous flow, the encounter is the punctuated inspection of these data checkpoints. In this case biometrics are usually updated when migrants encounter law enforcement at various checkpoints, who collect new data from them and try to retrace and record their movements. Each new encounter or checkpoint is added to the next in a series of event-encounters, thus increasing the possibility of tracking the individual's past motion and anticipating future motions or patterns of life. Probability and risk-based strategies are then used to determine when to initiate another encounter, redirect migrants, or allow movement to continue to circulate. As Secure Communities executive director David Venturella testified to

Congress, "We have adopted a risk-based strategy that focuses, first, on criminal aliens who pose the greatest threat to our communities. To manage this increased workload and prudently scale the system capabilities, we are classifying all criminal aliens based on the severity of the crimes they have been convicted of."[48] Data power is the kinopower of the checkpoint: to let flows circulate in an open but highly modulated and bounded informatic milieu.

The second major information checkpoint boundary is the use of biometric RFID cards to continuously track and modulate the circulation of biosocial motion across the border. In 1995 the INS and US Customs Service designed the Secure Electronic Network for Travelers Rapid Inspection, or SENTRI. It was first implemented in Otay, California, in 1996, in El Paso in 1999, and then in San Yisador, the busiest border crossing in the world, in 2000. Today SENTRI is used by twelve major ports of entry along the US-Mexico border and is under the control of the DHS.[49] SENTRI uses IDENT and several other criminal, law enforcement, customs, immigration, and terrorist biometric databases to store and track the biometric data of travelers. Travelers can voluntarily pay to go through an extensive criminal background check, provide a digital ten-fingerprint scan, an iris scan, and a personal interview with a CBP officer to apply for expedited low-risk processing. These preapproved travelers are then given RFID cards to put in their car window. As they approach the border these RFID cards confirm their biometric information at the port of entry before they arrive, allowing them pass through quickly. SENTRI cards also allow citizens to bypass airport security checkpoints at selected airports and participate in the Global Entry program that allows for expedited returns through Customs. Biometric RFID passports are now available to allow travelers from selected developed countries to stay in the United States up to ninety days without a visa. Such biometric RFID border systems now exist in countries all over the world.[50]

The first kinetic function of the biometric RFID card is similar to the first function of the immigrant database. Biometric RFID cards rely on the creation and maintenance of enormous databases that isolate a series of data points from the continuous flows of mobile bodies. Just as the body of the high-risk migrant is transformed into a series of biometric data points, so the low-risk business traveler is also transformed into fingerprints, iris images, numbers, dates, and so on. In the first case, however, the biometric database and RFID chip are used to hunt down, raid, detain, and expedite the removal of unwanted migrants. In the second case the same database-card system is used to preapprove, track, facilitate, and expedite the passage of a desired business class or "kinetic elite."[51] There is no contradiction to this social kinetic technology, just as there is no contradiction when a river bifurcates and moves faster in some areas and slower in others. It is the same kinetic regime of database-linked RFID chips that determines the kinetic risk probability of a given social flow. Modern borders are the modulation and management of these two kinds of flows: securitized flows to be slowed and detained, and economic flows to be sped up and facilitated. They are two sides of the same border regime.

The second kinetic function of the biometric RFID card is to provide elasticity. Biometric checkpoints are based on elastic risk assessments that change and respond in real time to the fluctuation of events and global flows, and to the changes in biometric data itself during each encounter when it is collected. Since the movement of both high- and low-risk travelers is tracked by the same biometric-RFID technologies, this allows the border to expand and contract where and when it is most needed. It can contract around low-risk flows and expand around high-risk flows.

Since the in(fo)dividual is nothing other than a series of distinctly isolatable data points, biometric databases can also be searched based on independent variables such as skin color, eye color, and previous pattern-of-life points. If the DHS is searching for a terrorist suspect, biometric databases, filled with the information of both migrants fingerprinted by law enforcement and business travelers, can be searched according to the risk factors of independent variables—a facial pattern, a kinetic history, an eye color, a skin color, a common name, and so on. The "terrorist" subject thus comes into being as a kinformational border mosaic of data points before any actual suspects are matched to it within a degree of statistical certainty. The border between citizen and terrorist can thus appear at any bio- or kinometric point whatever.

With the use of RFID cards at the US-Mexico border, patrols can simultaneously track low-risk social motions in real time and focus their efforts of intervention on securitizing those in the slow lane whose biometry has not yet been recorded. However, since the checkpoint does not have a perfect database or border guard, it compensates for this with algorithmically determined "random" border inspections. Although the vast majority of port-of-entry traffic passes through, the kinetic function of the random search is precisely to demonstrate the possibility that the border can appear at any moment to control movement at any point whatever in the flow. No flow is safe, no matter how low risk.

In fact, this kinetic logic is visually demonstrated in the symbol for biometrics (figure 10.1).

The image used to indicate biometric RFID is a single continuous flow interrupted by a point. The informational checkpoint is precisely this

Figure 10.1: Biometric Passport Symbol.

isolation of a series of data points in the continuous flow of social motion. In the image, the flow is temporarily bifurcated around the checkpoint and reconnected with its previous trajectory. As SENTRI or e-passport travelers move, their motion is temporarily redirected through the port of entry as their data is quickly scanned. Afterward, the checkpoint quickly reconnects the flow with its original trajectory. This is the ideal geometry of the checkpoint: a flow punctuated by a series of possible points of intervention.

Conclusion

Contemporary life is bordered from all around and in every direction. From the biometric data that divides the smallest aspects of our bodies to the aerial drones that patrol the immense expanse of our domestic and international airspace, we are defined by borders. The twenty-first century will thus be the century of borders not simply because more techniques of social division exist today than ever before, but because the entire history of border technologies has now re-emerged and combined to form the most complex hybrid divisions civilization has ever known. Borders can no longer simply be understood as the geographical divisions between nation-states. Their form and function has become too complex, too hybrid. What we need now is a theory of the border that can make sense of this hybridity.

The age of globalization has given rise to an apparent contradiction: more people are on the move than ever before in history, and yet the disparities of wealth and the number of borders have never been greater. This so-called contradiction stems from a fundamental misunderstanding about the nature of borders. If a border is a geographically fixed national line largely intended to stop movement and there are so many of them today, then of course global mobilization and mass migration seem like contradictions. However, this contradiction is produced, like all contradictions, by a logic of stasis. Borders, this book argues, are neither statist, nor fixed, nor designed to stop human movement. Borders are not permeable membranes that people pass through. They are themselves mobile processes designed to redirect, recirculate, and bifurcate social motion—not stop it. Thus globalization appears exactly as it is: an intensification of social division through bordered circulation. There is no contradiction.

Rather than viewing borders as the result or outcome of preestablished social entities like states, this book reinterprets the history of social life from the perspective of the continual and constitutive motion of the borders that organize and divide society. Societies and states are the products of (b)ordering, not the other way around. Accordingly, this book begins not with normative principles derived from political philosophy, but from the material and social technologies that define the conditions under which such principles and states emerge in the first place.

This new starting point of political theory allows us to overcome three important problems set out at the beginning of this book. First, it overcomes the problem of statism that reduces all border phenomena to geographical nation-states. Opposed to this, this book examines the material phenomena of social division in general as the constitutive force of societies. Second, this new starting point also overcomes the opposite problem of multidisciplinary approaches to border studies that focus strictly on the regional and empirical specificity of borders. Instead, this book deploys a critical limology that has allowed us to provide a theoretical framework based on the discovery of several major historical border regimes that organize the distribution of empirical border phenomena. This also allows us to overcome a third problem of restricting border history to the nineteenth century and onward. If border regimes precede the nation-state, then so does their history. Accordingly, the present work provides a social history of borders beginning with the first human societies up to the present.

The important payoff and consequence of this conceptual (Part I) and historical (Part II) theory of the border is that it provides us with the tools to analyze contemporary borders in a new way—from the perspective of the primacy of bordered motion. This is possible because the border is not only a historical phenomenon but also a contemporary one, produced under certain social conditions that have persisted throughout history according to different regimes, to varying degrees, and in unique combinations. Contemporary borders are a hybrid mix of all of them.

Analyzing contemporary borders according to the primacy of movement thus makes two important contributions. First, it allows us to see that contemporary borders are not a secondary phenomenon produced by states; rather, the process of bordering is the primary condition by which things like societies and states are established in the first place. Borders are an essential part of how societies move. Second, it allows us to see that contemporary borders are poorly understood according to a single axis of analysis. Borders are always a mixture of territorial, political, juridical, and economic regimes of division. All four are operative at the same time to different degrees.

However, there is still much work to be done in three major areas. The first area is historical. This book has limited its historical scope for the sake of clarity and brevity to analyzing only four major border regimes—the fence, the wall, the cell, and the checkpoint—during their general period of social dominance. Once each of these four border regimes emerged historically, they tended to persist and mix with one another, creating all manner of hybrid combinations. Social division is always multiple; it is always a question of bifurcation. Thus what remains to be done in future work is to analyze the border regimes presented in this book, and new ones, according to their full historical and kinetic mixture or hybridization, which this book has only presented alone during their period of relative dominance.

The second area is geographical. This book has examined a long but narrow selection of border history—focusing mainly on the West. Such a move risks perpetuating a pernicious Eurocentrism, even if the history presented is hardly a flattering one. However, by focusing critically on the West in this way my hope is that a certain lie of stability and fixity, which often grounds hegemony and empire, has been exposed—and along with it the claim of Western cultural superiority. This is hardly sufficient to fully overcome the perceived superiority of Western culture, but it is a start. My hope for future studies along these lines would therefore be threefold: a further demonstration of the failures of these regimes, the colonial impact and adoption of these regimes outside Europe, and the emergence of other non-Western border regimes along different geographical timelines.

The third area is contemporary. This book has used its conceptual and historical framework to analyze only one major contemporary border, the US-Mexico border. Many other major and interesting border regimes remain to be analyzed within this framework: the Israel-Palestine border, postapartheid South African borders, the Kashmir border, the India-Pakistan border, southern European borders, and many others. Although the proper names of these borders refer to states, this does not mean that the kinopolitical analysis of them is state-centric. In fact, it means the opposite. As Part III of this book has shown in the case of the US-Mexico border, border regimes are prior to states and are mixed or hybrid. Every state and state border is crisscrossed and composed of numerous other kinds of border mobilities that cannot be understood by state or political power alone. Critical limology reveals that the state is the product of these more primary process of multiple bordering regimes. Therefore, future research into contemporary border regimes, even if it begins with a seemingly state centered name like the "Israeli security wall," should aim to reveal at least three things: the historical admixture of border regimes in the present, their constitutive relationship to contemporary social motion, and the breakdowns that expose the primacy of motion and mobility in border regimes—and thus the possibility of moving otherwise. There are so many new borders today that much work remains to be done to reinterpret them according to the primacy of motion and their hybrid mix of border regimes.

The fourth area is subversive. In addition to limiting its historical and contemporary scope, this book also limits its treatment of certain subversive efforts to undermine border power. This is the case largely because these subversive movements were already treated in *The Figure of the Migrant* in the pedetic motion of the four major figures of the migrant. However, despite this treatment, further elaboration is still possible. For example, with respect to the US-Mexico border alone, an entire typology could be drawn up of the ways various migrant figures constantly subvert the border's power and invent alternative forms of motion and social distribution.

There is much more work to be done in the kinopolitical analysis of the border. The aim of this book has been to prepare the way for further analysis by creating a general conceptual and historical framework proper to the border and based on social motion that can be used to perform further historical and contemporary analysis of borders elsewhere. No doubt the present age of borders will require such new forms of theoretical action.

NOTES

INTRODUCTION

1. From the Latin *finis*, to border.
2. Etienne Balibar, "What Is a Border?," in *Politics and the Other Scene* (London: Verso, 2002), 75–86.
3. The English word "border" comes from the Proto-Indo-European root **bherdh-*, "to cut, split, or divide."
4. Border theory has traditionally concerned itself primarily with the borders between states. See John House, "The Frontier Zone: A Conceptual Problem for Policy Makers," *International Political Science Review* 1 (1980): 456–477; Victor Prescott, *Political Frontiers and Boundaries* (London: Allen & Unwin, 1987); Oscar Martinez, "The Dynamics of Border Interaction: New Approaches to Border Analysis," in *World Boundaries*, vol. 1, *Global Boundaries*, ed. Clive Schofield (London: Routledge, 1994), 1–15; Anthony Giddens, *The Nation-State and Violence* (Berkeley: University of California Press, 1987), 50; Richard Hartshorne, "Geographic and Political Boundaries in Upper Silesia," *Association of American Geographers* 23. 4 (1933): 195–228; Jacques Ancel, *Les frontières: Étude de géographie politique*, Recueil des cours vol. 55 (Paris, 1936); Jacques Ancel, *Géopolitique* (Paris: Delagrave, 1936); Friedrich Ratzel, *Politische Geographie* (Leipzig: R. Oldenbourg, 1897).
5. "A border should thus be more broadly interpreted than as an object alone." Henk van Houtum, "The Mask of the Border," in *The Ashgate Research Companion to Border Studies*, ed. Doris Wastl-Walter (Farnham, Surrey, England: Ashgate, 2011), 50.
6. For Ratzel there are three border zones, two peripheral, and one central zone where two states mingle. Ratzel, *Politische Geographie*, cited in Victor Prescott, *The Geography of Frontiers and Boundaries* (Chicago: Aldine, 1965), 17.
7. The word "define" comes from the word "fin," meaning to limit or border.
8. For a description of several of these alternative societies and political figures see Thomas Nail, *The Figure of the Migrant* (Stanford: Stanford University Press, 2015).
9. Chris Rumford, "Seeing Like a Border," in Corey Johnson, Reece Jones, Anssi Paasi, Louise Amoore, Alison Mountz, Mark Salter, and Chris Rumford, "Interventions on Rethinking 'the Border' in Border Studies," *Political Geography* 30.2 (2011): 61–69; 68.
10. David Newman, "On Borders and Power: A Theoretical Framework," *Journal of Borderlands Studies* 18.1 (2003): 13–25; 16.
11. Borders often happen far away from territorial limits and fluctuate based on risk assessments "processes of searching and scanning, detention and deportation that

are located far away from the visible policing of the border line. In effect, within these global and data-driven systems, border lines are drawn via the association rules between items of data." Alison Mountz, "Border Politics: Spatial Provision and Geographical Precision," in Johnson et al., "Interventions," 64. See also Didier Bigo, "When Two Become One: Internal and External Securitizations in Europe," in *International Relations Theory and the Politics of European Integration: Power, Security, and Community*, ed. M. Kelstrup and M. C. Williams (London: Routledge, 2000); and Mathew Coleman, "Immigration Geopolitics beyond the Mexico-US Border," *Antipode* 39.1 (2007): 54–76.

12. Newman, "On Borders and Power," 16.

13. Newman, "On Borders and Power," 16.

14. Manuel Castells, *The Rise of the Network Society* (Malden, MA: Blackwell, 1996), 376.

15. For examples of the metaphorical usage of concepts of mobility and fluidity see John Urry, *Sociology beyond Societies: Mobilities for the Twenty-First Century* (London: Routledge, 2000), 2. Zygmunt Bauman notes the effort "to deploy 'fluidity' as the leading metaphor for the present stage of the modern era." Zygmunt Bauman, *Liquid Modernity* (Hoboken, NJ: Wiley, 2013), 2.

16. By saying the border is not a metaphor I mean that the mobility of the border is not "like" something else that actually moves—implying that the border has no actual movement, but only a metaphorical, ideal, or representational one. This does not mean that there is no such thing as metaphor—only that linguistic metaphor presupposes matter that moves. This is directly attested to in the original Greek meaning of the word "metaphor" as "transport." Metaphor is a kinetic process by which the features of one material thing are literally or affectively transported to another. The danger is that the original kinetic definition has been lost in favor of an idealist and representational model that simply compares essences by analogy. If a soldier is the human brick stacked into the military wall, it is not because the soldier is like a brick or the brick is like the soldier, but that both actually move according to the same border regime. They share the same affective capacity without being modeled on one another. For more on this idea of affect vs. metaphor see Gilles Deleuze and Félix Guattari, "Becoming Intense, Becoming Animal," in *A Thousand Plateaus: Capitalism and Schizophrenia*, trans. Brian Massumi (Minneapolis: University of Minnesota Press, 1987).

    Furthermore, if the soldier is not only matter in motion but also a figure imbued with social meaning as a civic figure, a hero, a righteous warrior, a manly protector, this is the case because both the motion and the ideal "meanings" of the figure are part of the same coconstitutive regime of motion. Matter and meaning are not modeled on one another or reducible to one another, but enter into the same specific historical regimes of motion that regulate and circulate their shared trajectories. In this sense kinopolitics is a rejection of both materialist and idealist forms of explanatory reductionism.

17. Ancel, *Les Frontières*, 52.

18. Nick Vaughan-Williams, *Border Politics: The Limits of Sovereign Power* (Edinburgh: Edinburgh University Press, 2009), 1.

19. Borders have always been mobile. Their management has always been crucial. This is not a new phenomenon—as some have argued. "If the major focus of past research into borders was concerned with the way in which they were demarcated and delimited, it is the management of the border regime which is of greater

importance today." Newman, "On Borders and Power," 16. See also Johnson et al., "Interventions."

20. For a summary of historical positions affirming a difference between natural and artificial borders see Prescott, *Political Frontiers and Boundaries*, 51. See also Ancel, *Les Frontières*, 51 ("frontière naturelle").

21. Wendy Brown, *Walled States, Waning Sovereignty* (New York: Zone Books, 2010).

22. The border "wall" will be further developed in chapter 3.

23. This argument is fully defended in Part III.

24. "Doors and bridges can be as apt a metaphor for borders as are walls and barriers, but neither should it be forgotten that while walls can be knocked down as quickly as they are constructed, so too doors can be slammed shut as easily as they are opened." Newman, "On Borders and Power," 19. See also Henk Van Houtum and Anke Strüver, "Borders, Strangers, Bridges and Doors," *Space and Polity* 6.2 (2002): 141–146.

25. Newman, "On Borders and Power," 15.

26. See Giorgio Agamben, *Homo Sacer*, trans. Daniel Heller-Roazen (Stanford: Stanford University Press, 1998).

27. See Henri Bergson, *Matter and Memory*, trans. N. M. Paul and W. S. Palmer (New York: Zone Books, 1988), 179–223; and Nail, *Figure of the Migrant*, 12: "The problem with this spatial logic, according to the Greek philosopher Zeno, is that we would have to traverse an infinite distance of intervals in order to arrive anywhere. Thus, movement would be impossible. The same result occurs, according to Zeno, when we understand movement as a series of temporal now-points or instants. If every unit of time is infinitely divisible, it will take an infinity of time to move from one point to any other. The problem is that movement cannot be divided without destroying it. By thinking that we can divide movement into fixed, immobile stages based on departures and arrivals, we spatialize and immobilize it. Movement, according to such a definition, is just the *difference* between divisible points of space-time, but there is no real continuity."

28. "All borders, each act of debordering and rebordering, and every border crossing are constitutive of social relations, and, as such, help us orientate ourselves to the world." Chris Rumford, "Theorizing Borders," *European Journal of Social Theory* 9.2 (2006): 155–169; 167.

29. "There is a tendency to privilege space and spatialities in geographical analysis of borders." Linn Axelsson, "Temporalizing the Border," *Dialogues in Human Geography* 3.3 (2013): 324–326; 324.

30. Rumford, "Theorizing Borders," 166.

31. "Borders as dividers of space." Alexander Diener and Joshua Hagen, *Borders: A Very Short Introduction* (New York: Oxford University Press, 2012), 2.

32. David Newman, "Boundaries," in *A Companion to Political Geography* ed. John A. Agnew, Katharyne Mitchell, and Gerard Toal (Malden, MA: Blackwell, 2003), 134.

33. Mountz, "Border Politics," 66–67.

34. A more detailed explanation will be provided in chapter 2.

35. See Nail, *Figure of the Migrant*, 24: "Instead of analyzing societies as primarily static, spatial, or temporal, kinopolitics or social kinetics understands them primarily as "regimes of motion." Societies are always in motion: directing people and objects, reproducing their social conditions (periodicity), and striving to expand their territorial, political, juridical, and economic power through diverse forms of expulsion. In this sense, it is possible to identify some- thing like a political theory of movement."

36. Johnson et al., "Interventions," 61.

37. See Etienne Balibar, "The Borders of Europe," in *Cosmopolitics: Thinking and Feeling beyond the Nation*, ed. Pheng Cheah and Bruce Robbins (Minneapolis: University of Minnesota Press, 1998), 216–229.

38. See Axelsson, "Temporalizing the Border," 324; and Johnson et al., "Interventions."

39. Newman, "Boundaries," 134.

40. Johnson et al., "Interventions," 62.

41. Immanuel Kant, *Critique of Pure Reason*, trans. Werner S. Pluhar (Indianapolis: Hackett, 1996), 20.

42. Kant, *Critique of Pure Reason*, 21.

43. Kant, *Critique of Pure Reason*, 21.

44. Kant, *Critique of Pure Reason*, 22.

45. For an excellent example of counterborder movements see Audra Simpson, *Mohawk Interruptus: Political Life across the Borders of Settler States* (Durham: Duke University Press, 2014).

46. Critical limology is also "critical" in the sense of showing that the history of dominant border regimes is not a necessary one. Since the conditions are not essential or universal ones—but historical and mobile—the concrete borders can be otherwise than they are.

47. Most of border theory before 1980 has been a history of state borders.

48. For an example of this sort of historical work on the concept of territory see Stuart Elden, *The Birth of Territory* (Chicago: University of Chicago Press, 2013).

49. "As with the idea of 'Neo-Medievalism,' history may give us some clues as to what to expect" [of the future of post-Westphalian borders]." John Williams, *The Ethics of Territorial Borders: Drawing Lines in the Shifting Sand* (Houndmills, Basingstoke, Hampshire: Palgrave Macmillan, 2006), 17–18.

50. For an example of this see Wendy Brown, *Walled States, Waning Sovereignty* (New York: Zone Books, 2010). Her argument is that walls are emerging as desperate and failed attempts to deal with increasing nonborder phenomena. But historically, walls have never worked. It is not as if at one point walls worked and now because of disease, migration, smuggling, and transborder organizations and so on, they do not. Many of these same phenomena existed historically to some degree. Walls have never fully worked for keeping people out.

51. The kinopolitical structure of these alternatives is exemplified, but not certainly not exhausted, in *The Figure of the Migrant*.

CHAPTER 1

1. Adam Smith, *The Wealth of Nations* (1776; repr. Lawrence: Digireads.com Publishing, 2009), book II, introduction, 162.

2. David Harvey, *The New Imperialism* (Oxford: Oxford University Press, 2003); Silvia Federici, *Caliban and the Witch* (New York: Autonomedia, 2004); Saskia Sassen, *Expulsions: Brutality and Complexity in the Global Economy* (Cambridge, MA: Belknap Press of Harvard University Press, 2014); Saskia Sassen, "A Savage Sorting of Winners and Losers: Contemporary Versions of Primitive Accumulation," *Globalizations* 7.1–2 (2010): 23–50; Fredy Perlman, *The Continuing Appeal of Nationalism* (Detroit: Black & Red, 1985); Massimo De Angelis, "Marx and Primitive Accumulation: The Continuous Character of Capital 'Enclosures,'" *The Commoner*, http://www.commoner.org.uk/02deangelis.pdf, accessed April 10, 2015.

3. Karl Marx, *Capital: A Critique of Political Economy*, trans. Ben Fowkes (London: Penguin, 1990), 1:786.

4. A "politics of mobility" has also been proposed in Tim Cresswell, "Towards a Politics of Mobility," *Environment and Planning. D, Society & Space* 28.1 (2010): 17–31. Cresswell advocates for the historical and contemporary study of what he calls "constellations of movement." This is what I am calling "regimes of social motion."

5. This approach has also been proposed by Peter Merriman. In particular, he rejects geography's privileging of space and time and proposes instead a "geography of mobility," which he applies to the case of "driving mobilities." "Mobility and movement," in geography, he argues, "are positioned as important, but they are frequently thought of as functions of space and time. In contrast, [Merriman] seek[s] to suggest a way forward which does not seek to apprehend events—and, in particular, movements—as if they necessarily unfold in or produce ontologies situated in space and time (or space-times), and [he] map[s] out an approach which seeks to reveal how other primitive ontological constituents continually erupt into being and are no less important to situating the unfolding of particular events.... Movement, affect, sensation, rhythm, vibration, energy, force, and much more, then, might be taken to be fundamental to understanding how life unfolds, and we might even go as far as to suggest that space-time is a Western fiction, a series of stories we like to tell ourselves, which in turn structure how we think about the world." Peter Merriman, *Mobility, Space, and Culture* (New York: Routledge, 2012), 2.

6. In my definition of "society" I follow John Urry's definition of the "social as mobility." John Urry, *Sociology beyond Societies: Mobilities for the Twenty-First Century* (London: Routledge, 2000), 2.

7. Fulit dynamics also has its conceptual origin in the work of Lucretius, as Michel Serres argues in *The Birth of Physics*, trans. Jack Hawkes, ed. David Webb (Manchester: Clinamen Press, 2000).

8. In fluid dynamics the density, pressure, and velocity of fluids are assumed to be well defined at infinitesimally small points, which vary continuously.

9. See Victor Prescott, *The Geography of Frontiers and Boundaries* (Chicago: Aldine, 1965), 9–32; and Jacques Ancel, *Les frontières: Étude de géographie politique*, Recueil des cours, vol. 55 (Paris, 1936), 52.

10. For a detailed philosophical history of statistics see Ian Hacking, *The Taming of Chance* (Cambridge: Cambridge University Press, 1990).

11. Harvey's discovery of circulation also had an influence on political theories of circulation as a movement of "social health" in the work of Thomas Hobbes and others. See Jürgen Overhoff, *Hobbes's Theory of the Will: Ideological Reasons and Historical Circumstances* (Lanham, MD: Rowman & Littlefield, 2000); and Richard Sennett, *Flesh and Stone: The Body and the City in Western Civilization* (New York: Norton, 1994).

12. "What emerges in the seventeenth century, all at once, is not so much the applied sciences, the practice of exactitude and precision, as the general philosophy of its possibility." Serres, *The Birth of Physics*, 141.

13. Serres, *The Birth of Physics*, 141.

14. Nikos Papastergiadis argues that the migrant is defined by an "endless motion, [which] surrounds and pervades almost all aspects of contemporary society." *The Turbulence of Migration: Globalization, Deterritorialization, and Hybridity* (Cambridge: Polity Press, 2000), 1. Similarly, Dimitris Papadopoulos and Vassilis Tsianos argue that "the practices of contemporary transnational migration force us to revise Deleuze & Guattari's split between nomadism and migration. Nomadism's dictum 'you never arrive somewhere' constitutes the matrix

of today's migrational movements." "The Autonomy of Migration: The Animals of Undocumented Mobility," in *Deleuzian Encounters: Studies in Contemporary Social Issues*, ed. Anna Hickey-Moody and Peta Malins (Basingstoke, UK: Palgrave Macmillan, 2007), 224.

15. Papastergiadis, Gloria Anzaldúa, Homi Bhabha, and others argue that we should understand the migrant in terms of hybridity. See Papastergiadis, *The Turbulence of Migration*, 168–88; Gloria Anzaldúa, *Borderlands: The New Mestiza = La Frontera* (San Francisco: Spinsters / Aunt Lute, 1987); Homi Bhabha, *The Location of Culture* (London: Routledge, 1994).

16. Michel Serres develops a similar theory of vortices: "The vortex conjoins the atoms, in the same way as the spiral links the points; the turning movement brings together atoms and points alike." *The Birth of Physics*, 16. Deleuze and Guattari then further develop this under the name of "minor science" in *A Thousand Plateaus: Capitalism and Schizophrenia*, trans. Brian Massumi (London: Continuum, 2008), 361–62.

17. The kinetic roots of the word junction come from the Proto-Indo-European root *yeug-, "to join, to yoke."

18. John Lowe and S. Moryadas, *The Geography of Movement* (Boston: Houghton Mifflin, 1975), 54.

19. Lowe and Moryadas have been thoroughly critiqued in Tim Cresswell, *On the Move: Mobility in the Modern Western World* (Hoboken, NJ: Taylor & Francis, 2012), 27–29.

20. Peter Haggett puts movement first, but only arbitrarily: "It is just as logical to begin with the study of settlements as with the study of routes. We choose to make that cut with movement." *Locational Analysis in Human Geography* (New York: St. Martin's Press, 1966), 31.

21. Many US detention centers will pay one dollar per hour for detained migrants' labor even though their legal status forbids them from working. "Punishment and Profits: Immigration Detention," Aljazeera.com, 2012, http://www.aljazeera.com/programmes/faultlines/2012/04/201241081117980874.html.

22. Department of Homeland Security, Office of Inspector General, "Immigration and Customs Enforcement's Tracking and Transfers of Detainees," 2009, 2, http://www.oig.dhs.gov/assets/Mgmt/OIG_09-41_Mar09.pdf, accessed April 10, 2015.

23. Saskia Sassen offers a similar definition of expulsion: "people, enterprises, and places expelled from the core social and economic orders of our time." *Expulsions*, 1.

24. There are even "quite a few things the tourist could complain about." Zygmunt Bauman, *Globalization: The Human Consequences* (New York: Columbia University Press, 1998), 98.

25. OED online.

26. See chapter 4 for detailed examples of these social points.

27. The word "mark" comes from the Old French word *marchier* "to walk; to travel by foot," from the PIE root *merg-, meaning "boundary" or "border."

28. For a detailed history and analysis of this border procession see Jean-Louis Durand, *Sacrifice et labour en Grèce ancienne: Essai d'anthropologie religieuse* (Paris: Découverte, 1986).

29. François Polignac, *Cults, Territory, and the Origins of the Greek City-State* (Chicago: University of Chicago Press, 1995), 41–42.

30. Rom the PIE root *ter- meaning "boundary marker" and the root of the words "terminate" and "exterminate."

31. Siculus Flaccus, *De Condicionibus Agrorum*, 11.

32. Ovid, *Fasti*, book II, February 23: The Terminalia, http://www.poetryintranslation.com/PITBR/Latin/OvidFastiBkTwo.htm#_Toc69367696.

33. George C. Homans, *English Villagers of the Thirteenth Century*, 2nd ed. (Cambridge, MA: Harvard University Press, 1991), 368.

34. The word "limit" comes from the Latin word *limes* (plural: *limites*) meaning "path, track, trail or a line left by the passage of something." Oxford Latin Dictionary.

35. Thus, in Pokorny's etymology the word "limit" comes from the PIE root *el-*, "to bow or to bend." http://indo-european.info/pokorny-etymological-dictionary/index.htm.

36. http://en.wiktionary.org/wiki/patte. The word "patrol" comes from the Frankish *patta-*, "paw, sole of the foot," from the Proto-Germanic *pat-*, "to walk, tread, go, step," and likely, from the PIE root *pat-*, "path, to go."

37. The word "boundary" also has a kinetic origin in three related meanings of the English word "bound." First, the noun "bound" comes from the Old French *bonde* meaning "limit or boundary stone" (modern French *borne*), variant of *bodne*, from the medieval Latin *bodina*, also meaning "boundary." Second, the adjective "bound," meaning "to be ready to go," comes from PIE root *bheue-* "to be, exist, dwell." And third, the past participle "bound" comes from the word "bind," from the PIE root *bhendh-* meaning "to bind, compel, or bond, or bend." The English word "boundary" thus resonates with these three meanings. As a function or "synonym" for the border, the word "boundary" plays an important meaning in relation to the mark and the limit.

38. This is the sense in which the adjective "bound" also resonates with its PIE root *bheue-* "to be, exist, dwell."

39. From the same PIE root as bound and bind (*bhendh-*) also comes the Germanic root *band-*, whose derivatives such as "band," "bond," and "bend" all refer to a mobile "unified social group." http://www.etymonline.com/index.php?term=band.

40. Band: A thin strip of flexible material used to encircle and bind one object or to hold a number of objects together.

41. Ovid, *Fasti*, book II, February 23: The Terminalia. http://www.poetryintranslation.com/PITBR/Latin/OvidFastiBkTwo.htm#_Toc69367696.

42. See Frederick J. Turner, *The Frontier in American History* (New York: Holt, Rinehart and Winston, 1962).

43. Frantz Fanon, "Concerning Violence," in *The Wretched of the Earth*, trans. Constance Farrington (London: Penguin, 1967), 29–30. Originally published as *Les damnés de la terre* (Paris: Maspero, 1961).

44. The German geographer Friedrich Ratzel proposed the idea of borders as having two periphery zones and one central zone where two states mingle, in his book *Politische Geographie* (Leipzig: R. Oldenbourg, 1897). The idea is also discussed in Prescott, *Geography of Frontiers*, 17. See also Peter Nyers, "Moving Borders: The Politics of Dirt," *Radical Philosophy* 174 (2012): 2–6; David Newman, "On Borders and Power: A Theoretical Framework," *Journal of Borderlands Studies* 18.1 (2003): 13–25 ("Hybridization takes place in contact zones" [16]); Malcolm Anderson, *Frontiers: Territory and State Formation in the Modern World* (Cambridge: Polity Press, 1996), 9; and Turner, *Frontier in American History*.

45. See Isaiah Bowman, *The Pioneer Fringe* (New York: American Geographical Society of New York, 1931).

46. See Frederick J. Turner, *The Significance of the Frontier in American History* (Ann Arbor: University Microfilms, 1966).

47. See Neil Smith, *The New Urban Frontier: Gentrification and the Revanchist City* (London: Routledge, 1996).

48. Thomas Nail, *The Figure of the Migrant* (Stanford: Stanford University Press, 2015), 37. The frontier zone is the place where the process of expansion by expulsion occurs. See also Part II of *The Figure of the Migrant* more generally for the theory and history of social expansion by expulsion that defines the disjoining frontier zone of societies and its subjective effects on the figure of the migrant.

49. This is what Marx calls "social metabolism." *Capital*, 1:283.

CHAPTER 2

1. Gordon Childe, *Man Makes Himself* (New York: New American Library, 1951), 59.

2. The first "great migration" of human movement occurred almost two million years ago when *Homo erectus* moved out of Africa into the Middle East. Although it is strange to call this a migration since it took thousands of years of *Homo erectus* simply following the migration of wild game moving north (at about 1 km a year) to avoid rising temperatures and the desertification of Africa. Whether we call this migration or not, *Homo erectus* and early *Homo sapiens* were initially nonsedentary hunter-gatherers who increasingly settled down in societies. For a fully developed historical account of this movement see Patrick Manning, *Migration in World History* (New York: Routledge, 2005), 16–39.

3. For an interesting discussion of the "degrees of mobility in neolithic" see Douglass Bailey, Alasdair Whittle, and Vicki Cummings, *(Un)Settling the Neolithic* (Oxford: Oxbow, 2005), 1.

4. Here I follow Manuel De Landa's definition of territorialization. "The other dimension [processes of territorialization] defines variable processes in which these components become involved and that either stabilize the identity of an assemblage, by increasing its degree of internal homogeneity or the degree of sharpness of its boundaries, or destabilize it." Manuel De Landa, *A New Philosophy of Society: Assemblage Theory and Social Complexity* (London: Continuum, 2006), 12.

5. Bernard Cache, *Earth Moves: The Furnishing of Territories*, trans. Anne Boyman, ed. Michael Speaks (Cambridge, MA: MIT Press, 1995), 11.

6. I defined social force thus in *The Figure of the Migrant* (Stanford: Stanford University Press, 2015):

> By social force, I mean that which *describes* the motion of society. I do not mean the vital or metaphysical *cause* of motion. As Bergson argues, force "is known and estimated only by the movements which it is supposed to produce in space . . . [but it is] one with these movements." There is no secret cause or "action at a distance" behind different types of movement. There are simply different types or tendencies in social movement. The theory of social forces describes them.
>
> A social force is not the same as a physical force. In physics, the concept of force does not describe social actors, their relations, or causes. It deals only with material bodies *as material*. But political philosophy deals with material bodies as territorial, political, juridical, economic, and so on. Human beings do not necessarily desire, believe, or collectively act in the ways that particles do in physics. Social forces are thus not modeled on physical forces but describe entirely different types of forces.
>
> In a specifically kinopolitical analysis, the dominant types of social motion, their direction, and relation are what are of interest. In kinopolitics, some types of social movement are more or less directed inward toward a

dominant social center, or outward away from one, or in a legal tension with others, and so on. For example, a "social center" does not have to be geometrically or exactly in the center of a territory, city, or village. A social center relates to the relatively high degree of power, influence, or prestige of a social institution—power exerted by individuals at the top of a social hierarchy. The type and degree of social motion directed by this power center exert a social "force" insofar as the social motion collectively mobilizes people politically, legally, economically, and so on. (40)

7. The first definition of the word "fence" comes from its etymological origins in the PIE root *gwhen-, to strike.

8. Cache, *Earth Moves*, 24.

9. "The wall delimits and the window selects." Cache, *Earth Moves*, 28.

10. Lewis Mumford, *The City in History: Its Origins, Its Transformations, and Its Prospects* (New York: Harcourt, Brace & World, 1961), 7.

11. Mumford, *City in History*, 7.

12. Mumford, *City in History*, 7.

13. Mumford, *City in History*, 10.

14. "The Neolithic period is pre-eminently one of containers: it is an age of stone pottery utensils, of vases, jars, vats, cisterns, bins, barns, granaries, houses, not least great collective containers like irrigation ditches and villages." Mumford, *City in History*, 16.

15. The word "corral" comes from the PIE root *kers-, meaning "to run."

16. The hunting interpretation proposed by Maitland was adopted by Dussaud and later by Field, but was supplanted by the herd corral theory, which gained wider acceptance. Cited in A. Holzer, U. Avner, N. Porat, and L. K. Horwitz, "Desert Kites in the Negev Desert and Northeast Sinai: Their Function, Chronology and Ecology," *Journal of Arid Environments* 74.7 (2010): 806. See also René Dussaud, "Les releves du Capitaine Rees dans le désert de Syrie," *Syria* 10.2 (1929): 151; Henry Field, "North Arabian Desert Archaeological Survey, 1925–50," in *Papers of the Peabody Museum of Archaeology and Ethnology* 45.2 (Cambridge: Peabody Museum, 1960), 129–131; O. Eissfeldt, "Gabelhurden im Ostjordanland," *Kleine Schriften* 3 (1960): 61–70; A. S. Kirkbride, "Desert 'Kites,'" *Journal of the Palestine Oriental Society* 20 (1946): 1–5; W. A. Ward, "The Supposed Asiatic Campaign of Narmer," *Mélanges de l'Université Saint-Joseph de Beyrouth* 45 (1969): 208; Y. Yadin, "The Earliest Record of Egypt's Military Penetration into Asia," *Israel Exploration Journal* 5 (1955): 5–10.

17. J. C. Echallier and F. Braemer, "Nature et functions de 'desert kites': Donnees et hypotheses nouvelles," *Paléorient* 21.1 (1995): 35–63.

18. David Kennedy, "Kites: New Discoveries and a New Type," *Arabian Archaeology and Epigraphy* 23.2 (2012): 145–155.

19. E. K. Barth, "Trapping Reindeer in South Norway," *Antiquity* 7 (1983): 109–115.

20. V. N. Yagodin, "'Arrow-Shaped' Structures in the Aralo-Gaspian Steppe," in *The Harra and the Hamad: Excavations and Surveys in Eastern Jordan*, ed. A. V. G. Betts (Sheffield: Gontinuum International Publishing Group, 1998), 207–223.

21. See G. G. Frison, *Prehistoric Hunters of the High Plains* (New York: Academic Press, 2004); Frison, *Survival by Hunting: Prehistoric Human Predators and Animal Prey* (Berkeley: University of California Press, 1991); Bryan Hockett and Timothy W. Murphy, "Antiquity of Communal Pronghorn Hunting in the North-Central Great Basin," *American Antiquity* 74.4 (2009): 708–734.

22. G. S. Goon, *The Hunting People* (London: Nick Lyons, 1976), 111–115.

23. Holzer et al., "Desert Kites," 806.
24. Dani Nadel, Guy Bar-Oz, Uzi Avner, Elisabetta Boaretto, and Dan Malkinson, "Walls, Ramps and Pits: The Construction of the Samar Desert Kites, Southern Negev, Israel," *Antiquity* 84.326 (2010): 977.
25. Kennedy, "Kites," 149.
26. The word "palisade" comes from the Latin word *pālus* meaning "stake, pole, or pile," from the PIE root **pag-* meaning "to fasten."
27. For an extensive report on Neolithic palisades in Europe see Alex Gibson, *Behind Wooden Walls: Neolithic Palisaded Enclosures in Europe* (Oxford: Archaeopress, 2002).
28. Dušan Borić, "First Households and 'House Societies' in European Prehistory," in *Prehistoric Europe: Theory and Practice*, ed. Andrew Jones (Chichester: Wiley-Blackwell, 2008), 114.
29. This is perhaps the kinetic basis of future kinship relations theorized by Claude Lévi-Struass as the *société à maisons,*" or "house society." Claude Lévi-Strauss, *The Way of the Masks*, trans. Sylvia Modelski (Seattle: University of Washington Press, 1982).
30. Some holes were admittedly small storage pits, but others may well have been sockets for posts. See Gordon Childe, "Cave Men's Buildings," *Antiquity* 24 (1950): 7.
31. Borić, "First Households," 114.
32. Dimitrij Mlekuž, "Bodies, Houses and Gardens: Rhythm Analysis of Neolithic Life-Ways," *Documenta Praehistorica* 37 (2010): 199.
33. Ian Hodder, "Architecture and Meaning: The Example of Neolithic Houses and Tombs," in *Architecture and Order: Approaches to Social Space*, ed. Pearson Parker and Colin Richards (London: Routledge, 1994), 80. Amy Bogaard writes, "Functional interdependence between small-scale crop and animal husbandry practices is key to understanding early farming and broader changes in society, especially increasing household autonomy." Amy Bogaard, "Garden Agriculture' and the Nature of Early Farming in Europe and the Near East," *World Archaeology* 37.2, „Garden Agriculture" (2005): 178. See also K. V. Flannery, "The Origins of the Village Revisited: From Nuclear to Extended Households," *American Antiquity* 67 (2002): 417–433.
34. Jean-Jacques Rousseau, "Discourse on Inequality," in *Basic Political Writings*, trans. and ed. Donald A. Cress, 2nd ed. (New York: Hackett, 2011), 69; modified translation.
35. Jessica Smyth, "Tides of Change? The House through the Irish Neolithic," in *Tracking the Neolithic House in Europe: Sedentism, Architecture and Practice*, ed. Daniela Hofmann and Jessica Smyth (New York: Springer, 2013), 308. See also J. Kiely, "A Neolithic House at Cloghers Co. Kerry," in *Neolithic Settlement in Ireland and Western Britain*, ed. I. Armit, E. Murphy, E. Nelis, and D. Simpson (Oxford: Oxbow, 2003), 182–187.
36. John Barrett, *Fragments from Antiquity: An Archaeology of Social Life in Britain, 2900–1200 BC* (Oxford: Blackwell, 1994), 143–145.
37. Bogaard, "Garden Agriculture."
38. According to the OED.
39. For an extensive list of palisaded enclosures and types in Neolithic Germany see Gibson, *Behind Wooden Walls*, 59–92.
40. Julian Thomas, *Understanding the Neolithic* (London: Routledge, 2002), 134.
41. Thomas, *Understanding the Neolithic*, 51.
42. Thomas, *Understanding the Neolithic*, 84–85.

43. "In this context, it is highly significant that the classification which Colin Richards used to detect spatial patterning in the Grooved Ware at Durrington Walls was based upon two binary oppositions: bounded/unbounded and decorated/undecorated." Thomas, *Understanding the Neolithic*, 84–85. See also C. C. Richards and J. S. Thomas, "Ritual Activity and Structured Deposition in Later Neolithic Wessex," in *Neolithic Studies*, ed. R. Bradley and J. Gardiner (Oxford: British Archaeological Reports no. 133, 1984), 189–218.

44. On the Black Sea coast and in northeast Bulgaria there are multiple palisaded, re-palisaded, occupied, and abandoned structures of rectangular buildings. The sites were continually being repurposed. Alasdair Whittle, *Europe in the Neolithic: The Creation of New Worlds* (Cambridge: Cambridge University Press, 1996), 90.

45. Whittle, *Europe in the Neolithic*, 191.

46. Whittle, *Europe in the Neolithic*, 132.

47. Poul Otto Nielsen, "Causewayed Camps, Palisade Enclosures and Central Settlements of the Middle Neolithic in Denmark," *Journal of Nordic Archaeological Science* 14 (2004): 19–33.

48. "I discount defense and fortification. Had these been major factors, one could expect more of this kind of site right through the Neolithic / Copper Age sequence. A different approach might be to regard these sites as places of social pre-eminence, where labour could be mobilized for impressive collective undertakings." Whittle, *Europe in the Neolithic*, 190.

49. Whittle, *Europe in the Neolithic*, 276.

50. "I suggest that the primary role of most enclosures was formally to bound a special space, to separate inside from outside, and to invest the activities associated with the various parts of the special space with appropriate significance." Whittle, *Europe in the Neolithic*, 286 n. 144.

51. See Thorkild Jacobsen, *The Treasures of Darkness: A History of Mesopotamian Religion* (New Haven: Yale University Press, 1976).

52. Robin Skeates, "The Neolithic Ditched Enclosures of the Tavoliere, South-East Italy," in *Enclosures in Neolithic Europe: Essays on Causewayed and Non-causewayed Sites*, ed. Gillian Varndell and Peter Topping (Oxford: Oxbow Books, 2002), 51–58.

53. Skeates, "Neolithic Ditched Enclosures," 55.

54. People emphasized the sense of bounded space by digging ditches or erecting palisades around settlements. See Mlekuž, "Bodies, Houses and Gardens," 196, fig. 1.

55. Glyn Daniel, *The Megalith Builders of Western Europe* (London: Hutchinson, 1958), 128.

56. Vyacheslav Mizin, "Stone Cairns and Simulacra: Navigation, Folklore, and Tradition in the Arctic," *Time and Mind: The Journal of Archaeology, Consciousness and Culture* Volume 6—Issue 3 November 2013: 313–330.

57. See Uzi Avner, "Current Archaeological Research in Israel: Ancient Agricultural Settlement and Religion in the Uvda Valley in Southern Israel," *Biblical Archaeologist* 53.3 (1990): 125–141.

58. Jacobsen, *Treasures of Darkness*, 3.

59. See Whittle, *Europe in the Neolithic*.

60. Mumford, *City in History*, 7–9.

61. See Whittle, *Europe in the Neolithic*.

62. Daniel, *Megalith Builders*, 15–24.

63. See Avner, "Current Archaeological Research."

64. Avner, "Current Archaeological Research," 138.

65. Avner, "Current Archaeological Research," 138.

66. Avner, "Current Archaeological Research," 138.
67. For example, in Sinai many of the roadside cairns are darkened on the inside from blood sacrifices or oil libations. "The faces of the inner stones were usually blackened, but no remains of burnt charcoal were found nearby. The stains may have come from libations of oil or blood on the piles, such as those performed by Moses at the foot of Mount Sinai (Exodus 24:6). It is believed that the crenellations commemorated acts of pilgrimage and were sanctified by libation. This example is located in Nahal Shaharut." Avner, "Current Archaeological Research," 137.
68. Roger Joussaume, *Dolmans for the Dead* (Syracuse, NY: Cornell University Press, 1985), 257.
69. Steven Rosen, "Desert Pastoral Nomadism in the Longue Durée: A Case Study from the Negev and the Southern Levantine Deserts," in *The Archaeology of Mobility: Old World and New World Nomadism*, ed. H. Barnard and Willeke Wendrich (Los Angeles: Cotsen Institute of Archaeology, University of California, 2008), 122.

CHAPTER 3
1. Gordon Childe, *Man Makes Himself* (New York: New American Library, 1951), 115.
2. Gordon Childe, "The Urban Revolution," *Town Planning Review* 21.1 (1950): 3–17.
3. These two kinetic functions are also related to the dual meaning of the modern English word "wall," which refers to both an internal and an external wall. Historically, the word "wall" is a seventeenth-century combination of two older English words: "wall" and "mure." The English word "mure" is now obsolete, according to the OED, even though it is still used in the English word "mural" and "immure." In many languages, however, this split remains active. For example, it can be found in the German words *wand* and *mauer*; the Spanish words *pared* and *muro*; and the French words *paroi* and *mur*. To understand the two kinetic functions of the wall it is important to recover the split meaning within the English word "wall."
4. "They assume precisely this form of bricks that ensures their integration into the higher unity." Gilles Deleuze and Félix Guattari, *Anti-Oedipus: Capitalism and Schizophrenia*, trans. Robert Hurley, Helen R. Lane, and Mark Seem (Minneapolis: University of Minnesota Press, 1983), 199.
5. Deleuze and Guattari, *Anti-Oedipus*, 196.
6. See Aurangzeb Khan and Carsten Lemmen, "Bricks and Urbanism in the Indus Valley Rise and Decline," July 24, 2014, *History and Philosophy of Physics*, http://arxiv.org/abs/1303.1426.
7. Euclid, *Elements*, book I, definition 15 and 16. My italics. Translation by Richard Fitzpatrick. http://isites.harvard.edu/fs/docs/icb.topic1047845.files/Elements.pdf
8. Euclid, *Elements*, book I, postulate 3.
9. The etymology of the word *mūrus* emphasizes the process of "fixing or building" (from *mei-), and not the "governing or ruling" (from *wal-) of the wall.
10. Plutarch, *Moralia*, volume 1, "How a Man May Become Aware of His Progress in Virtue," in *Plutarch's Complete Works*, vol. 2 (Princeton, NJ: Princeton University Press, 1909), 134.
11. Khan and Lemmen, "Bricks and Urbanism."
12. Lemmen, "Bricks and Urbanism," 6. The map clearly shows an explosion of brick usages after 3200 BCE.
13. See M. L. Smith, "The Archaeology of South Asian Cities," *Journal of Archaeological Research* 14.2 (2006): 97–142.

14. Martin Brice, *Stronghold: A History of Military Architecture* (London: Batsford, 1984), 40.
15. See Richard Gabriel, *The Great Armies of Antiquity* (Westport, CT: Praeger, 2002), 48–58. The world's first armies appeared in Sumer and Akkad between 3500 and 2200 BCE.
16. Lewis Mumford, *The City in History: Its Origins, Its Transformations, and Its Prospects* (New York: Harcourt, Brace & World, 1961), 60.
17. Aristotle, *Politics*, book VII, chapter 11, 1331.
18. See Richard Gabriel and Dennis E. Showalter, "Assyria: 890 to 612 BCE," in *Soldiers' Lives through History* (Westport, CT: Greenwood Press, 2007).
19. Cited in Toby Wilkinson, *The Rise and Fall of Ancient Egypt* (New York: Random House, 2010), 306.
20. Polybius, *The Histories of Polybius*, vol. 3, Loeb Classical Library, translated by W.R. Paton (Cambridge, MA: Harvard University Press, 1923), section 24.
21. Se Mumford, *City in History*, 39–60.
22. As Paul Virilio calls it throughout: Paul Virilio, *Speed and Politics: An Essay on Dromology*, trans. Mark Polizzotti (New York: Columbia University Press, 1986).
23. Thorsten Opper, *Hadrian: Empire and Conflict* (Cambridge, MA: Harvard University Press, 2008), 108–109.
24. See Alfred Bradford and Pamela Bradford, *With Arrow, Sword, and Spear: A History of Warfare in the Ancient World* (Westport, CT: Praeger, 2001), 65.
25. J. S. Wacher, *The Roman World* (London: Routledge, 1987), 157.
26. Mumford, *City in History*, 101.
27. The broad streets of Ur and little Lagash were used as a cardinal axis for soldiers. As Lewis Mumford writes, "The broad street had come in before the invention of wheeled vehicles, for it was probably first laid out for sacred processions and for marching soldiers. The frequent orientation of the main avenues to the points of the compass perhaps indicates the growing dominance of the sky gods." *City in History*, 73.
28. Mumford, *City in History*, 46.
29. Paul Virilio, *Bunker Archaeology*, trans. George Collins (New York: Princeton Architectural Press, 1994), 38.
30. André Leroi-Gourhan, *Gesture and Speech* (Cambridge, MA: MIT Press, 1993), 332.
31. On the difference and connection between the horizontal and vertical grid-wall see Spiro Kostof, *The City Shaped: Urban Patterns and Meanings through History* (Boston: Little, Brown, 1991), 138–139.
32. Mumford, *City in History*, 27.
33. See C. J. Gadd, *Hammurabi and the End of His Dynasty* (Cambridge: University Press, 1965).
34. Cited in Oswald Dilke, *The Roman Land Surveyors: An Introduction to the Agrimensores* (Newton Abbot: David and Charles, 1971), 20.
35. Mumford, *City in History*, 64.
36. Heather Baker, "Babylonian Land Survey in Socio-political Context," in *The Empirical Dimension of Ancient Near Eastern Studies*, ed. Gebhard J. Selz (Vienna: LIT Verlag, 2011), 297.
37. Duncan Melville, "Old Babylonian Weights and Measures," http://it.stlawu.edu/~dmelvill/mesomath/obmetrology.html.
38. Herodotus, *The History of Herodotus*, book 2, 109. Translated by S. Rappoport (The Grolier Society Publishers, London).
39. Cited in Dilke, *Roman Land Surveyors*, 21.

40. Dilke, *Roman Land Surveyors*, 22.
41. See H. W. Fairman, *Town Planning in Pharaonic Egypt* (Liverpool: University Press, 1949).
42. Mumford, *City in History*, 81.
43. Mumford, *City in History*, 207.
44. See Sir Henry Geroge Lyons, *The Cadastral Survey of Egypt 1892-1907* (Cairo: National Print. Dept, 1908)
45. See Ellen Morris, *The Architecture of Imperialism: Military Bases and the Evolution of Foreign Policy in Egypt's New Kingdom* (Leiden: Brill, 2005).
46. Dilke, *Roman Land Surveyors*, 23–25.
47. Mumford, *City in History*, 192.
48. Dilke, *Roman Land Surveyors*, 23.
49. Strabo, *Geography*, vol. 1, book 4, chapter 1, section 5.
50. Strabo, *Geography*, vol. 2, book 12, chapter 4, section 7.
51. Aristophanes, *Birds*, 1290.
52. See Kostof, *The City Shaped*, 95–158.
53. Mumford, *City in History*, 192.
54. Dilke, *Roman Land Surveyors*, 31–33.
55. Dilke, *Roman Land Surveyors*, 15.
56. Virgil, *Aeneid*, book 5, 746.
57. Jacques Ancel, *Géopolitique* (Paris: Delagrave, 1936), 33.
58. Siculus Flaccus, *De condicionibus agrorum*, in Campbell, *Writings of the Roman Land Surveyors*, 102–33, 104, 105; Siculus Flaccus, *De Condicionibus Agrorum*, lines 104–105.
59. Siculus Flaccus, *De Condicionibus Agrorum*, lines 120–121.
60. Brice, *Stronghold*, 48.
61. Brice, *Stronghold*, 49.
62. While the origin of the rampart begins with the encircling wall of the ancient city, not all ramparts are continuous circles.
63. Gilles Deleuze and Félix Guattari, *A Thousand Plateaus: Capitalism and Schizophrenia*, trans. Brian Massumi (Minneapolis: University of Minnesota Press, 1987), 431 n. 14.
64. Mumford, *City in History*, 36.
65. Childe, "The Urban Revolution," 7.
66. Mumford, *City in History*, 37. See also Childe, "The Urban Revolution."
67. Mumford, *City in History*, 37.
68. See Mircea Eliade, *Patterns in Comparative Religion* (New York: Sheed & Ward, 1958).
69. *The Epic of Gilgamesh*, tablet I i:1–19. Andrew George (Penguin Classics, 2003).
70. Mumford, *City in History*, 35.
71. Brice, *Stronghold*, 35.
72. Brice, *Stronghold*, 35.
73. Brice, *Stronghold*, 35.
74. Plato, *Laws*, book V, 745c. My italics. Plato, *Complete Works*, edited by John Cooper (Cambridge: Hackett Publishing Company, 1997).
75. Plato, *Laws*, book VI, 778e–779d.
76. Plato, *Laws*, book VI, 778e–779d.
77. "With respect to walls, those who say that a courageous people ought not to have any, pay too much respect to obsolete notions; particularly as we may see those who pride themselves therein continually confuted by facts." Aristotle, *Politics*, book VII, chapter XI.

78. "Wisdom is a most sure stronghold which never crumbles away nor is betrayed. Walls of defense must be constructed in our own impregnable reasonings." Diogenes Laertius relaying the thoughts of Antisthenes a rhetorician and student of Gorgia in *Lives of Eminent Philosophers,* book VI, chapter 1, line 13. (Harvard University Press, Loeb Classical Library, 1925).

79. See John Protevi, *Political Physics: Deleuze, Derrida, and the Body Politic* (London: Athlone Press, 2001), 115–117.

80. Dilke, *Roman Land Surveyors,* 87.

81. Olwen Brogan, "The Roman *Limes* in Germany," *Archaeological Journal* 92 (1935): 1; C. R. Whittaker, *Frontiers of the Roman Empire: A Social and Economic Study* (Baltimore: Johns Hopkins University Press, 1994), 200; and Edward N. Luttwak, *The Grand Strategy of the Roman Empire from the First Century A.D. to the Third* (Baltimore: Johns Hopkins University Press, 1976), 19. On military handbooks, see Brian Campbell, "Teach Yourself How to Be a General," *Journal of Roman Studies* 77 (1987): 13–29.

82. André Piganiol, "La notion de limes," *Quintus Congressus Internationalis Limitis Romani Studiosorum* (Zagreb: Jugoslavenka Akademija Znanosti, 1963), 122.

83. Brice, *Stronghold,* 59.

84. David Breeze, *The Northern Frontiers of Roman Britain* (London: Batsford, 1982), 84.

85. Brice, *Stronghold,* 59.

86. See David Divine, *The North-west Frontier of Rome: A Military Study of Hadrian's Wall* (London: Macdonald, 1969).

87. Procopius, *Anecdota,* XXIV, 12, in *Procopius,* trans. H. B. Dewing, Greek-English ed., 7 vols. (London: William Heinemann, 1954), vol. 6.

88. Fergus Millar, *The Roman Empire and Its Neighbours* (New York: Delacorte Press, 1968), 105.

89. Brice, *Stronghold,* 60.

90. Brice, *Stronghold,* 56.

91. Brice, *Stronghold,* 56.

92. Breeze, *Northern Frontiers,* 161; and John Cecil Mann, "The Frontiers of the Principate," *Aufstieg und Niedergang der Römischen Welt* 2 (1974): 508.

93. Barry Cunliffe, *Greeks, Romans, and Barbarians: Spheres of Interaction* (New York: Methuen, 1988), 3.

94. M. G. Lay, *Ways of the World: A History of the World's Roads and of the Vehicles That Used Them* (New Brunswick, NJ: Rutgers University Press, 1992), 93.

95. Mumford, *City in History,* 71–72.

96. Paul Virilio, *Negative Horizon: An Essay in Dromoscopy,* trans. Michael Degener (London: Continuum, 2006), 57.

97. Franz Kafka, "A Message from the Emperor," trans. Mark Harman, http://www.nybooks.com/blogs/nyrblog/2011/jul/01/message-emperor-new-translation/.

98. "An army is always strong enough when it can go and come, extend itself and draw itself back in, as it wishes and when it wishes." Paul Virilio attributes this phrase to the ancient Chinese strategist Se Ma in Virilio, *Negative Horizon,* 58.

99. Lay, *Ways of the World,* 56.

100. Paved roads first emerged in the center of ancient cities like Ur in the Middle East, about 4000 BCE. See Richard Kirby, *Engineering in History* (New York: McGraw-Hill, 1956).

101. Cited in Lay, *Ways of the World,* 50.

102. See L. S. De Camp, *The Ancient Engineers* (Garden City: Doubleday, 1963).

103. Lay, *Ways of the World,* 50.

104. Lay, *Ways of the World*, 45.

105. Lay, *Ways of the World*, 45.

106. See Lionel Casson, *Travel in the Ancient World* (Baltimore: Johns Hopkins University Press, 1994).

107. Herodotus, *The History of Herodotus*, vol. 2, book VIII, line 98.

108. As the Delphic Oracle told, "When all was lost, a wooden wall should still shelter the Athenians." Those noncombatants who put their trust in palisades died in the fire. Those Athenians like Themistocles, who believed the Oracle was referring to the wooden war galleys, took the fleet to sea and defeated the Persians at Salamis. See Brice, *Stronghold*, 45.

109. "By 2000 BCE metal tools allowed many ancient cities to create flagstones for paving local streets and paths. Around this time the Minoans of Crete created the largest and most innovative paved road. This first major road way from the capital at Knossus to the sea port of Leben was the most advanced and successful early road because it was so architecturally similar to a horizontal wall. Instead of simply setting down irregularly cut flat stones on the earth, it was made of thick (200mm) evenly cut sandstone pieces bound together by a clay-gypsum mortar, and a 4 m wide surface of basaltic flagstones flanked by mortared pieces of lime-stone, and lined with side drains. This Minoan technique would not be improved upon for over three millennia," Lay, *Ways of the World,* 52.

110. Lay, *Ways of the World*, 52.

111. Lay, *Ways of the World*, 53.

112. Raymond Chevallier, *Roman Roads* (Berkeley: University of California Press, 1976), 65.

113. Pliny the Elder, *Historia Naturalis*, 18, 111; Lay, *Ways of the World*, 59.

114. Lay, *Ways of the World*, 55.

115. "And after Phrygia succeeds the river Halys, at which there is a gate which one must needs pass through in order to cross the river, and a strong guard-post is established there." Herodotus, *The Histories of Herodotus*, book V, line 52.

116. Herodotus, *The Histories of Herodotus*, book I, line 180.

117. Natalie May, "Gates and Their Functions in Mesopotamia and Ancient Israel," in *The Fabric of Cities: Aspects of Urbanism, Urban Topography and Society in Mesopotamia, Greece and Rome*, ed. Natalie May and Ulrike Steinert (Boston: Brill, 2014), 77–121; 79.

118. Mumford, *City in History*, 71–72.

119. Virilio, *Speed and Politics*, 33.

120. Mumford, *City in History*, 66.

121. For a detailed historical analysis of these functions in the ancient near east see May, "Gates and Their Functions."

122. Plutarch, *Lives*, Romulus, chapter 1.

123. See J. Laet, *Portorium: Étude sur l'organisation douaniere chez les Romains, surtout à l'époque du haut-empire* (New York: Arno Press, 1975).

124. See Brice, *Stronghold*, 60.

125. Mumford, *City in History*, 28.

CHAPTER 4

1. Alexander Diener and Joshua Hagen, *Borders: A Very Short Introduction* (New York: Oxford University Press, 2012), 38.

2. Peter Sahlins, *Boundaries: The Making of France and Spain in the Pyrenees* (Berkeley: University of California Press, 1989), 6.

3. Lucien Febvre, "Frontière: The Word and the Concept," in *A New Kind of History: From the Writings of Febvre*, ed. Peter Burke (London: Routledge, 1973), 213.

4. Perry Anderson, *Passages from Antiquity to Feudalism* (London: NLB, 1974), 153.

5. Clifford Backman, *The Worlds of Medieval Europe* (New York: Oxford University Press, 2003), 178.

6. Anderson, *Passages*, 151.

7. Anderson, *Passages*, 148.

8. Anderson, *Passages*, 152. My italics.

9. From the root -*legh*, to lay down.

10. For an in-depth kinetic analysis of human joints see Vincenzo Parenti-Castelli and Nicola Sancisi, "Synthesis of Spatial Mechanisms to Model Human Joints," in *21st Century Kinematics*, ed. J. M. McCarthy (London: Springer-Verlag, 2013). Another example of spatial motion is what is called in mechanics "Bennett's linkage." Bennett's linkage is a spatial four-bar linkage with hinged joints that have their axes angled in a particular way that makes the system movable. See K. H. Hunt, *Kinematic Geometry of Mechanisms* (Oxford: Clarendon Press; New York: Oxford University Press, 1979).

11. Michel Foucault, *The History of Sexuality*, vol. 1: *An Introduction*, trans. Robert Hurley (New York: Vintage, 1990), 87.

12. Foucault, *The History of Sexuality*, 86.

13. Bodin, *Les six livres*, book III, chapter VI. Jean Bodin, *The Six Bookes of a Commonweale: A Facsimile Reprint of the English Translation of 1606*, trans. Richard Knolles, ed. Kenneth Douglas McRae (Cambridge, MA: Harvard University Press, 1962).

14. Bodin, *Les six livres*, book I, chapter VII.

15. Bodin, *Les six livres*, introduction, xix. See also P. Duféy, *Michel de L'Hôpital: Oeuvres complètes* (Paris, 1824–26), vol. 1, no. 4.

16. Ronnie Ellenblum, "Were There Borders and Borderlines in the Middle Ages? The Example of the Latin Kingdom of Jerusalem," in *Medieval Frontiers: Concepts and Practices*, ed. David Abulafia and Nora Berend (Aldershot, Hants, England: Ashgate, 2002), 109.

17. Ellenblum, "Borders and Borderlines," 114.

18. Kim Willsher, "History of Tattoos Stretches Back 5,000 years: Even Otzi, the Frozen Neolithic Man, had 57," *Guardian*, May 4, 2014, http://www.rawstory.com/rs/2014/05/04/history-of-tattoos-stretches-back-5000-years-even-otzi-frozen-neolithic-man-have-57/.

19. Pierre Clastres, *Society against the State: Essays in Political Anthropology* (New York: Zone Books, 1987), 188.

20. See Deborah Steiner, *The Tyrant's Writ: Myths and Images of Writing in Ancient Greece* (Princeton, NJ: Princeton University Press, 1994), 154–166.

21. Plato, *Laws*, 854d.

22. Steiner, *The Tyrant's Writ*, 155.

23. Plato, *The Republic*, 359d–e.

24. Jonathan Bloom, *Paper before Print: The History and Impact of Paper in the Islamic World* (New Haven: Yale University Press, 2001), 203.

25. Dard Hunter, *Papermaking: The History and Technique of an Ancient Craft* (New York: Dover, 1978), 4.

26. Valentin Groebner, *Who Are You? Identification, Deception, and Surveillance in Early Modern Europe*, trans. Mark Kyburz and John Peck (Brooklyn, NY: Zone Books, 2007), 159.

27. Groebner, *Who Are You?*, 156.

28. Groebner, *Who Are You?*, 156, 157.

29. Groebner, *Who Are You?*, 157.

30. For an elaboration of this point see Groebner, *Who Are You?*, 171–221.

31. Groebner, *Who Are You?*, 171.

32. Groebner, *Who Are You?*, 157.

33. Groebner, *Who Are You?*, 156.

34. Groebner, *Who Are You?*, 159.

35. Groebner, *Who Are You?*, 161.

36. Groebner, *Who Are You?*, 162.

37. Groebner, *Who Are You?*, 171.

38. "Carrying a *passeport*, an authorized, sealed document furnishing personal details about their bearer, was now no longer a privilege, but an obligation." Groebner, *Who Are You?*, 175,

39. Maurice Hartoy, *Histoire du passeport français, depuis l'antiquité jusqu'à nos jours: Histoire Législative et doctrinale, analyse et critique, renseignements pratiques* (Paris: Champion, 1937), 34–35.

40. Groebner, *Who Are You?*, 172.

41. Groebner, *Who Are You?*, 172.

42. Groebner, *Who Are You?*, 175.

43. Joseph Byrne, *Encyclopedia of the Black Death* (Santa Barbara, CA: ABC-CLIO, 2012), 37.

44. Byrne, *Encyclopedia of Black Death*, 37–38. See also Carlo Cipolla, *Public Health and the Medical Profession in the Renaissance* (Cambridge: Cambridge University Press, 1976); and Ann Carmichael, *Plague and the Poor in Renaissance Florence* (Cambridge: Cambridge University Press, 1986), 116.

45. Groebner, *Who Are You?*, 178–179.

46. Groebner, *Who Are You?*, 179.

47. Frank Aydelotte, *Elizabethan Rogues and Vagabonds* (Oxford: Clarendon Press, 1913). See also A. L. Beier, *Masterless Men: The Vagrancy Problem in England 1560–1640* (London: Methuen, 1985).

48. Cited by Groebner, *Who Are You?*, 191.

49. Groebner, *Who Are You?*, 191.

50. Groebner, *Who Are You?*, 200.

51. All cited in Groebner, *Who Are You?*, 201.

52. Bodin, *Six Livres*, book VI, chapter 1.

53. Michel Foucault, *Discipline and Punish: The Birth of the Prison*, trans. Alan Sheridan (New York: Pantheon Books, 1977), 147. My italics.

54. Foucault, *Discipline and Punish*, 170.

55. Foucault, *Discipline and Punish*, 148. My italics.

56. Foucault, *Discipline and Punish*, 172.

57. Emilia Jamroziak and Karen Stöber, *Monasteries on the Borders of Medieval Europe: Conflict and Cultural Interaction* (Turnhout: Brepols, 2013), 2.

58. Lewis Mumford, *The City in History: Its Origins, Its Transformations, and Its Prospects* (New York: Harcourt, Brace & World, 1961), 246.

59. Mumford, *City in History*, 247.

60. Cited in Mumford, *City in History*, 247. See also Bernard and Jean Mabillon, *Opera Omnia* (Paris: Apud Gaume Fratres, 1839), 663.

61. Augustine, *The Monastic Rules* (Hyde Park, NY: New City Press, 2004), chapter 1.

62. Saint Anthony, *Sermons for Sundays and Festivals* (Padova: Messaggero di Sant'Antonio, 2007).

63. John 14:2.

64. Augustine, *Political Writings*, ed. E. M. Atkins and Robert Dodaro (Cambridge: Cambridge University Press, 2001), 123–124.

65. Foucault, *Discipline and Punish*, 221.

66. Foucault, *Discipline and Punish*, 143.

67. Darlene Hedstrom, "The Geography of the Monastic Cell in Early Egyptian Monastic Literature," *Church History* 78.4 (2009): 767.

68. Hedstrom, "Geography of Monastic Cell," 380.

69. Robert Markus, *The End of Ancient Christianity* (Cambridge: Cambridge University Press, 1990), 71.

70. Hedstrom, "Geography of Monastic Cell," 385.

71. Cited in Hedstrom, "Geography of Monastic Cell," 383.

72. Anderson, *Passages*, 134.

73. Backman, *Worlds of Medieval Europe*, 73.

74. "While the dominant strand of monasticism came from the Mediterranean, another strand came from the Celtic people of, what is today, northwestern France and the British Isles. For the Celts, monasticism offered an escape from rural misery and clan warfare. By 600 CE Ireland had well over a hundred thriving monasteries and abbeys—the most fully monasticized region in Europe." Backman, *Worlds of Medieval Europe*, 76.

75. This social legislation is financed by the renounced wealth of its monks.

76. Since Saint Pachomius, the "father of cenobitic monasticism," also spent time in the Roman army, Marilyn Dunn suggests that this cellular structure may have even been partially inspired by Roman army barracks. Marilyn Dunn, "The Development of Communal Life," in *The Emergence of Monasticism: From the Desert Fathers to the Early Middle Ages* (Malden, MA: Blackwell, 2000), 29.

77. For floor plans and additional details of the cellular structure of Carthusian charterhouses see Roger Palmer, *English Monasteries in the Middle Ages: An Outline of Monastic Architecture and Custom from the Conquest to the Suppression* (London: Constable, 1930).

78. *Codex Theodosianus*, ed. T. Mommsen and P. Meyer (Berlin: Weidmann, 1905), 9.3.1.

79. Edward Peters, "Prison before the Prison: The Ancient and Medieval Worlds," in *The Oxford History of the Prison: The Practice of Punishment in Western Society*, ed. Norval Morris and David J. Rothman (New York: Oxford University Press, 1995), 3–43.

80. J. M. Ferrante, "Images of the Cloister: Haven or Prison," *Mediaevalia* 12 (1989 for 1986): 57–66.

81. Guy Geltner, "Medieval Prisons: Between Myth and Reality, Hell and Purgatory," *History Compass* 4 (2006): 5.

82. Foucault, *Discipline and Punish*, 238.

83. Cited in Foucault, *Discipline and Punish*, 238.

84. J. B. Given, *Inquisition and Medieval Society: Power, Discipline, and Resistance in Languedoc* (Ithaca, NY: Cornell University Press, 1997).

85. Geltner, "Medieval Prisons," 10.

86. Given's work does much to correct Foucault's omission of the power of the medieval prisons and their distinctly pre-Enlightenment origins. See Given, *Inquisition and Medieval Society*.

87. Saint Benedictine, *Rule of Saint Benedict*, chapter 36: "On the Sick."

88. See G. B. Risse, *Mending Bodies, Saving Souls: A History of Hospitals* (New York: Oxford University Press, 1999).

89. Benedictine, *Rule of Saint Benedict*, chapter 36.

90. Roy Porter, *The Greatest Benefit to Mankind: A Medical History of Humanity* (New York: Norton, 1997), 127–128.

91. Foucault, *Discipline and Punish*, 161.

92. Foucault, *Discipline and Punish*, 149. Foucault argues that the main difference between medieval and eighteenth-century discipline was that medieval discipline had a negative function, "not to waste time," whereas by the eighteenth century it has a more positive function, "to become more productive" (154). While all the other basic characteristics are shared between medieval and eighteenth-century disciplinary power, "productivity" is not, because it is not, I argue, an aspect of juridical kinopower, which ends approximately in the seventeenth century. Productivity is an aspect of a different form of power: economic kinopower. What Foucault defines as "disciplinary power" is actually the historical transition or admixture between the decline of juridical kinopower and the rise of economic kinopower that occurs in the eighteenth century.

93. Foucault, *Discipline and Punish*, 150.

94. See John Scattergood, "Writing the Clock: The Reconstruction of Time in the Late Middle Ages," *European Review* 11.4 (2003): 453–474.

95. See Carmichael, *Plague and the Poor*, 108–126.

96. Byrne, *Encyclopedia of Black Death*, 305.

97. Byrne, *Encyclopedia of Black Death*, 305.

98. Byrne, *Encyclopedia of Black Death*, 326.

99. Byrne, *Encyclopedia of Black Death*, 325.

100. *Orders Conceived and Published by the Lord Major and Aldermen of the City of London, Concerning the Infection of the Plague* (London: Printed by James Flesher, 1665).

101. Byrne, *Encyclopedia of Black Death*, 326.

102. Byrne, *Encyclopedia of Black Death*, 208.

103. Byrne, *Encyclopedia of Black Death*, 210.

CHAPTER 5

1. For a closer study of these migratory figures see Thomas Nail, *The Figure of the Migrant* (Stanford: Stanford University Press, 2015), 145–178.

2. Giuliano Procacci provides the most convincing refutation of Pirenne and Sweezy's immobility thesis. "To assert that feudalism was an immobile historical formation, not itself capable of internal development but merely susceptible to external influence is precisely to pose the problem in terms of random contingency and not in terms of dialectical interaction." Giuliano Procacci, "A Survey of the Debate," *Società* 11 (1955): 129.

3. Eric Hobsbawm, "The General Crisis of the European Economy in the 17th Century," *Past and Present* 5.1 (1954): 33–53.

4. "A great number of peasants were driven into vagabondage or forced to become city plebeians by the destruction of their domiciles and the devastation of their fields in addition to the general disorder." Friedrich Engels, *The Peasant War in Germany*, trans. Moissaye Olgin (New York: International Publishers, 1966), 147.

5. Jacques Turgot, "Eloge de Vincent de Gournay," *Mercure*, August 1759, reprinted in Anne-Robert-Jacques Turgot, *Oeuvres De Turgot*, vol. 1 (Paris: Guillaumin, 1844), 288; Marquis de Mirabeau, *Philosophie rurale*, 1763 and *Ephémérides du Citoyen*, 1767.

6. Giorgio Agamben, *The Kingdom and the Glory: For a Theological Genealogy of Economy and Government*, trans. Lorenzo Chiesa and Matteo Mandarini (Stanford: Stanford University Press, 2011), 17.

7. See Giorgio Agamben, "Movement," transcribed and translated by Arianna Bove, http://www.generation-online.org/p/fpagamben3.htm; and Ernst Junger, "Total Mobilization," in *The Heidegger Controversy: A Critical Reader*, ed. Richard Wolin (Cambridge, MA: MIT Press, 1993).

8. Michel Foucault, *Security, Territory, Population: Lectures at the Collège de France, 1977–78*, trans. Alessandro Fontana (Basingstoke: Palgrave Macmillan, 2007), 20.

9. Cited in Dean Wilson, *The Beat: Policing a Victorian City* (Beaconsfield, Australia: Circa, 2006), 50.

10. "The mechanized movements of the body during drill, parade and the beat itself were entrenched in the officers, so that wearing plain clothes or any other attempts to conceal their identity could not erase the signature of uniformed service. Detective Inspector Andrew Lansdowne observed in his memoirs that the common definition of a police detective was one who 'marches along the streets with the measured tread of a bobby, warning all thieves of his approach, and making it clear to every criminal that a detective is near.' Thus, their physique, which displayed attributes essential to law enforcement, could also impair that very same goal." Haia Shpayer-Makov, "Shedding the Uniform and Acquiring a New Masculine Image: The Case of the Late-Victorian and Edwardian English Police Detective," in *A History of Police and Masculinities, 1700–2010*, ed. David G. Barrie and Susan Broomhall (Abingdon, Oxon: Routledge, 2012), 147.

11. "Mainly ex-soldiers . . . patrolled the main streets of the centre of the metropolis between 9 a.m. and 7 p.m." Clive Emsley, *Crime and Society in England, 1750–1900* (London: Longman, 1987), 229. "In France, exceptionally, the main roads were patrolled by a centralized, royal constabulary, the Maréchaussée. Armed and accoutered like cavalrymen, the cavaliers of the Maréchaussée were ex-soldiers and the institution had been established originally to police the royal armies." Clive Emsley, *Crime, Police, and Penal Policy: European Experiences, 1750–1940* (Oxford: Oxford University Press, 2007), 66.

12. Alan Williams, *The Police of Paris, 1718–1789* (Baton Rouge: Louisiana State University Press, 1979), 189.

13. Williams, *Police of Paris*, 189–190.

14. Jeremy Bentham, *An Introduction to the Principles of Morals and Legislation* (New York: Hafner, 1948), 112.

15. Foucault, *Discipline and Punish: The Birth of the Prison*, trans. Alan Sheridan (New York: Vintage, 1977), 286.

16. "When . . . people find no work and will not rebel against society, what remains for them but to beg? And surely no one can wonder at the great army of beggars, most of them able-bodied men, with whom the police carries on perpetual war." Karl Marx and Friedrich Engels, *Karl Marx, Frederick Engels*, vol. 4 (London: Lawrence & Wishart, 2014), 385.

17. The city of Berlin is divided into 118 precincts (*Reviere*), each under the supervision of a lieutenant. For the purposes of discipline and control, the precincts are grouped into thirteen districts (*Hooptmannschaften*), a captain in charge of each, and each containing from eight to ten precincts. See Raymond Fosdick, *European Police Systems* (Montclair: Patterson Smith, 1969), 115.

18. Jacques Rancière, *Dissensus: On Politics and Aesthetics*, trans. Steve Corcoran (London: Continuum, 2010), 36. My italics.

19. Criminality is not a new phenomenon, but modern policing creates a new type of border between legality and criminality.

20. Mark Neocleous, *The Fabrication of Social Order: A Critical Theory of Police Power* (London: Pluto Press, 2000), 82.

21. In the most systematic study of the Paris police before the revolution, Alan Williams concludes that the provision of security and the maintenance of order were the overriding concerns of the police force, with deterrent patrol as its main activity. See Williams, *Police of Paris*, 202; see also table 2, 68. "This is in part confirmed by Pierre Clément, in one of the earliest historical studies of the Old Regime police: crime and street disorders are cited as prime concerns, with deterrent patrol as the main police activity. In his memoir, Lenoir declares that crime control is the 'most immense and most important' of all police functions." Jean-Paul Brodeur, *The Policing Web* (Oxford: Oxford University Press, 2010), 10.

22. Cited in Neocleous, *Fabrication of Social Order*, 6.

23. Thomas Hobbes, *Leviathan*, ed. Richard Tuck (Cambridge: Cambridge University Press, 1991), 128.

24. Foucault, *Security, Territory, Population*, 98.

25. Foucault, *Security, Territory, Population*, 313. My italics.

26. Neocleous, *Fabrication of Social Order*, 3.

27. Justi, *Staatswirtshaft* and *Grundsatze der policeywissenschaft*, both cited in W. Small, *The Cameralists: The Pioneers of German Social Polity* (Kitchener, ON: Batoche, 2001), 307, 366, 437.

28. Neocleous, *Fabrication of Social Order*, 13.

29. See Francçois Quesnay (1694–1774), *Maximes générales du gouvemement économique d'un royaume agricole*, in *Physiocratie ou constitution naturelle du gouvernement le plus au humain*, ed. Pierre Samuel Du Pont de Nemours (Paris: Merlin, 1768), 99–122; republished in *François Quesnay et la physiocratie*, Vol 2 (Paris: Institut National d'Études Demographiques), 949–976.

30. Nicolas de la Mare, *Traité de la police* (Paris: Chez M. Brunet, 1719), 2.

31. Jean-Charles-Pierre Lenoir, *Ordonnance de M. Le Lieutenant Général De Police* (Paris: De l'Imprimerie royale, 1779), 34.

32. Foucault, *Security, Territory, Population*, 314–315.

33. Charles de Secondat baron de Montesquieu, *The Spirit of Laws*, trans. Thomas Nugent, vol. 2 (New York: Bell, 1892), book 26, 168.

34. Klaus Mladek, *Police Forces: A Cultural History of an Institution* (New York: Palgrave Macmillan, 2007), 51. My italics.

35. Foucault, *Security, Territory, Population*, 344–348.

36. See Immanuel Kant, "What Is Enlightenment?" in *Perpetual Peace and Other Essays on Politics, History, and Morals*, trans. Ted Humphrey (Indianapolis: Hackett, 1983).

37. "It will be necessary to arouse, to facilitate, and to *laisser faire*, in other words to manage and no longer to control through rules and regulations." Foucault, *Security, Territory, Population*, 352.

38. Montesquieu, *The Spirit of Laws*, book 12.

39. Günther Heinrich von Berg, *Handbuch des Teutschen Policeyrechts*, 2nd ed., vol. 1 (Hannover: Hahn, 1802), 13.

40. Karl Marx and Frederick Engels, "On Freedom of the Press, Proceedings of the Sixth Rhine Province Assembly" (1842), in *Collected Works*, vol. 1 (London: Lawrence & Wishart, 1975), 163.

41. Marx and Engels, "Freedom of the Press," 163.

42. Edwin Chadwick, "Preventive Police," *London Review*, 1829, 255.

43. Brodeur, *The Policing Web*, 68.

44. "Constables were to prevent crime through regular patrols that would make the criminals aware they were being watched and reassure law-abiding citizens that order was being maintained." Wilson, *The Beat*, 44.

45. "However, to project the necessary awe and clout, the officer had to have a physique that communicated the might possessed by the police and underscored their role in society. Police officers were expected to be strong in order to overpower persons if an offense was committed, to convey an image of manliness to deter potential offenders, and to be conspicuous in case help was needed." Shpayer-Makov, "Shedding the Uniform," 142.

46. "The posture and regulated gait of the constable were complemented by the system of beat patrol, which envisaged individual constables moving at a regular pace through space. The regularity and uniformity of the constable on the beat would be projected out onto the space through which he moved, police authorities hoped, bringing about control over public space through steady surveillance and physical example." Dean Wilson, "'Well-Set-Up Men': Respectable Masculinity and Police Organizational Culture in Melbourne 1853–c. 1920," in Barrie and Broomhall, *History of Police*, 167.

47. "Devised by a former officer of the London Metropolitan Police, police beats were introduced to Melbourne in 1854 and divided the city into discrete units to provide round-the-clock surveillance. The regularity of spatial division was to complement the regulated body of the constable. Beats were revised in 1859 including detailed maps of individual beats compiled by Superintendent Freeman, which he claimed 'relate with minuteness the manner in which they should be worked.' Individual beats were timed, the superintendent having noted where every constable would be at ten-minute intervals. By 1888 two miles per hour was assessed as the correct walking pace to observe 'people and places.' The beat system was envisaged as a giant outdoor incarnation of Bentham's panopticon—a massive vision-machine in motion constructed from a multitude of human moving parts." Wilson, "Well-Set-Up Men," 167.

48. "A massive vision-machine in motion constructed from a multitude of human moving parts." Wilson, "Well-Set-Up Men," 167.

49. "The beat system, in combination with the hierarchical and bureaucratic structure of the police organization, situated the average foot constable within a strict disciplinary regime . . . what is of significance here is the functioning of the beat system as a kind of internal panopticon which monitored not only the urban population but the police themselves. Experiments had already been trialed in the early 1850's to ensure constables patrolled their beats with regularity." Wilson, *The Beat*, 23–24.

50. "At present in the suburbs of the Metropolis the police patrol singly at the rate of three miles an hour, and the present arrangement as to single patrol is that the policemen shall pass every part of his beat once in a quarter of an hour. The defect of this arrangement is that depredators calculate upon the opportunities afforded to them during this quarter of an hour, and arrange for it; they watch for the approach of the patrol, and may hear his footfall." Edwin Chadwick, *The Health of Nations* (London: Longmans, 1965), 434–435. "A perfect knowledge is obtained every evening of the different routes and situations of the patroles:—they are narrowly watched, and their vigilance (wherever they are vigilant) is in too many instances defeated." Patrick Colquhoun, *A Treatise on the Police of the Metropolis* (London: J. Mawman, 1800), chapter 5, 222.

51. "Those who administer public power must have the power and the right to keep watch over the citizens' conduct; they have police power and police legislation." Johann Gottlieb Fichte, *Foundations of Natural Right*, trans. Michael Baur, ed. Frederick Neuhouser (Cambridge: Cambridge University Press, 2000), 146.

52. He watches rather than he acts and the more he watches and the less he needs to act. See Joseph Michel Antoine Servan, *Discours sur l'administration de la justice criminelle* (A Genève, 1767), 17. Cited by Brodeur, *The Policing Web*, 57.

53. Servan, *Discours*, 23.

54. Wilson, *The Beat*, 50.

55. "London's newly-formed police force of 1829 was distinguished from the old watch system by the introduction of an around-the-clock patrol, designed to prevent crime rather than simply arrest offenders after the fact. ... A regular uniformed police beat would make the 'criminal class' aware that they were under surveillance, while simultaneously deterring potential offenders from committing criminal acts." Wilson, *The Beat*, 45.

56. "Watch-houses are now placed at convenient distances all over the Metropolis; where a parochial constable attends, in rotation, every night, to receive disorderly and criminal persons, and to carry them before a Magistrate next morning.— In each watch-house also (in case of fire) the names of the turn-cocks, and the places where engines are kept, are to be found. This circumstance is mentioned for the information of strangers unacquainted with the Police of the Metropolis; to whom it is recommended, in case of fire, or any accident or disturbance requiring the assistance of the Civil Power, to apply immediately to the Officer of the night, at the nearest watch-house, or to the watchmen on the beat." Colquhoun, *Treatise on the Police*, 1215.

57. "To establish a Correspondence with the Magistrates in Town and Country, so as to be able more effectually to watch the motions of all suspected persons; with a view to quick and immediate detection; and to interpose such embarrassments in the way of every class of offenders, as may diminish crimes by increasing the risk of detection: All this, under circumstances where a centre-point would be formed, and the general affairs of the Police conducted with method and regularity:— where Magistrates would find assistance and information; where the greater offenses, such as the Coinage of base Money, and Lottery Insurances, would be traced to their source." Colquhoun, *Treatise on the Police*, 80.

58. *Commission into the State of the Melbourne Police*, 1855, 11. Cited in Wilson, *The Beat*, 50.

59. "How could rectitude possibly fear and hate the eye of such watchfulness?" Fichte, *Foundations of Natural Right*, 263.

60. Many police historians and theorists have drawn on Bentham's ideas to explain policing. Brodeur writes, "The main instrument of prevention was surveillance. In his eulogy of d'Argenson, Fontenelle gave an early expression to the Benthamian strategy of panoptic surveillance when he wrote that one of the functions of the police chief magistrate was "to be present everywhere without being seen." Brodeur, *The Policing Web*, 57. "The beat system was envisaged as a giant outdoor incarnation of Bentham's panopticon—a massive vision-machine in motion constructed from a multitude of human moving parts." Wilson, "Well-Set-Up Men," 167. "There is an obvious link between the police patrol and the disciplinary society, with the policeman as 'the personification of panopticism.' The very idea of patrol as a mechanism of crime prevention was that criminals would be deterred because they never knew whether or not a watchman or later a police officer might

be approaching, and that there was always one within easy reach should anyone call for assistance." F. M. Dodsworth, "The Idea of Police in Eighteenth-Century England: Discipline, Reformation, Superintendence, c. 1780–1800," *Journal of the History of Ideas* 69.4 (2008): 583–604, 594-595. "Paris had by one count 8,500 riots during the eighteenth century. In this scenario, the CP [*commissaire de police*] becomes something like a guard in Jeremy Bentham's Panopticon prison (or hospital, hospice, or school), representing 'the architecture of surveillance,' though without walls, which would make unnecessary vigilant, aggressive policing." John Merriman, *Police Stories: Building the French State, 1815–1851* (New York: Oxford University Press, 2006), 11.

61. Foucault, *Discipline and Punish*, 214.
62. "The practices employed by the functionaries of the criminal justice systems to achieve their aims were also similar: patrols, surveillance, registration, the collection of information, incarceration, and so forth." Emsley, *Crime, Police*, 273.
63. Emsley, *Crime, Police*, 131.
64. Wilson, "Well-Set-Up Men," 166.
65. Wilson, *The Beat*, 51.
66. Lenoir, *Ordonnance*, 66.
67. Lenoir, *Ordonnance*, 68–69.
68. Cited in Wilson, *The Beat*, 53. *Regulations*, 1877, 28.
69. Wilson, *The Beat*, 51.
70. Chadwick, *The Health of Nations*, 203.
71. Emsley, *Crime, Police*, 120.
72. Emsley, *Crime, Police*, 118.
73. Chadwick, "Preventative Policing," 282.
74. Fosdick, *European Police Systems*, 356.
75. Fosdick, *European Police Systems*, 348.
76. Fosdick, *European Police Systems*, 316.
77. Fosdick, *European Police Systems*, 280–281.
78. Foucault, *Security, Territory, Population*, 315.
79. "Napoleon wanted facts—facts about agriculture, the economy in general, the population, and what the population was thinking and doing. The various police institutions were one source for such information, particularly with reference to the movement of people and to popular opinion." Emsley, *Crime, Police*, 118.
80. Foucault, *Security, Territory, Population*, 326.
81. Foucault, *Security, Territory, Population*, 335.
82. Hobbes, *Leviathan: A Critical Edition*, ed. G. A. J. Rogers and Karl Schuhmann (London: Continuum, 2005), 200.
83. Jean-Jacques Rousseau, *The Social Contract and Discourses*, trans. G. D. H. Cole (London: J. M. Dent & Sons, 1920), 252.
84. Hobbes, *Leviathan*, 262.
85. Edwin Chadwick, *On the Evils of Disunity in Central and Local Administration* (London: Longmans, Green, 1885), 95.
86. Clive Emsley, *The English Police: A Political and Social History* (Hemel Hempstead: Harvester Wheatsheaf, 1991), 57.
87. David Garrioch, "The Paternal Government of Men: The Self-Image and Action of the Paris Police in the Eighteenth Century," in Barrie and Broom, *History of Police*, 38.
88. Cited in Charles Clarkson and J. H. Richardson, *Police!* (London: Field and Tuer, 1889), 3.

89. Emsley, *Crime, Police*, 66.

90. Didier Truchet, *Le droit public* (Paris: Presses universitaires de France, 2003).

91. Cited in Paul Virilio, *Speed and Politics: An Essay on Dromology* (New York: Columbia University Press, 1986).43.

92. Cited in Emsley, *Crime, Police*, 110–111.

93. Fichte, *Foundations of Natural Right*, 255.

94. Foucault, *Security, Territory, Population*, 18.

95. James C. Scott, *Seeing Like a State: How Certain Schemes to Improve the Human Condition Have Failed* (New Haven: Yale University Press, 1998), 61.

96. Montesquieu, *Spirit of the Laws*, chapter xxiv.

97. Chadwick, "Preventative Policing," 274.

98. Chadwick, *The Health of Nations*, 435.

99. Cited in Wilson, *The Beat*, 75.

100. Lenoir, *Ordonnance*, 53.

101. Wilson, *The Beat*, xvi.

102. "The move-on law, a combination of council regulation and the *Police Offences Act of 1865*, subsequently became a staple piece of legislation for policing the city." Wilson, *The Beat*, 62.

103. Cited in Wilson, *The Beat*, 62.

104. Cited in Wilson, *The Beat*, 62.

105. E. P. Thompson, *The Making of the English Working Class* (New York: Vintage, 1966).

106. Mladek, *Police Forces*, 257.

107. Rancière, *Dissensus*, 37.

108. Servan, *Discours*, 18–19.

109. Lenoir, *Ordonnance*, 267.

110. Jeremy Bentham, *A Manual of Political Economy* (n.p.: n.p., 1800), 40, http://soc-serv.mcmaster.ca/econ/ugcm/3ll3/bentham/manualpoliticaleconomy.pdf.

111. Cited in Wilson, *The Beat*, 64.

112. Brodeur, *The Policing Web*, 57.

113. Fichte, *Foundations of Natural Right*, 258.

114. "The right of association and public meeting.—By the decrees of July 28, to August 2, 1848, the clubs are subjected to a mass of police regulations, denying them almost every liberty. For instance, they are not allowed to pass resolutions in a legislative form, &c. By the same law, all non-political circles and private re-unions are thrown entirely under the supervision and caprice of the police." Karl Marx and Friedrich Engels, *Karl Marx, Frederick Engels: Collected Works* , vol. 10, (New York: International Publishers, 1975), 569.

115. "Some senior police officials believed deficiencies in the beat system could be rectified through the increased use of plain-clothes police and the substantial re-organisation of existing police beats. The utility of the plain-clothes patrol was expressed by Inspector Cawsey, who claimed that 'the thief cannot know where the plain clothes man is ... a plain clothes man may pop up at any moment.' Plain-clothes police functioning as 'rovers' were thought to overcome the predictability of the uniformed beat." Wilson, *The Beat*, 71.

116. Neocleous, *Fabrication of Social Order*, 4.

117. "'A man in uniform will hardly ever take a thief' explained Superintendent Andrew McLean to a parliamentary committee some five years after the new police were created. In the same forum, the commissioners of the Metropolitan Police reported an assessment that three-quarters of the 'beggars and felons' apprehended were taken by officers 'in plain clothes.'" Emsley, *Crime, Police*, 110.

118. Lenoir, *Ordonnance*, 154.

119. Brodeur, *The Policing Web*, 52.
120. Emsley, *Crime, Police*, 106.
121. "This idea of the detective's visible autonomy was reflected in practice by his 'right' to plain clothes. The literary detective was also depicted as a renegade: the demarcation from a form of criminal was at times dangerously close. Indeed, at times, the boundaries between whether the detective was a formal law enforcer or law unto himself seemed far from clear." Susan Broomhall and David G. Barrie, introduction to *History of Police*, 15.
122. Fichte, *Foundations of Natural Right*, 263.
123. Lenoir, *Ordonnance*, 110.
124. Saint-Just, *Rapport sur les factions de l'étranger* (Paris: De l'Imprimerie Nationale, 1794).
125. "Concerns from the 1870's with the 'larrikin' problem led police to increasingly prefer surreptitious modes of policing, involving irregular beats and plain-clothes patrols, to detect disorderly conduct in public spaces." Wilson, *The Beat*, 68.
126. Emsley, *Crime and Society*, 225.
127. Thomas Hobbes, *De Cive*, chapter XIII, no. VII. Thomas Hobbes, The English Works of Thomas Hobbes of Malmesbury: Vol. 2, edited by John M. O'Sullivan, and William Molesworth (London: John Bohn, 1840).

CHAPTER 6

1. G. E. Aylmer, "The Meaning and Definition of 'Property' in Seventeenth-Century England," *Past and Present* 86 (February 1980): 87–97.
2. Johann Frederick Fichte, *Foundations of Natural Right*, trans. Michael Baur, ed. Frederick Neuhouser (Cambridge: Cambridge University Press, 2000), 195.
3. Cited by Mark Neocleous, *The Fabrication of Social Order: A Critical Theory of Police Power* (London: Pluto Press, 2000), 39. See also William Blackstone, *Commentaries on the Laws of England*, vol. 4 (London: Dawsons, 1966), 162. Blackstone defines "public police" as involving the citizens conforming to "the rules of propriety, good neighbourhood, and good manners" and being "decent, industrious, and inoffensive in their respective stations."
4. Ellen Wood, *The Origin of Capitalism: A Longer View* (London: Verso, 2002), 101.
5. Colquhoun cited by Neocleous, *Fabrication of Social Order*, 53.
6. Fichte, *Foundations of Natural Right*, 183.
7. Jürgen Habermas, *The Structural Transformation of the Public Sphere: An Inquiry into a Category of Bourgeois Society*, trans. Thomas Burger (Cambridge, MA: MIT Press, 1989), 110.
8. See David Hume, *A Treatise of Human Nature*, Part II, section VI, no. I; Georg Hegel, *Outlines of the Philosophy of Right*, trans. and Stephen Houlgate (Oxford: Oxford University Press, 2008), 61.
9. Colin Gordon, "Governmental Rationality: An Introduction," in *The Foucault Effect: Studies in Governmentality: with Two Lectures by and an Interview with Michel Foucault*, ed. Graham Burchell, Colin Gordon, and Peter Miller (Chicago: University of Chicago Press, 1991), 31.
10. Hegel, Lectures of 1819–1820, cited in Georg Hegel, *Elements of the Philosophy of Right*, ed. Allen Wood (Cambridge: Cambridge University Press, 1991), 453.
11. Hegel, *Elements*, paragraph, 244.
12. Neocleous, *Fabrication of Social Order*, 81.
13. Patrick Colquhoun, *A Treatise on the Police of the Metropolis* (London: J. Mawman, 1800), 94–95.

14. Alexander Diener and Joshua Hagen, *Borders: A Very Short Introduction* (New York: Oxford University Press, 2012), 40.

15. Diener and Hagen, *Borders*, 41.

16. E. J. Hobsbawm, *Nations and Nationalism since 1780: Programme, Myth, Reality* (Cambridge: Cambridge University Press, 1990), 80.

17. See Hobsbawm, *Nations and Nationalism*.

18. Diener and Hagen, *Borders*, 42.

19. Diener and Hagen, *Borders*, 43.

20. Diener and Hagen, *Borders*, 43.

21. Georges Lefebvre, *The French Revolution from 1793 to 1799*, trans. John Hall Stewart and James Friguglietti (London: Routledge, 1962), 295.

22. John Torpey, *The Invention of the Passport: Surveillance, Citizenship and the State* (Cambridge: Cambridge University Press, 2000), 2.

23. On the "departmentalization" of France, see Isser Woloch, *The New Regime: Transformations of the French Civic Order, 1789–1820s* (New York: Norton, 1994), 27. See also Isser Woloch, "Napoleonic Conscription: State Power and Civil Society," *Past and Present* 111 (1986): 101–129.

24. Torpey, *Invention of the Passport*, 3.

25. See Barry Hindess, "Divide and Rule: The International Character of Modern Citizenship," *European Journal of Social Theory* 1.1 (1998): 57–70.

26. Torpey, *Invention of the Passport*, 78.

27. See Torpey, *Invention of the Passport*, especially 53.

28. Cited in Torpey, *Invention of the Passport*, 38. "In an article of 22 July 1854 in *La Lumiere* (page 156), one Richebourg claims to have introduced the idea of the passport photograph."

29. Torpey, *Invention of the Passport*, 38.

30. Daniel Headrick, *When Information Came of Age: Technologies of Knowledge in the Age of Reason and Revolution, 1700–1850* (Oxford: Oxford University Press, 2000), 83.

31. Quetelet, "Recherches sur le penchant au crime aux différens âges," *Nouveaux mémoires de l'Académie royale des Sciences et Belles-Lettres de Bruxelles*, 1832, 1.

32. Benedict Anderson, *Imagined Communities: Reflections on the Origin and Spread of Nationalism* (London: Verso, 1991), 143.

33. Michel Foucault, *Security, Territory, Population: Lectures at the Collège de France, 1977–78*, ed. and trans. Michel Senellart, François Ewald, and Alessandro Fontana (Basingstoke: Palgrave Macmillan, 2007), 106.

34. Hobsbawm, *Nations and Nationalism*, 97.

35. "This concern with immigrants and their impact on the total population was reflected again in the 1890 census, in the more elaborate maps, charts, and sections on the foreign-born population. Maps and tables also showed the distribution in the United States of 'Natives of the Germanic Nations' and of 'Greco-Latins.' . . . These reports suggest the continuing concerns with preserving a national identity as a basically northern European people." Clara Rodriguez, *Changing Race: Latinos, the Census, and the History of Ethnicity in the United States* (New York: New York University Press, 2000), 79.

36. Torpey, *Invention of the Passport*, 34.

37. Torpey, *Invention of the Passport*, 32.

38. Grégoire Chamayou, *Manhunts: A Philosophical History* (Princeton, NJ: Princeton University Press, 2012), 81.

39. Torpey, *Invention of the Passport*, 47.

40. Ian Hacking, *The Taming of Chance* (Cambridge: Cambridge University Press, 1990), 16–26; Hobsbawm, *Nations and Nationalism*, 81.

41. Cited in Kathrin Levitan, *A Cultural History of the British Census: Envisioning the Multitude in the Nineteenth Century* (New York: Palgrave Macmillan, 2011), 17.

42. Levitan, *British Census*, 17–18.

43. Levitan, *British Census*, 17–18.

44. Levitan, *British Census*, 19.

45. Hacking, *The Taming of Chance*, 18.

46. Levitan, *British Census*, 29.

47. Levitan, *British Census*, 28 n. 90.

48. Olivier Razac, *Barbed Wire: A Political History* (New York: New Press, 2002), 12.

49. Razac, *Barbed Wire*, 95.

50. Walter P. Webb, cited in Claude Folhen, *La vie quotidienne au Far-West 1860–1870* (Hachette: Literature, 1974), 86.

51. Letter of Jefferson to William Henry Harrison, February 27, 1803, cited in Nelcya Delanoe, *L'entaille rouge: Des terres indiennes à la démocratie américaine, 1776–1996* (Paris: Albin Michel, 1996), 54.

52. Delanoe, *L'entaille rouge*, 72.

53. Robert Antelme, *L'espece humaine* (Paris: Gallimard, 1957), 34.

54. Stanislas Kozak, cited in Marcel Ruby, *Le livre de la deportation* (Paris: Robert Laffont, 1995), 379.

55. For a detailed account of this process see Hannah Arendt, *The Origins of Totalitarianism* (New York: Harcourt, 1976), 267–302.

56. Aleksandr Solzhenitsyn, *The Gulag Archipelago*, trans. Thomas P. Whitney, vol. 3 (New York: Harper & Row, 1978), 527.

57. Razac, *Barbed Wire*, 99–114.

58. Razac, *Barbed Wire*, 99–114.

59. On this thesis I follow the work of Hacking, *The Taming of Chance* and Headrick, *When Information Came of Age*.

60. Headrick, *When Information Came of Age*, 8.

61. Hacking, *The Taming of Chance*.

62. Headrick, *When Information Came of Age*, 1–14.

63. Headrick, *When Information Came of Age*, 17.

64. Information borders are divisions or space-time bits taken from continuous social flows. Historically, the process of modern social division begins with large and less numerous groupings of data: census, births, deaths, marriages, and so on. But over the course of this period, the data becomes smaller and more numerous. More and more microdivisions are made into the continuity of social flows: biometric data, daily patterns of movement, consumption patterns, down to the most minute and subtle eye motions tracked on computer screens. However, we should not confuse high-definition digital images, sounds, RFID points, and constant video surveillance for the kinetic "continuity" of "individuals." Information and data only appear "continuous" because there is so much of it. But the difference between analog and digital remains infinite, just as in statics and fluid dynamics, in the sciences. Upon close enough inspection, digitalization is ontologically pixilated into discrete discontinuous "dividuals." Thus, modern limology does not contrast the "individual" with the "dividual" or the "continuous" with the "discrete": the modern individual is fundamentally kinometric (data in motion). Motion *is* divided motion. Individuals are "in(fo)dividuals" or "kindividuals."

65. Headrick, *When Information Came of Age*, 79.

66. RFIDs are not continuously streams of movement, but simply appear as such because they have many more plotted digitally plotted points in a series—in which a signal is transmitted and returned. See Louise Amoore, *The Politics of Possibility: Risk and Security beyond Probability* (Durham, NC: Duke University Press, 2013), 105–106.
67. Fichte, *Foundations of Natural Right*, 257. Translation modified.
68. Fichte, *Foundations of Natural Right*, 257.
69. Fichte, *Foundations of Natural Right*, 262–263.
70. Fichte, *Foundations of Natural Right*, 257.
71. Fichte, *Foundations of Natural Right*, 258–259.
72. Fichte, *Foundations of Natural Right*, 258–259.
73. Fichte, *Foundations of Natural Right*, 259.
74. Fosdick, *European Police Systems*, 324–325.
75. Grégoire Chamayou, "Fichte's Passport: A Philosophy of the Police," trans. Kieran Aarons, *Theory and Event* 16.2 (2013): 5.
76. Chamayou, "Fichte's Passport," 6.

CHAPTER 7

1. US Immigration, "The Costs and Benefits of Border Security," http://www.usimmigration.com/cost-benefits-border-security.html.
2. Ronald Rael, "Border Wall as Architecture," *Environment and Planning D: Society and Space* 29.3 (2011): 409–420.
3. Craig Glenday, *Guinness World Records 2009* (Random House Digital, 2009), 457.
4. David Bacon, *The Right to Stay Home: How US Policy Drives Mexican Migration* (Boston: Beacon Press, 2013), 11.
5. Joseph Nevins, *Operation Gatekeeper and Beyond: The War on "Illegals" and the Remaking of the U.S.-Mexico Boundary* (New York: Routledge, 2010), 23–24.
6. Nevins, *Operation Gatekeeper*, 18–22.
7. US Customs and Border Protection, "DHS and DOI Sign Agreement for Mitigation of Border Security Impact on the Environment," http://www.cis.org/sites/cis.org/files/articles/2010/border-mitigation.pdf.
8. Congressional Research Service, "Border Security: Barriers along the U.S. International Border," https://www.fas.org/sgp/crs/homesec/RL33659.pdf, 24.
9. Peter Nyers, "Moving Borders: The Politics of Dirt," *Radical Philosophy* 174 (July–August 2012): 4.
10. Jason Beaubien, "Border Fence Yields Showdown at Smuggler's Gulch," National Public Radio, February 6, 2009, http://www.npr.org/templates/story/story.php?storyId=100336089.
11. Nyers, "Moving Borders," 4.
12. In the 1940s Border Patrol officials in Calexico erected a chain-link fence, salvaged from a Japanese American internment camp, along 5.8 miles of the boundary line to prevent illegal immigrant entries. See Kelly Hernandez, *Migra! A History of the U.S. Border Patrol* (Berkeley: University of California Press, 2010), 130; Rachel St. John, *Line in the Sand: A History of the Western U.S.-Mexico Border* (Princeton, NJ: Princeton University Press, 2011), 204.
13. Mohammad Chaichian, *Empires and Walls: Globalization, Migration, and Colonial Domination* (Leiden: Brill, 2013), 229.
14. Cited in Chaichian, *Empires and Walls*, 230.
15. July 9, 1951, memo from Chief Patrol inspector, El Centro, to district Enforcement officer in Los Angeles (nArA 56084/946A, 9, 59A2034). Cited in Hernandez, *Migra!*, 131 n. 21.

16. Stephanie Simon, "Border-Fence Project Hits a Snag," *Wall Street Journal*, February 4, 2009, http://www.wsj.com/articles/SB123370523066745559.

17. Detention Watch Network, "The Money Trail," http://www.detentionwatchnetwork.org/node/2393.

18. "Only two miles long, the fence did not completely restrict border crossings, but it was a physically distinctive and visually imposing landmark that cut through the heart of Calexico-Mexicali." St. John, *Line in the Sand*, 145.

19. Congressional Research Service, "Border Security," 28.

20. Congressional Research Service, "Border Security," 28.

21. "In the period of 1800–1860, the total income of the United States rose 1,270.4 percent, whereas that of Mexico declined 10.5 percent. This had the effect of drawing Mexico's northern borderlands toward the United States and, as a result, facilitating the goals of those championing U.S. territorial expansionism as it weakened the ties between the population of Mexico's northern states and the country's center." Cited in Nevins, *Operation Gatekeeper*, 21.

22. This is a big claim, but not an incorrect one. See David Bacon, *Illegal People: How Globalization Creates Migration and Criminalizes Immigrants* (Boston: Beacon Press, 2008) and Bacon, *Right to Stay Home*.

23. "In this regard, 'hard' boundaries invite—indeed, they help make inevitable—many of the very transgressions that they exist to repel—whether they be in the form of 'exotic' ideas, illicit commodities, or unwanted peoples." Nevins, *Operation Gatekeeper*, 14.

24. Chacón Akers, Mike Davis, and Julián Cardona, *No One Is Illegal: Fighting Violence and State Repression on the U.S.-Mexico Border* (Chicago: Haymarket Books, 2006), 210.

25. Maria Sacchetii, "The Unforgotten," *Boston Globe*, July 2014, http://www.bostonglobe.com/metro/2014/07/26/students-make-efforts-identify-immigrants-buried-unmarked-graves-near-southwest-border/4iDqnsqHzu9m8N6pPZXffI/story.html.

26. "The 'Funnel Effect' and Recovered Bodies of Unauthorized Migrants Processed," Binational Migration Institute, October 2006, http://bmi.arizona.edu/sites/default/files/The%20Funnel%20Effect%20and%20Recovered%20Bodies.pdf.

27. Hernandez, *Migra!*, 130–131.

28. July 1, 1949, report, "Preliminary Estimate for Lighting of Boundary Fence, installing Protective devices, and Erection of observation Towers at Calexico, san ysidro, and nogales," file 56084/946A, box 9, acc 59A2034 NARA, 1. Cited by Hernandez, *Migra!*

29. "A Continued Humanitarian Crisis at the Border: Undocumented Border Crosser Deaths Recorded by the Pima County Office of the Medical Examiner, 1990–2012," Binational Migration Institute, University of Arizona, June 2013, 11, http://bmi.arizona.edu/sites/default/files/border_deaths_final_web.pdf.

30. "Meanwhile, U.S. officials continued to erect more substantial chain-link fences to channel human movement in more heavily populated areas." St. John, *Line in the Sand*, 204.

31. In addition, interviews conducted with current and former unauthorized migrants in 2009 found that one out of four illegal entrants from Mexico had entered illegally through a port, either hidden in a vehicle or using borrowed or fraudulent documents, and that aliens attempting illegal entry through a POE were half as likely to be apprehended as those crossing between the ports. See Jonathan Hicken, Mollie Cohen, and Jorge Narvaez, "Double Jeopardy: How U.S. Enforcement Policies Shape Tunkaseño Migration," in *Mexican Migration and*

the U.S. Economic Crisis, ed. Wayne A. Cornelius, David FitzGerald, Pedro Lewin Fischer, and Leah Muse-Orlinoff (La Jolla: University of California, San Diego Center for Comparative Immigration Studies, 2010), 60–61.

32. Reece Jones, *Border Walls: Security and the War on Terror in the United States, India, and Israel* (London: Zed Books, 2012), 118.

33. Karla Zablusdovsky, "Hunting Humans: The Americans Taking Immigration into Their Own Hands," *Newsweek*, July 23, 2014, http://www.newsweek.com/2014/08/01/texan-ranchers-hunt-daily-illegal-immigrants-260489.html.

34. Zablusdovsky, "Hunting Humans."

35. Zablusdovsky, "Hunting Humans."

36. The Minutemen were not literally trying to kill migrants in this example, but the turkey metaphor is explicitly related to hunting. Diana Welch, "This Ain't No Picnic: Minutemen on Patrol," *Austin Chronicle*, October 28, 2005, http://www.austinchronicle.com/news/2005-10-28/303805/.

37. Debbie Nathan, "Border Geography and Vigilantes," *NACLA* 34.2 (2000): 5.

38. Rael, "Border Wall as Architecture," 270.

39. Manuel Roig-Franzia, "Mexico Calls US Border Fence Severe Threat to Environment," *Washington Post*, November 16, 2007, www.washingtonpost.com/wp-dyn/content/article/2007/11/15/AR2007111502272.html.

40. See Bacon, *Right to Stay Home*; Bacon, *Illegal People*; Davis, *No One Is Illegal*.

41. Southern Poverty Law Center, "Close to Slavery: Guestworker Programs in the United States," 2013, http://www.splcenter.org/sites/default/files/downloads/publication/SPLC-Close-to-Slavery-2013.pdf.

42. See Bacon, *Right to Stay Home*; Bacon, *Illegal People*; Davis, *No One Is Illegal*.

43. Congressional Research Service, "Border Security: Immigration Enforcement between Ports of Entry," December 31, 2014, http://www.fas.org/sgp/crs/homesec/R42138.pdf, 35.

44. "U.S. border enforcement policy has unintentionally encouraged undocumented migrants to remain in the U.S. for longer periods and settle permanently in this country in much larger numbers." Half of the Mexico-based family members of unauthorized aliens interviewed by the UC, San Diego MMFRP (Mexican Migration Field Research Program) in 2009 indicated that they had a relative who had remained in the United States longer than they had intended because they feared they would be unable to re-enter the United States if they returned home; see Hicken, Cohen, and Narvaez, "Double Jeopardy," 57–58.

45. Detention Watch Network, "The Money Trail."

46. "During the Battle of Agua Prieta in November 1915, a battalion of U.S. soldiers posted in Douglas escorted refugees from the border to a fenced enclosure measuring two hundred by three hundred yards. By November 3 this camp housed 2,700 refugees, mostly women and children. While U.S. officials released "well-to-do" refugees, they continued to detain thousands of restricted immigrants such as indigent refugees and Chinese immigrants barred by U.S. immigration laws." St. John, *Line in the Sand*, 128.

47. See Giorgio Agamben, "What Is a Camp?," in *Means without End: Notes on Politics*, trans. Vincenzo Binetti and Cesare Casarino (Minneapolis: University of Minnesota Press, 2000), 37–48.

48. Kate Linthicum, "Expansion of Adelanto Immigrant Detention Center Underway," *Los Angeles Times*, July 8, 2014, http://www.latimes.com/local/la-me-ff-adelanto-immigration-20140709-story.html.

49. Thomas Nail, "Child Refugees: The New Barbarians," *Pacific Standard*, August 19, 2014.

50. Rob Reynolds, "US Border Sees Influx of Child Migrants," *Al Jazeera*, June 2104, http://www.aljazeera.com/indepth/features/2014/06/us-border-sees-influx-child-migrants-20146167848636918.html.

51. Reynolds, "US Border Sees Influx."

52. See Friedrich Nietzsche, *On the Genealogy of Morals*, trans. Walter Kaufmann (New York: Vintage Books, 1967).

53. Susanna Newbury, "Drawing a Line: Encounters with the U.S.-Mexico Border," KCET Los Angeles, November 13, 2012, http://www.kcet.org/arts/artbound/counties/san-diego/U.S.-Mexico-border-geography.html.

54. Article V, Treaty of Peace, Friendship, Limits and Settlement with the Republic of Mexico (Treaty of Guadalupe Hidalgo). February 2, 1848, United States Statutes at Large 9 (1848): 922, http://avalon.law.yale.edu/19th_century/guadhida.asp#art5.

55. St. John, *Line in the Sand*, 92.

56. Newbury, "Drawing a Line."

57. SueAnne Ware, "Borders, Memory and the Slippage In-Between," in *Fluctuating Borders: Speculations about Memory and Emergence*, ed. Rosalea Monacella and SueAnne Ware (Melbourne: RMIT University Press, 1999), 78–97.

58. Jessica Auchter, *The Politics of Haunting and Memory in International Relations* (New York: Routledge / Taylor & Francis Group, 2014), 101.

59. Associated Press, "5,100 Crosses at Mexico Border Mark Migrant Deaths," *San Diego Union Tribune*, October 30, 2009.

60. Ted Robbins, "U.S.-Mexico Border Crossing Grows More Dangerous," National Public Radio, September, 21, 2009, http://www.npr.org/2009/09/21/113035382/u-s-mexico-border-crossing-grows-more-dangerous.

61. Paul Ingram, "Marchers Call for Justice in Teen's Cross-Border Shooting Death," *Tucson Sentinel*, April 11, 2013, http://www.tucsonsentinel.com/local/report/041113_rodriguez_march/marchers-call-justice-teens-cross-border-shooting-death/.

62. Rev. John Stowe, "A Theological Perspective on Social Justice in the U.S.-Mexico Border Region," in *Social Justice in the U.S.-Mexico Border Region*, ed. Mark Lusk, Kathleen A. Staudt, and Eva Moya (Dordrecht: Springer, 2012), 93.

63. Ricardo Elford, "Discarded Migrants," *CMSM Forum*, Autumn 2010, http://www.archchicago.org/immigration/pdf/Immigration/Discarded_Migrants.pdf.

64. Mark Lusk, Kathleen Staudt, and Eva Moya, "Social Justice at the Border and in the Bordered United States: Implications for Policy and Practice," in Lusk, Staudt, and Moya, *Social Justice*, 263.

CHAPTER 8

1. Tony Payan, *The Three U.S.-Mexico Border Wars: Drugs, Immigration, and Homeland Security* (Westport, CT: Praeger Security International, 2006).

2. Andrew Stiles, "Building a Human Wall on the Border," *National Review*, July 2, 2013, Accessed from http://www.nationalreview.com/article/352539/building-human-wall-border-andrew-stiles.

3. See Joseph Nevins, *Operation Gatekeeper and Beyond: The War on "Illegals" and the Remaking of the U.S.-Mexico Boundary* (New York: Routledge, 2010); Chacón Akers, Mike Davis, and Julián Cardona, *No One Is Illegal: Fighting Violence and State*

Repression on the U.S.-Mexico Border (Chicago: Haymarket Books, 2006); Payan, *U.S.-Mexico Border Wars.*

4. Robert Farley, "Obama Says Border Patrol Has Doubled the Number of Agents since 2004," *politifact.com*, May 10, 2011, http://www.politifact.com/truth-o-meter/statements/2011/may/10/barack-obama/obama-says-border-patrol-has-doubled-number-agents/.

5. Chad C. Haddal, "Border Security: The Role of the U.S. Border Patrol," Congressional Research Service Report, March 3, 2010, http://assets.opencrs.com/rpts/RL32562_20100303.pdf.

6. Lois Lorentzen, *Hidden Lives and Human Rights in the United States: Understanding the Controversies and Tragedies of Undocumented Immigration* (Santa Barbara: Praeger, 2014), 166. See also David Spener, *Clandestine Crossings: Migrants and Coyotes on the Texas-Mexico Border* (Ithaca, NY: Cornell University Press, 2009).

7. Timothy J. Dunn and José Palafox, "Militarization of the Border," in *The Oxford Encyclopedia of Latinos and Latinas in the United States*, ed. Suzanne Oboler and Deena J. González (New York: Oxford University Press, 2005).

8. According to the OED.

9. US Customs and Border Protection, "Border Patrol History," http://www.cbp.gov/border-security/along-us-borders/history.

10. Plutarch, *Moralia*, "How a Man May Become Aware of His Progress in Virtue," in *Plutarch's Complete Works*, vol. 2 (Princeton, NJ: Princeton University Press, 1909), 134.

11. US Customs and Border Protection, "Laredo North Station," http://www.cbp.gov/border-security/along-us-borders/border-patrol-sectors/laredo-sector-texas/laredo-north-station.

12. Dunn and Palafox, "Militarization of the Border."

13. Dunn and Palafox, "Militarization of the Border."

14. José Gonzalez, "The Dynamics of an ICE Raid," https://shusterman.com/pdf/dynamicsofaniceraid.pdf.

15. Margot Mendelson, Shayna Strom, and Michael Wishnie, "Collateral Damage: An Examination of ICE's Fugitive Operations Program," Migration Policy Institute, February 2009, http://www.migrationpolicy.org/research/ice-fugitive-operations-program.

16. "The Obama administration claimed that it was only seeking criminals for deportation, and that participation in the program was voluntary. But when New York state and Massachusetts formally refused to participate, DHS announced that participation in Secure Communities was mandatory and implemented the program everywhere." David Bacon, *The Right to Stay Home: How US Policy Drives Mexican Migration* (Boston: Beacon Press, 2013), 175.

17. Bacon, *Right to Stay Home.*

18. Bacon, *Right to Stay Home*, 147.

19. Bacon, *Right to Stay Home*, 146.

20. National Immigration Forum, "Fact Sheet: Operation Stonegarden," February 17, 2010.

21. Immigration Policy Center, "Falling through the Cracks," http://www.immigrationpolicy.org/just-facts/falling-through-cracks.

22. Marc Lacey, "Border Deployment Will Take Weeks," *New York Times*, August 1, 2010.

23. Chad C. Haddal, Yule Kim, and Michael John Garcia, "Border Security: Barriers along the U.S. International Border," Congressional Research Service Report, March 16, 2009, https://www.fas.org/sgp/crs/homesec/RL33659.pdf.

24. Haddal, Kim, and Garcia, "Border Security."

25. Haddal, Kim, and Garcia, "Border Security."

26. Matthew Carr, *Fortress Europe: Dispatches from a Gated Continent* (New York: New Press, 2012), 233.

27. Mohammad Chaichian, *Empires and Walls: Globalization, Migration, and Colonial Domination* (Leiden: Brill, 2013), 227.

28. Military Surplus Supplier, http://www.calumetindustries.com/index.php?s=aluminum.

29. Telephone conversation with CBP, November 30, 2005. Cited in Haddal, Kim, and Garcia, "Border Security," 22.

30. The drop in apprehensions occurs in tandem with the construction of walled urban areas and increased border patrol numbers. "The total number of agents nationally also grew, from 4,028 in fiscal year 1993 to 21,394 in fiscal year 2012. The greatest rise in the number of Border Patrol agents occurred in the Southwest border sectors, from South Texas to California, from a total of 3,444 agents in fiscal year 1993 to 18,412 in fiscal year 2012. Today, the Border Patrol's Tucson sector has the largest number of agents in the Southwest, 4,176 in fiscal year 2012, compared with 287 in fiscal year 1993. Tucson had 92,639 apprehensions in 1993, a high of 616,346 in 2000 and 120,00 in 2012. The San Diego sector, which reported the most apprehensions in the nation in 1993, 531,689 (El Paso was No. 2), saw its number of arrests drop to 120,000 in 2012." Diana Washington Valdez, "Hold the Line: El Paso Operation Changed Enforcement Method along US-Mexico border," *El Paso Times*, September 29, 2013, http://www.elpasotimes.com/news/ci_24199714/controversial-el-paso-border-patrol-enforcement-operation-succeeded.

31. See Haddal, Kim, and Garcia, "Border Security," ii.

32. Haddal, Kim, and Garcia, "Border Security."

33. Alan Taylor, "On the Border," *Atlantic*, May 6, 2013, http://www.theatlantic.com/photo/2013/05/on-the-border/100510/.

34. M. G. Lay, *Ways of the World: A History of the World's Roads and of the Vehicles That Used Them* (New Brunswick, NJ: Rutgers University Press, 1992), 93.

35. I. S. Griffith and N. D. Zimmerly, "Engineers Support U.S. Border Patrol," *Engineer* 44.3 (2014): 16–19, http://0-search.proquest.com.bianca.penlib.du.edu/docview/1625137769?accountid=14608.

36. Department of Homeland Security, US Customs and Border Protection, US Border Patrol, "Final Environmental Assessment: Baboquivari Road Project along the U.S./Mexico International Border in Arizona," December 2014, http://www.cbp.gov/sites/default/files/documents/FEA%20TCA%20BBQ%2041515.pdf.

37. Krista Schlyer, *Continental Divide: Wildlife, People, and the Border Wall* (College Station: Texas A&M University Press, 2012), 142.

38. United States Department of the Interior Bureau of Land Management Case File # 53512, "Improvement and Construction, Operation, and Maintenance of Proposed All-Weather Road in the El Centro Station Area of Responsibility, U.S. Customs and Border Protection, U.S. Border Patrol, El Centro Sector," December 2013, http://www.blm.gov/pgdata/etc/medialib/blm/ca/pdf/elcentro/nepa/bp.Par.7200.File.dat/blm_fonsidr_westdesert_roadway.pdf.

39. "Operation Gatekeeper: An Investigation into Allegations of Fraud and Misconduct," US Department of Justice, Office of the Inspector General, 1998, http://www.justice.gov/oig/special/9807/gkp19.htm.

40. Richard Misrach, "Border Signs," *California Sunday Magazine*, 2014, https://stories.californiasunday.com/2014-11-02/richard-misrach-border-signs/.

41. Lisa Seghetti, "Border Security: Immigration Inspections at Ports of Entry," Congressional Research Service, January 26, 2015, https://www.fas.org/sgp/crs/homesec/R43356.pdf, 15.
42. Seghetti, "Border Security," 12.
43. Nicholas Genova, "Migrant 'Illegality' and Deportability in Everyday Life," *Annual Review of Anthropology* 31 (2002): 419–447.

CHAPTER 9

1. William Robinson, "The New Global Capitalism and the War on Immigrants," Truth-Out.org, September, 13 2013, http://www.truth-out.org/news/item/18623-the-new-global-capitalism-and-the-war-on-immigrants#; and T. Golash-Boza, "The Immigration Industrial Complex: Why We Enforce Immigration Policies Destined to Fail," *Sociology Compass* 3 (2009): 295–309, http://www.huffingtonpost.com/todd-miller/border-security_b_3580252.html.
2. Laura Sullivan, "Prison Economics Help Drive Ariz. Immigration Law," National Public Radio, October 28, 2010; CRIMINAL: How Lockup Quotas and 'Low-Crime Taxes' Guarantee Profits for Private Prison Corporations," *In the Public Interest*, September 19, 2013, http://www.inthepublicinterest.org/criminal-how-lockup-quotas-and-low-crime-taxes-guarantee-profits-for-private-prison-corporations/.
3. On the creation and usage of the term "illegal" see David Bacon, *Illegal People: How Globalization Creates Migration and Criminalizes Immigrants* (Boston: Beacon Press, 2008); Julie Dowling and Jonathan Inda, *Governing Immigration through Crime: A Reader* (Stanford: Stanford University Press, 2013); Catherine Dauvergne, *Making People Illegal: What Globalization Means for Migration and Law* (Cambridge: Cambridge University Press, 2008).
4. Pew Research Center, "Modes of Entry for the Unauthorized Migrant Population," May 22, 2006, http://www.pewhispanic.org/2006/05/22/modes-of-entry-for-the-unauthorized-migrant-population/.
5. See Ronald Mize and Alicia Swords, *Consuming Mexican Labor: From the Bracero Program to NAFTA* (Toronto: University of Toronto Press, 2011).
6. See David Bacon, *The Right to Stay Home: How US Policy Drives Mexican Migration* (Boston: Beacon Press, 2013), 148–193.
7. The Southern Poverty Law Center, "Close to Slavery: Guestworker Programs in the United States," updated 2013 report, http://www.splcenter.org/sites/default/files/downloads/publication/SPLC-Close-to-Slavery-2013.pdf.
8. Anna Gorman, "Tougher Rules on Policing Illegal Immigrants," *Los Angeles Times*, October 14, 2009.
9. See generally Oversight Hearing on the Executive Office of U.S. Attorneys, House Subcommittee on Commercial and Administrative Law, 110th Congress (2008) (written statement of Heather Williams, First Ass't Fed. Public Defender, Dist. Ariz., Tucson), http://judiciary.house.gov/hearings/pdf/Williams080625.pdf; Federal Criminal Enforcement and Staffing: "How Do the Obama and Bush Administrations Compare?," *Trac Reports*, February 2, 2011, http://trac.syr.edu/tracreports/crim/245/.
10. "At Nearly 100,000 Immigration Prosecutions Reach All Time High," *Trac Reports*, November 25, 2013, http://trac.syr.edu/immigration/reports/336/.
11. American Civil Liberties Union, "Warehoused and Forgotten: Immigrants Trapped in Our Shadow Private Prison System," June 2014, https://www.aclu.org/sites/default/files/assets/060614-aclu-car-reportonline.pdf.

12. The above statistics are all from Associated Press, "Immigrants Face Long Detention, Few Rights: Many Detainees Spend Months or Years in US Detention Centers," NBC News, March 15, 2009, http://www.nbcnews.com/id/29706177/#.Up-sKpF4Gf0.

13. "Of the detainee population of 32,000, 18,690 immigrants have no criminal conviction. More than 400 of those with no criminal record have been incarcerated for at least a year." Department of Homeland Security, Office of Inspector General, "Immigration and Customs Enforcement's Tracking and Transfers of Detainees," 2009, 2, http://www.oig.dhs.gov/assets/Mgmt/OIG_09-41_Mar09.pdf.

14. "Lost in Detention," *PBS Frontline*, aired October 18, 2011, http://video.pbs.org/video/2155873891/.

15. See American Civil Liberties Union, "Warehoused and Forgotten."

16. Spencer S. Hsu and Sylvia Moreno, "Border Policy's Success Strains Resources," *Washington Post*, February 2, 2007, http://www.washingtonpost.com/wp-dyn/content/article/2007/02/01/AR2007020102238.html; Human Rights First, "U.S. Detention of Asylum-Seekers: Seeking Protection, Finding Prison," June 2009, http://www.humanrightsfirst.org/wp-content/uploads/pdf/090429-RP-hrf-asylum-detention-report.pdf.

17. American Civil Liberties Union, "Warehoused and Forgotten," 3.

18. American Civil Liberties Union, "Warehoused and Forgotten."

19. Eric Holder, Attorney General, US Department of Justice, "Remarks at the Annual Meeting of the American Bar Association's House of Delegates," August 12, 2013, http://www.justice.gov/iso/opa/ag/speeches/2013/ag-speech-130812.html.

20. American Civil Liberties Union, "Warehoused and Forgotten."

21. American Civil Liberties Union, "Warehoused and Forgotten," 34.

22. American Civil Liberties Union, "Warehoused and Forgotten," 3.

23. North Carolina Department of Public Safety, "24 Hours in Prison," http://www.doc.state.nc.us/DOP/HOURS24.htm.

24. American Civil Liberties Union, "Warehoused and Forgotten."

CHAPTER 10

1. Jens Manuel Krogstad and Jeffery Passel, "5 Facts about Illegal Immigration in the U.S.," Pew Research Center, November 18, 2014.

2. Data from US Census Bureau 2006, 2010, and 2013 American Community Surveys (ACS), 2000 Decennial Census, and Campbell J. Gibson and Emily Lennon, "Historical Census Statistics on the Foreign-Born Population of the United States: 1850–1990," Working Paper No. 29, US Census Bureau, Washington, DC, February 1999, www.census.gov/population/www/documentation/twps0029/twps0029.html.

3. Krogstad and Passel, "5 Facts."

4. Kristin F. Butcher and Anne Morrison Piehl, "Why Are Immigrants' Incarceration Rates So Low? Evidence on Selective Immigration, Deterrence, and Deportation," NBER Working Paper No. 13229, National Bureau of Economic Research, Cambridge, MA, July, http://www.nber.org/papers/w13229.

5. Anita Khashu, "The Role of Local Police: Striking a Balance between Immigration Enforcement and Civil Liberties," Police Foundation, April 2009, 25.

6. See Khashu, "Role of Local Police." Local police have problems with federal immigration enforcement.

7. Khashu, "Role of Local Police," 21–22.

8. Khashu, "Role of Local Police," 18, 169.

9. Khashu, "Role of Local Police," executive summary.

10. Hispanics constitute approximately 60 percent of all undocumented persons, but well over 90 percent of those subjected to INS enforcement actions are Hispanic. Carmen Joge and Sonia M. Pérez, *The Mainstreaming of Hate: A Report on Latinos and Harassment, Hate Violence, and Law Enforcement Abuse in the '90s* (Washington, DC: National Council of La Raza, 1999), 26, http://www.civilrights.org/publications/justice-on-trial/race.html.

11. See, for example, John R. Tester, Dwain W. Warner, and William W. Cochran, "A Radio-Tracking System for Studying Movements of Deer," *Journal of Wildlife Management* 28.1 (1964): 42–45.

12. Robert L. Schwitzgebel, "Man and Machine," *Psychology Today*, April 1969.

13. Alicia Caldwell, "ZDHS Is Using GPS-Enabled Ankle Bracelets to Track Immigrant Families Crossing the Border," *Huffington Post*, December 24, 2014, http://www.huffingtonpost.com/2014/12/24/dhs-is-using-gpsenabled-a_n_6379132.html.

14. Yvonne Jewkes and Jamie Bennett, *Dictionary of Prisons and Punishment* (Cullompton: Willan, 2008), 82–84.

15. See Khashu, "Role of Local Police."

16. Lonnie J. Westphal, "The In-Car Camera: Value and Impact," *Police Chief* 71.8 (August 2004), http://www.policechiefmagazine.org/magazine/index.cfm?fuseaction=display&article_id=358.

17. Westphal, "In-Car Camera."

18. Lisa Seghetti, "Border Security: Immigration Enforcement between Ports of Entry," Congressional Research Service Report, December 31, 2014, 18, https://www.fas.org/sgp/crs/homesec/R42138.pdf.

19. Testimony of CBP assistant commissioner Mark Borkowski before the House Committee on Homeland Security, Subcommittee on Border and Maritime Security, "After SBInet: The Future of Technology on the Border," 112th Congress, 1st sess., March 15, 2011.

20. Seghetti, "Border Security," 19.

21. David Perera, "CBP Awards Integrated Fixed Towers Procurement to Texas Firm," *Fierce Homeland Security*, February 28, 2014, http://www.fiercehomelandsecurity.com/story/cbp-awards-integrated-fixed-towers-procurement-texas-firm/2014-02-28.

22. The Associated Press, "Drone Carrying Drugs Crashes Near U.S.-Mexico Border," BBC News, January 22, 2015, http://www.bbc.com/news/world-latin-america-30931367.

23. CBP Office of Congressional Affairs, March 19, 2013; and CBP Office of Air and Marine, "2011 Air and Marine Milestones and Achievements," http://www.cbp.gov/xp/cgov/border_security/am/operations/2011_achiev.xml.

24. Northern border unmanned aerial systems (UAS) are based in Grand Forks, ND; Southwest border UAS are based in Sierra Vista, AZ (four systems) and Corpus Christi, TX (one system); and maritime UAS are based in Corpus Christi, TX (one system) and in Cape Canaveral, FL (two systems).

25. Associated Press, "Border Patrol Forced to Negotiated through Rough Terrain," NBC News, November 21, 2005, http://www.nbcnews.com/id/10137304/ns/us_news-security/t/border-patrol-forced-negotiate-tough-terrain/#.VOTsBEKzj0c.

26. Associated Press, "Jackals in the Night: Border Patrol's Helicopter Unit Keeps Watch in California Mountains," Fox News, April 25, 2008, http://www.foxnews.

com/story/2008/04/25/jackals-in-night-border-patrol-helicopter-unit-keeps-watch-in-california/.

27. "U.S. Customs and Border Protection's Unmanned Aircraft System Program Does Not Achieve Intended Results or Recognize All Costs of Operations" (Project Number 13-135-AUD-DHS), December 15-17, 2014, https://www.oig.dhs.gov/assets/Mgmt/2015/OIG_15-17_Dec14.pdf.

28. Schied, memorandum.

29. Andrew Becker, "New Drone Report: Our Border Is Not as Secure as We Thought," April 4, 2013, http://www.thedailybeast.com/articles/2013/04/04/new-drone-report-our-border-is-not-as-secure-as-we-thought.html.

30. "USAF Drone Operators Insignia Patch," *Afghanistan War*, September 12, 2012, http://afghancentral.blogspot.com/2012/09/usaf-drone-operators-insignia-patch.html.

31. Associated Press, "Half of U.S.-Mexico Border Now Patrolled Only by Drone," *Guardian*, November 13, 2014, http://usa.news.net/article/2274725/us-drones-patrol-half-of-mexico-border.

32. Grégoire Chamayou, *A Theory of the Drone*, trans. Janet Lloyd (New York: New Press, 2015).

33. Michael Berry and Nabiha Syed, "The FAA's Slow Move to Regulate Domestic Drones," *Washington Post*, September 24, 2014, http://www.washingtonpost.com/news/volokh-conspiracy/wp/2014/09/24/the-faas-slow-move-to-regulate-domestic-drones/.

34. US Government Accountability Office, "Border Patrol: Checkpoints Contribute to Border Patrol's Mission, but More Consistent Data Collection and Performance Measurement Could Improve Effectiveness," August 2009, http://www.gao.gov/new.items/d09824.pdf.

35. ACLU, "The Constitution in the 100-Mile Border Zone," https://www.aclu.org/immigrants-rights/constitution-100-mile-border-zone.

36. US Customs and Border Protection, "Office of Border Patrol—Sectors and Stations," Accessed at http://ecso.swf.usace.army.mil/maps/SectorP.pdf.

37. ACLU, "100-Mile Border Zone."

38. US Government Accountability Office, "Border Patrol."

39. US Government Accountability Office, "Border Patrol."

40. In *City of Indianapolis v. Edmond*, 531 U.S. 44 (2000).

41. Cindy Casares, "Border Patrol Takes 'No' for an Answer at Internal Checkpoints," *Texas Observer*, March 7, 2013.

42. ACLU, "U.S. Border Patrol Interior Checkpoints: Frequently Asked Questions," ACLU Border Litigation Project, https://www.aclusandiego.org/wp-content/uploads/2014/11/Border-Patrol-Checkpoint-FAQs.pdf.

43. US Department of Homeland Security, "Privacy Impact Assessment for the Automated Biometric Identification System (IDENT)," December 7, 2012, http://www.dhs.gov/sites/default/files/publications/privacy-pia-nppd-ident-06252013.pdf.

44. Of the total 24,310 workers checked, 17 percent quit, were fired, or were arrested as a result of Operation Vanguard.

45. US Immigrations and Customs Enforcement, "Law Enforcement Support Center," http://www.ice.gov/lesc.

46. Although under Secure Communities most migrants were being deported, regardless of criminal background.

47. US Department of Homeland Security, "Privacy Impact Assessment."

48. David Venturella, "Testimony to House Subcommittee on Homeland Security Appropriations, Committee on Appropriations," May 12, 2009, 943.
49. US Customs and Border Protection, "SENTRI: Secure Electronic Network for Travelers Rapid Inspection," http://www.cbp.gov/travel/trusted-traveler-programs/sentri.
50. See Matthew B. Sparke, "A Neoliberal Nexus: Economy, Security and the Biopolitics of Citizenship on the Border," *Political Geography* 25.2 (2006): 151–180.
51. Peter Adey, "Divided We Move': The Dromologics of Airport Security and Surveillance," in *Surveillance and Security in Everyday Life*, ed. Torin Monahan (New York: Routledge, 2006), n.p.

INDEX

elimination of provincial borders within, 145

Law on Suspects (1793), 150

plain clothes police, 135

police patrol as border, 115–6, 125, 126, 246n21

renovation of Paris, 131

spying during French Revolution, 136

traffic regulation in, 129–31

frontier, in kinopolitics, 40–2

frontières plastiques (Ancel), 6

Frontier in American History, The (Turner), 41

funnel effect, of US-Mexico border, 172–6, 255n31, 256n44

geodesy and surveyors, 71–5

geomorphology, 6

Germany

concentration camps and denationalization of people, 154

and labor circuit, 146

landlord permits, 98

police patrol as border, 127

Glidden, J. F., 153

Gordon, Colin, 141–2

Goseck Circle, Germany, 54

Great Wall of China, 8

"Great Wall of China, The" (Kafka), 66

Greece. *See* ancient Greece

Groebner, Valentin, 94, 98

ground sensors, 212

Guattari, Félix, 65–6

Habermas, Jürgen, 141

Hacking, Ian, 156

Hadrian's Wall, Scotland, 8, 38, 80, 86–7

Halley, Edmond, 25

Hammurabi, King, 72

Harshorn, Richard, 12

Harvey, William, 25, 229n11

Haussmann, Baron, 131

Headrick, Daniel, 156, 157

health borders, 97

Health of Nations, The (Chadwick), 132

Hedstrom, Darlene, 100

Hegel, G.W.F., 142, 143

henge enclosures. *See* sacred palisade fences

Herodotus, 72–3, 83, 85, 93

Hippocrates, 107

Hippodamus, 73–4

Hobbes, Thomas, 137

Hobsbawm, Eric, 110–1

Holder, Eric, 199

Holdich, Thomas, 12, 25

horarium (timetable), 105–6, 160, 201

hospital, as confinement cell, 103–4, 106

human cattle pens. *See* immigrant detention centers, in US

human corralling. *See* funnel effect, of US-Mexico border

Humane Borders, 182

hunting traps. *See* corral fences

hybrid transition zones, 8, 26

ICAD database. *See* Integrated Computer Assisted Detection (ICAD) database

ICE. *See* Immigration and Customs Enforcement (ICE)

IDENT. *See* Automated Biometric Identification System (IDENT)

identification cells, 92–8

identification cells, of US-Mexico border regime, 194–6

identity formation, in community palisades, 57

immigrant detention centers, in US, 30, 171, 177–8, 194, 197–200, 230n21

immigrant military-prison-industrial-detention complex, 193, 202

Immigration and Customs Enforcement (ICE). *See also* Operation Secure Communities (ICE)

Enforcement and Removal Operations (ERO), 186

hotline for reporting illegal aliens, 208

Law Enforcement Support Center (LESC), 217

stacking process of, 186–7

use of electronic monitoring, 207

use of raids, 186–7, 218

Immigration and Nationality Act, amendments to (1996), 197

Immigration and Naturalization Services (INS), 174, 186, 210, 216, 218

in-car police cameras, 208–9

in(fo)dividuals, 114, 156, 216, 219, 253n64

information checkpoints, 155–61
  checkpoints, overview, 110–5
  and in(fo)dividuals, 156, 253n64
  inspection function of, 157–60
  isolation of data points, 156–7
  summary conclusion, 161
  traceability of mobility, 160–1
  in US-Mexico border regime, 216–20
INS. *See* Immigration and Naturalization
  Services (INS)
inspection and checkpoints. *See* information checkpoints
Integrated Automated Fingerprint
  Identification System, 216–7
Integrated Computer Assisted Detection
  (ICAD) database, 210
Integrated Surveillance Information
  System (ISIS), 210
intensive division, 3, 34
Inter-faith Immigrant Coalition, 182
interior checkpoints, in US-Mexico
  border regime, 41, 214–6
iris scans, 216–7
ISIS. *See* Integrated Surveillance
  Information System (ISIS)
Israel, breach of security fence, 26
Italy, bills of health, 97

jail, origin of term, 102
Janin, Louis François, 152–3
Jefferson, Thomas, 154
Jericho, 67
Johnson, Corey, 10
Jones, Reece, 10
junctions, in kinopolitics, 27–8, 32–5
juridical power, 1–2, 12, 16. *See also*
  cells, as border regime; *headings at*
  US-Mexico border
jurisdiction, in letters, 95–6
Justi, Johann Heinrich Gottlob von, 118

Kafka, Franz, 66
Kant, Immanuel, 10, 13
Kerlikowske, R. Gil, 213
kindividuals. *See* in(fo)dividuals
kinopolitics, defined, 24, 229n5. *See also*
  border kinopower
kinopticism, distinguished from panopticism, 124, 210
kites. *See* corral fences

labor circuit, defined, 30–1
laissez passer, in capitalism, 112, 114, 120
La Mare, Nicolas de, 118, 120
landing mats. *See* corrugated-steel walls,
  of US-Mexico border regime
land surveying, 71–5
Law Enforcement Support Center (LESC)
  (ICE), 217
Laws (Plato), 78–9, 93
leakage, of borders, 13
Lefebvre, Georges, 145
legal contracts, 89
legal enclosure, in letters, 95–6
Leibniz, G. W., 151
Lenoir, Jean Charles Pierre, 118, 125,
  132, 133, 135
Leroi-Gourhan, André, 71
letter, as identification cell, 93–6, 156
Leviathan (Hobbes), 129
Levitan, Kathrin, 151–2
life and death flows. *See* burial borders;
  tombs, as megalithic boundary
limit, in kinopolitics, 37–9
limites. *See* territorial walls
limit vs. nonlimit junctions, 32–3, 35
linkage, of cells, 92
local law enforcement, and immigrant
  detention, 193–4, 197–8, 200–1
Locke, John, 139
loop space, 9
Louis XI, King, 96–7
Louis XIV, King, 115–6
Lowe, John, 27–8

MacKie, Euan, 61
madness, 104
manhunt apparatus, 51, 98, 150,
  173, 174–5. *See also headings at*
  US-Mexico border
march, defined, 36–8
mark, defined, 36–8
Marx, Karl, 22–4, 29, 116, 121,
  134, 245n16
McLean, Andrew, 135, 250n117
mechanical clocks, 106
megalithic boundaries, 57–62
Merriman, Peter, 229n5
Mesopotamia, 64, 65
  city gates in, 86
  cuneiform tablets, 72

Rumford, Chris, 5, 9
RVSS. *See* remote video surveillance systems (RVSS)

sacred and profane flows. *See* sacred palisade fences; temples, as megalithic boundary
sacred palisade fences, 53–4, 77
Sanctorius, 25
San Diego-Tijuana border, 179–80, 188–9
SBI. *See* Secure Border Initiative (SBI)
SBInet, 210–1
Schmitt, Carl, 8
Schwitzgebel, Ralph, 206–7
Schwitzgebel, Robert, 206–7
Scotland
    Antonine Wall, 80
    Brodgar temple, 61
    Hadrian's Wall, 8, 38, 80, 86–7
    Skara Brae, 61
    Standing Stones of Henness, 61
Secure Border Initiative (SBI), 210–1
Secure Electronic Network for Travelers Rapid Inspection (SENTRI), 218–20
Secure Fence Act (2006), 169–70, 176
security checkpoints, 138–55
    checkpoints, overview, 110–5
    national security checkpoints, 143–55
    private property, 138–43
    summary conclusion, 161
    in US-Mexico border regime, 209–16
security fence functions, of US-Mexico border, 176–8
sedentism, 47–8, 65
Servan, Antoine, 123, 133
Sesostris III, 78
ships, as wooden walls, 83, 240n108
siege towers, 75–6
Sinai region, 61, 236n67
Skara Brae, Scotland, 61
Skeates, Robin, 57
Smith, Adam, 22
Smith, M. L., 67
social cohesion/coercion, in community palisades, 55–7
Social Contract, The (Rousseau), 129
social division. *See* border as social division; *specific border regimes*
social elasticity, defined, 111–2

social expansion, defined, 34
social expulsion, defined, 34
social flows, 24–6
social force, defined, 232n6
social motion. *See* border kinopower
social space, defined, 9, 227n35
social transportation, 82
soldiers, as military wall, 69–71, 80
Southern Poverty Law Center, 196
Spain, passport requirements, 97–8
spy checkpoints, 134–7, 209, 250n115, 251n121
stacking of bricks, 65
stake fences. *See* palisade fences
Standing Stones of Henness, Scotland, 61
statism, 15–6, 222
statistics
    measurement of flows, 25, 26
    in police patrols, 128
stela. *See* territorial markers, as megalithic boundary
Stonehenge, England, 54
Strabo,, 74, 84
student visas, 195–6
Sumerian Ziggurats, 68
superhenges. *See* sacred palisade fences
superintendence, origin of term, 124. *See also* police checkpoints
surveyors. *See* geodesy and surveyors
Swift & Company, 187
Switzerland, beggar's permits, 97

tactical interior checkpoints, in US-Mexico border regime, 215–6
taxation
    and city port walls, 85, 86–7
    and geodesy, 72–3
    and social kinetics of walls, 66
    and transport walls, 81, 83, 84
temples, as megalithic boundary, 59–61, 100
tensional social motion, defined, 90. *See also* cells, as border regime; *headings at* US-Mexico border
territorial boundary monuments, 178–9
territorialization, defined, 48, 232n4
territorial markers, as megalithic boundary, 61–2
territorial ports, 86–7

security function of, 176–8
social kinetics of, 171–2
US-Mexico border, as wall border
    regime, 183–92
  corrugated-steel walls, 188–90
  port walls, 190–2
  US enforcement operations, 184–8
US-Mexico border regime, overview
  as checkpoint against terrorism, 171
  deaths of immigrants due to,
      173–4, 179–80
  holes in, 26, 170, 172
  social circulation of labor and
      customs, 8
  summary conclusion, 165–7
  as zone of contestation, 167–8
US National Security Agency, 137

VADER (Vehicle and Dismount
    Exploitation Radar), 213
Vaughan-Williams, Nick, 7
Venturella, David, 217–8
Vickers, Michael, 174–5
vigilante migrant hunting
    groups, 174–5
vine arbor siege walls (*vinea*), 75
Virgil, 74
Virilio, Paul, 82, 85
virtual fence, in US-Mexico border
    regime, 210–2
visas, 192, 194–6
von Berg, Heinrich, 121

walls, as border regime, 64–87. *See
    also* US-Mexico border, as wall
    border regime
  history of, 228*n*50
  military, 68–79, 237*n*27
  origin of term, 236*n*3
  port, 81–7
  rampart, 76–80
  social kinetics of, 65–8
  summary conclusion, 87
war on immigration, in US (1990s),
    183, 202
watchhouses, 121, 122, 123–4. *See also*
    police checkpoints
watermarks, in letters, 94–5
water walls. *See* aqueducts
Wealth of Nations (Smith), 22
Whittle, Alasdair, 56
Willacy County Correctional Center,
    Texas, 198–9
Williams, Alan, 115
Williams, John, 16
wisdom, as walled stronghold, 79, 239*n*78
Woodhenge, England, 54
workers' visas, 195–6
workplace raids. *See* Immigration and
    Customs Enforcement (ICE)
World War I/II, 154

Zeno, 9, 227*n*27
zone, defined, 41
zone of experimentation (Bowman), 41–2